BRIAN TANNEBAUM

THE PRACTICE

BRUTAL TRUTHS ABOUT LAWYERS AND LAWYERING

Cover design by Elmarie Jara/ABA Publishing.

Printed in the United States of America.

18 17 16 15 14 5 4 3 2 1

ISBN: 978-1-62722-001-9

e-ISBN: 978-1-62722-002-6

Discounts are available for books ordered in bulk. Special consideration is given to state bars, CLE programs, and other bar-related organizations. Inquire at Book Publishing, ABA Publishing, American Bar Association, 321 N. Clark Street, Chicago, Illinois 60654-7598.

www.ShopABA.org

For Lisa, Alexa, and Marissa

My girls

CONTENTS

Chapter 7
Of Course, Social Media   131

Chapter 8
Referrals, and the Feeding and Proper Care of
Referral Sources   159

Chapter 9
Money   183

Chapter 10
What Law School Doesn't Teach You about the Practice   215

Chapter 11
Reevaluating the Whole Thing

Epilogue

Acknowledgments

Notes

Index

FOREWORD

Had we met at any time during my law school years, Brian Tannebaum and I would not have recognized each other as part of the same species. Tannebaum would not have regarded my accomplishment of completing 25 full seasons of Madden NFL 2002 while playing out the string at Harvard Law School as proper training for a career as a legal practitioner. The fact that I had secured a job at a prestigious Manhattan law firm long before leading the New York Giants to six consecutive video Super Bowl victories wouldn't have changed his impression.

I would have viewed Tannebaum's accomplishment of graduating from Stetson Law School and starting a successful small law practice as one regards a dog that can leap twice its own height to secure a Frisbee. Cute, and certainly something I could not do, but something that speaks more about the height of the Frisbee than the skill of the dog.

Of course, Tannebaum and I would not have met, or had any cause to interact, over the normal course of our careers. Part of the joy of going to Harvard or Stetson is that you can always feel superior to your opposite number on the other side of the spectrum. A Harvard guy and a Stetson guy walk into a courtroom, both leave the room feeling they've won regardless of the outcome of the case. There's no punchline there because I'm not making a joke. Lawyers are a strange bunch.

The funny thing that happened on the way to our lives being blissfully ignorant of each other was that the economy tanked, and the legal job market collapsed. Well, that was funny to us in our own ways. Suddenly a whole bunch of law graduates realized they had no idea how to run a business. They realized they had no idea how to service clients. They realized they had no idea how to build a practice without a bloated corporate structure spoon-feeding them the answers in six minute increments.

Above the Law, the website I work for, at the time of the financial crisis catered to an audience of Biglaw associates and law students who wanted to be them. But after the crisis, those entry-level positions in the Biglaw world simply ceased to exist. Sure, the Harvard Law guys were largely okay: you can write *Harvard Law* in crayon and generally get an interview somewhere. But you weren't going to be just fine if you finished in the bottom third of your class at Duke Law, or the bottom half at Vanderbilt Law, or were outside the top 25% at the University of Florida Levin College of Law. Kids who wanted nothing more than to take the highest paying corporate law job on offer suddenly had to fend for themselves against people who had actually trained to be legal *practitioners*, instead of legal employees.

In 2011, Above the Law was looking for more columnists who could speak directly to the "small law" practitioner experiences and skills our readers needed in the "new normal" of the legal job market. In 2011, Brian Tannebaum was looking to blow up the Biglaw wanna-bes who thought that they just needed to "slum it" in solo practice before Wall Street law firms started hiring again. He wanted to say something to the people who thought law practice would be easy if they weren't getting paid as much for it.

A mutual friend introduced us over email. I can't reprint the first email Tannebaum sent me. He earned the nickname "T-Bomb" from the readers for a reason. I also shouldn't reprint the second, or the third. But the fourth one, the fourth email in a thread that involved me begging him to send around some writing samples, read: "I can send you some writing samples of legal documents I've written, but I FIGURED SENDING YOU A BLOG POST THAT LOOKS SOMEWHAT LIKE SOMETHING I MAY WRITE IN THE FUTURE WOULD BE APPROPRIATE, as I haven't seen much in the way of legal prose at ATL, unless I need to start clicking on some pictures or something."

Real talk from a real practitioner. This book is comprised of the stuff that they really don't teach you about in a school for lawyers. It's as good an answer as any to the derisive question from an elitist commenter on any law blog: "What is a Stetson?"

-Elie Mystal: Editor, *Above the Law*.

INTRODUCTION

I love practicing law. I don't love it every day. I don't know that anyone in any profession or job loves what they do every single day. I tell people that I love what I do about 28 days a month. That's pretty good for a lawyer, as many of my colleagues are miserable all the time. After 19 years I think it's impossible to be happy every day in any job. People look at what I do—representing people in trouble—and think it's fascinating. It's the interesting topic at cocktail parties and other social gatherings. The show *Law & Order* was so popular it spun off several different series, all surrounding the daily grind of the criminal justice system. Has anyone ever seen a TV show called *Commercial Litigation*? Some days what I do is fascinating; other days it's enough to make me wish I worked at a wine bar, or a T-shirt shop in the Florida Keys.

Being a lawyer requires thought. It requires thought even when you're not actually talking to a judge or a client. Lawyers who represent people with serious problems take those problems home at night. If you're a lawyer who hasn't awoken in the middle of the night with a theory about a case or the thought that you forgot to do something in a case, I envy you.

I don't feel like I've been practicing law that long. It's not that 19 years is a terribly long time, but so much has changed since I began practicing. E-mail was around in the beginning, but the only e-mail I had was an interoffice address. We could receive messages from our supervisors, and were able to communicate with secretaries and other lawyers. We had beepers or "pagers." Instant communication meant you would receive a message that simply said "5-1 911." That meant "get to courtroom 5-1 immediately." I had no alphanumeric way of communicating. We had to know phone numbers. A certain phone number meant the boss wanted to speak to you, while another meant it was time to talk about lunch. Cell phones were around, but they did nothing else but serve as a telephone. Many young lawyers didn't have one. A morning at work began with listening to voice mails more than sorting through e-mail.

All documents were printed and faxed. There was no scan-to-e-mail. There was no Wi-Fi. If lawyers wanted to work remotely, they would hide out, not at a coffee shop, but in the local law school library—where they could find case law in books and dump quarters in the copy machine.

We had a dress code. Ties, jackets, lawyer uniforms. Jeans were discouraged. We didn't pride ourselves on having practices where we didn't meet with clients and therefore could run around town in shorts and T-shirts. I didn't know Starbucks or the concept of working out of a coffee shop.

I started as an assistant public defender, the type of job that young Biglaw associates and even others going into small-firm civil practice often look at with disdain, until they realize later that the promises of going to court as a law firm associate are just that—empty promises. When I started, the economics were different. Biglaw associates in South Florida were starting at $50,000–55,000. I started at $32,500 (which included a $4,500 raise for passing the bar exam).

It wasn't until about 2000 that I first heard the news of a Biglaw firm paying a six-figure salary to a first-year associate. I remember the number: $105,000. That changed everything. Starting salaries for prosecutors and public defenders went up a little—now around $42,000, 19 years later—while Biglaw is hovering at $160,000. While in 1994 lawyers were deciding whether to go to Biglaw for $20,000 more, now the gap is $120,000.

In 1994 a lawyer qualified to get an offer from Biglaw would only be making a $20,000 decision, but when the difference became six figures, the state attorney and public defender's office—while the best place for trial experience—could no longer compete with those whose number-one priority was not learning to be a lawyer, but paying off ridiculous student loans.

Those of you who read my columns on *Above the Law* and elsewhere may have read comments arguing that I am envious of Biglaw or bitter that I never worked there, but my story evidences otherwise.

I am the first lawyer in my family. Growing up I never experienced law until I received a traffic ticket. I don't remember my parents ever involved in any legal proceedings except for meeting with a lawyer to write their wills. The first time I ever went to court I was telling a judge I wasn't speeding. I was a great student until the middle of junior high school, when I started to lose interest in academics. In high school I did so poorly that when I went to my guidance counselor to ask my rank (I actually did it as a joke), she replied "You really want to know?" I was 555 out of 860.

My cousin graduated with me and went on to Harvard. Some friends went to Michigan, and those other good out-of-state state schools, while many of my friends made their alumni parents proud and went to Florida and Florida State. I only got into the University of South Florida, which isn't even in South Florida. It's in Tampa. It was so named because when it was founded it was the southernmost state university in Florida. No one in my family was excited about m going to USF. What was I going to do with a degree from USF? They didn't even have a football team.

I did OK at USF. My success was outside the classroom. I became student body president and met people that are still today in leadership positions throughout Florida. I realized then, and now, that my network would win out over a grade in a class any day. While serving as student body president, I worked on the campaign of then U.S. Senator Lawton Chiles, who was elected governor of Florida. I had one year left of college and then I was going to go to Tallahassee and work for him. My life was set. That was my goal.

During the campaign I became close friends with the 1969 (the year I was born) student body president, Steve Anderson. He was the chair of the Chiles campaign in Tampa and a prominent lawyer with a good law firm—his law firm. I had thought of going to law school but was concerned I would not be accepted anywhere. It seemed easier to just hang out in Tallahassee with politicians and maybe become a lobbyist or something. I relayed my goal to Steve to which he responded, "I can get you a job there, but I'm going to make sure it doesn't happen, because I want you to go to law school." Steve saw me as a future colleague in Tampa, but I knew I wanted to eventually return to my native Miami. That struggle lasted many years. Steve was, and is, like a second father to me, and if anything could keep me in Tampa, it would be him.

With the directive of my mentor Steve, during my senior year at USF I worked harder than I ever had, and brought my GPA up to a respectable level. I took the LSAT, did well enough not to be laughed at, and applied to a few law schools. My goal was to come home to Miami, go to the University of Miami School of Law, and build a network in Miami that would help me when I became a lawyer. Miami Law put me on the wait list. Stetson accepted me. Stetson? Well, my future wife was there, but I wanted to come home. I needed not only to go to law school—I needed to start getting to know the people running my hometown. I had been away for four years and if I didn't come home now, I would never be able to establish myself in Miami.

Stetson was the first school to accept me. They would be the only school to accept me. I moved from Tampa to St. Petersburg with the hope that Miami would take me. The day before classes started at Stetson, I called Miami Law: "No." After a semester at Stetson I would be on academic probation, facing dismissal from the only law school that accepted me. My father had no sympathy. "I don't need to motivate you; that's the only school you got into. If you don't bring your grades up, you're not going to be a lawyer." So I did.

I also tried out for the trial team, something for which Stetson was gaining a national reputation. I resisted until three days before the tryouts, which required making a closing argument before a group of trial team alumni based on a hypothetical. I went to the campus (we still didn't have e-mail), picked up the packet containing the hypothetical and instructions, and put together a closing argument.

That Saturday 75 people tried out. Twelve would be selected. We were told to come back to campus later that afternoon and there would be a board on an easel in the courtyard announcing the new team. There was no text, no website—we had to actually get up and go to the campus. Imagine that. I took a walk from my apartment across the street and saw the easel from a distance. Upon approaching, I saw the two columns of six names:

12. Brian Tannebaum

That year Stetson became the first school to win all five national trial competitions. I participated in one of them: the American Bar Association (ABA) National Criminal Justice Trial Advocacy Competition at the John Marshall Law School in Chicago. The final round was Stetson versus Harvard. One of the judges for that round, the legendary Albert Krieger, would later become my friend, mentor, referral source, and co-counsel.

My law school grades would never be great. I would graduate in the top 69 percent of my class. When the recruiters came to interview I signed up for two interviews—one with a Biglaw firm (again, another joke of mine) and the other with the Miami-Dade County state attorney's office.

My interview with the state attorney's office didn't go well; they didn't like my attitude, nor that I did not think exigent circumstances applied to avoid getting a warrant if there was marijuana in a locker in the airport. My trial team coach, himself both a former prosecutor and public defender, asked me to consider the Miami-Dade County public defender's office. He had a connection—the elected public defender—and thought I would enjoy the office. I agreed to consider it because I wanted to go back to Miami, and wasn't sure I would be called back for another interview with the prosecutor's office.

I eventually received the traditional call to meet with the elected state attorney, which meant an offer was forthcoming, and did receive an offer from the public defender. I didn't know what to do. I asked my dad and he gave me a very simple answer: "Which people do you like more?" Even though the interview was much more rigorous and the people a bit nasty, I had a sense about the public defender's office.

When I first started law school, I didn't know what lawyers other than prosecutors and criminal defense lawyers did on a daily basis. When I started law school, I did so with the long-term goal of becoming a criminal defense lawyer. I thought being a lawyer meant representing clients, often in court. I had no concept of Biglaw until I got to law school. While in law school I worked with Steve Anderson for a while, and later did a clinic at the state attorney's office. At Steve's firm I sat in an office and did research. At the state attorney's office I was in court. There was no comparison. I was not going to be happy sitting in an office, regardless of the view or quality of the furniture.

I left the public defender's office in 1997, not simply for more money, but because I was bored. I wanted a new challenge. I wanted to learn federal practice, I wanted to run my own firm. Since 1997 I have been a private practitioner. I worked for a small firm, I was of counsel to another small firm, and I've had my partnership since 2002. I began in private practice doing exclusively criminal defense, and seven years later began representing lawyers in bar discipline matters. I've had great months and years, and others that made me think about closing up shop. The year after September 11 was a particular disaster, as law enforcement concentrated less on typical crime, and more on finding Osama bin Laden. People also saw hiring counsel as a luxury because they were holding on to their money.

This book is a collection of much of what I have written at both *Above the Law* and my blog, *My Law License*. Some posts were written after research and review of other writings. Others—the ones that received the most feedback—were written while I was angry, or annoyed, or dealing with one of those typical things that lawyers deal with in practice. They are in no particular order, but they are categorized by topic, including the type of lawyer you want to be, when and how to make the switch to small law, the Great Office Debate, old-school networking, marketing in real life and on social media, the feeding and proper care of referral sources, what law school doesn't teach you about clients and reevaluating the whole thing.

People ask me "Why do you write?" People assume I write for attention, or because it makes me money. These people can't understand why anyone would do anything other than for attention or money. These are also the people that went to law school for attention and money, not to represent clients. They are the disillusioned ones. The ones that thought good grades and pedigree schools were a guaranteed ticket to success in the practice, but still haven't seen the benefits.

I have no guaranteed ticket to success in the practice. I didn't get to a point of loving what I do because it was owed to me due to grades or where I went to law school. I can only tell you what I've done right, and the mistakes I've made. Some of this may not work for you, or it may change your life.

I hope you like the book, but in reality, I really don't care.

CHAPTER 1

WHAT TYPE OF LAWYER DO YOU WANT TO BE?

We are in a generation where a great deal of people went to law school not to become lawyers, but to make money. When your goal in finding a job is to make money, you'll generally do anything. When your goal is to try cases or negotiate contracts, you'll look for something that allows you to try cases or negotiate contracts. Sometime in the late 1980s, in what I call the "L.A. Law generation" (from the show of the same name), people got the idea that all lawyers were rich, had high-rise offices with mahogany furniture, and spent their days having fun and eating well. When the jobs weren't there upon graduation, it was time to "take anything." While there is merit to doing anything you have to do (legally) to feed yourself or your family, the law school graduate who is willing to take anything is going to be in a worse position than the one who is willing and able to hold out for something tailored to their goals.

On April 21, 2010, I posted the question "Is Looking for 'Any Job I Can Get' Hurting You?" I wrote about Donald Trump's daughter Ivanka. Anyone who has watched her career realizes she is no idiot daughter. She works. Yes, she has a great name, went to the finest schools, and likely a few doors were opened for her just based on who her father is. But she said something important during an interview. She was asked "What is the biggest mistake people make when they come to you for a job—what don't they do right?" Ivanka said, "They don't know what they want. People are casting their net far too wide in this climate because they're looking for any opportunity."

I've heard this before, and I hear it a lot now. I hear law school graduates say they are looking for "anything," and I hear lawyers say that law students are looking for "anything." What does that get you? If you appear desperate, what will be the result? You'll get little to nothing.

I know, there are no jobs, there are loans that need to be repaid, bills that need to be paid, entitlements that need to be fulfilled. But why not narrow the search?

I have these conversations with unemployed lawyers. I ask "What are you looking for?" And they reply, "Anything." I don't get it. If you want to do plaintiff's personal injury work, isn't your job search better conducted by focusing on that area of law? What result do you expect if your interest is family law and you are telling a partner in an employment law firm that you "just need a job" and will do "anything"? Why would they hire you?

If you are looking for a job to make money, why not just do something else rather than take a law job doing something you hate? Is it that important to be paid for legal work even though your life is miserable? Is your ego more important than your happiness?

I know you went to law school to become a lawyer (well, I know some did), but you didn't spend three years studying, then another few months studying to take the bar, for the purpose of taking "anything."

SOME OF US GET TIRED OF HEARING . . .

Although there is a whole new generation of bloggers that are told success is having enough keywords in a post to generate search engine optimization (SEO), putting the blog high up on the Google chain and causing the flood gates to open with client calls, one of the true signs of a successful blog is that it generates discussion and debate. One of the staples of blogging is angering people. I blog, and I anger people. One, or maybe both, of those are reasons the American Bar Association (ABA) asked me to put together this book.

Contrary to what the marketers sell, good blogging isn't just reposting stories about auto accidents or a recent arrest with links to your website. Good blogging contains opinions, and opinions generate opinions, conversation, interest, and maybe an inquiry from a journalist, fellow lawyer, or client. Maybe.

Much of my blog posts are my opinion. This comes from experience, and I hope that someone, or even a few people, takes something from it that helps them. But I'm not writing for you, and I'm not here to be "nice" or tell you things that will make you feel better. I didn't start blogging to coddle the unemployed lawyers who went to law school only for the end goal of graduating and receiving their six-figure Biglaw check.

I prefer the truth. Always have. So when I wrote that post about whether looking for "any job I can get" is hurting you, I was happy to read comments like this:

> It was not much fun reading some of the "There will be no jobs/ Do you REALLY want to be a lawyer?" posts, especially as graduation/get a job/pass the bar pressure started to build.
>
> Your emphasis on knowing what you want to do, getting to know the local legal community, and improvising on the job search (on a post last summer) was extremely valuable to me. Although it wasn't possible for me to work for free for a local attorney, in the hopes of getting a future job, I was able to negotiate with the three-attorney

firm where I'd clerked since my first summer for continued employment. I don't make ideal money. I don't do ideal work. But I JUST started practicing, so I don't have the relationships with other lawyers and the courts that justify the big dollars. There are no perfect clients—just the ones who pay, and pay less for my time than my bosses'.

I can credit you with making crystal clear the importance of a realistic and flexible view of what I would be able to do with my degree and license. I don't see you as preaching from your very comfy chair with your feet up at all. You're further down the road trying to share your experience navigating this career. So I'll say a big fat "THANKS" for all the free, honest advice.

And I'm happy to read this comment as well:

No offense, but I'm so sick of the high and mighty job advice from people who got out of it and market not legal services but advice to all the other disgruntled lawyers. We may be BS artists, but the problem is we recognize it in you, BT. You have to get what you can get, and some of us get tired of hearing about how you should only do what you are passionate about, yada, yada, yada. You are dreaming! Moreover, you're just selling bullshit. So, give us all a break.

This is the type of dissenting view that is the enemy of those who spend their days convincing lawyers like me that I need to develop a personal brand. Sit on Twitter for five minutes and you'll see lawyers tweeting out platitudes about themselves and other niceties, avoiding any dissenting opinion, criticism, or debate. Most of them barely practice law, or haven't practiced in years, so debating anything regarding the legal profession is either done on the surface or ignored because it's "negative."

I am a lawyer. I advocate. People disagree with me—normally the lawyers standing across the courtroom. I can take it. I actually like it. Without it, things would be pretty boring. So I don't get offended when people comment to tell me they hate me, that they don't want to hear it anymore, or that I don't know what I'm talking about.

It's OK, really.

SOMETHING LEBRON SAID

One thing that hasn't changed in terms of how to be successful is watching and listening to successful people to see and hear how they reached their status. Today we hear that in the legal profession it's simply a good website and good search terms, but when my Miami Heat won the 2012 NBA Championship, I heard a short comment from LeBron James that stuck with me.

It is no surprise that I am a big fan of divisive people. I love watching the hate, the squirming when these people are successful, the "yeah, but . . ." commentary. I love watching losers nip at the feet of winners. Lawyers love to do this.

Find an article about a successful lawyer and watch the comments from other lawyers (they're the ones using the stage name "Anonymous"). If a lawyer wins a case, the other lawyers of course could have won the same case. If a lawyer gets a big settlement, he probably has an unhappy home life. This mentality isn't limited to lawyers, but lawyers do love to rationalize their own lack of success by attacking the success of other lawyers.

And so you all hate LeBron. I have news for you: while he and the Heat were celebrating with the trophy (and a $150,000 bar tab, I hear), he wasn't thinking abouthow miserable you are and how much you don't like him. As Bruce Jenkins wrote in the *San Francisco Chronicle*:[1] "As the celebration unfolded in Miami, LeBron James reveled in the NBA championship that eluded him for so long. He wore smiles of youthful exuberance and knew, in his heart, that his critics had run out of ammunition."

I like to do things differently. I like to watch successful people and try to learn something from them. I know, it's odd. I probably should sit around with the losers and wonder along with them why failure and mediocrity is conspiring against so many lawyers.

But I don't.

I watch successful people, I talk to them, I ask questions. I listen. You may like to curse the darkness because it makes you feel better to be critical of success than to try and mirror it.

In all the celebration, in all the excitement and anxiety of watching the NBA finals, there was one moment when I caught a glimpse of the essence of true success. It was during the post-game-five interview, when LeBron said this: "I'm happy now that eight years later, nine years later since I've been drafted, that I can finally say that I'm a champion, and I did it the right way. I didn't shortcut anything. You know, I put a lot of hard work and dedication in it, and hard work pays off."

Eight, nine years? The "right way"? No shortcuts? Hard work and dedication? How does this square with building a fake image on the Internet overnight and banking cash immediately? Eight or nine years to become the best? *Years*?

Yeah, LeBron switched teams. Boo hoo. He went somewhere he thought he could be a champion. Doesn't seem like a bad move at this point. Maybe you should do the same. The bad news from LeBron for all you trying to convince the Google searchers you're the best overnight, is that becoming the best takes time. It takes work, it takes more than just telling people you are the best. Even with the iPhone and your cool creative marketer, there are no shortcuts. You've all been lied to.

LeBron is a champion. He is a winner. He worked to get to this point in his career. His image was created by his work on (and off) the court. He believes there are no shortcuts. He's right, which is probably why you hate him so much.

WHAT IS YOUR CODE OF ETHICS?

Of course becoming the lawyer you want to be requires you to be something other than a beating heart with a JD. You have to stand for something more than your "brand" or what's in your bank account. It's called a code of ethics.

As lawyers we are all required to follow the ethics rules of our state bar associations. Most are the same: watch the conflicts, communicate with your clients, don't get arrested, operate with a good faith basis in litigation, the trust account money isn't yours, advertise within the confines of certain language, and rat on your colleagues if you see them doing something wrong (that always gets a good laugh).

I wonder though, if lawyers operate under their own personal code of ethics. Today's young lawyers, desiring more "work/life balance" and finding Biglaw less interested in how great they think they are and their entitlement to a funnel of money to pay off their student loans, are on the Internet doing Google searches like "how to make money as a lawyer" and "how to market yourself as a lawyer." Law is a business. That law is a profession is nothing more than a nice topic for ethics seminars and for older lawyers to whine about. The young lawyer is more focused on web marketing and flexible payment plans.

I have a personal code of ethics, that has developed with certain experiences and the natural progression of maturing as a lawyer. Here it is:

1. **My client does not dictate how I treat opposing counsel.** When I ask for something, too many lawyers tell me, "I have to ask my client/the victim." These requests are generally related to time extensions and issues of rescheduling. I'm not interested in how "aggressive" your client wants you to be. You, as opposing counsel, and I, have lives. We have families, illnesses, vacations, and just other things going on. I won't outsource my courtesy to my client's wishes, even if you do. And I won't be "mean" to the prosecutor to put on a show for my client.

2. **I will never take your case just because you "think it's a great case for me."** Let's be honest. Some lawyers decide to take a case if only one requirement is met: the client writes a check. Yes, in the beginning, I took cases I didn't want to take. I represented clients I didn't want to represent. As time went on, I learned that sometimes the best case is the one you don't take. To some, this is not an option. That's too bad. And it's something to reconsider. Being a lawyer is not a commitment to misery in search of the almighty dollar.

3. **I will deal with difficult clients, but not those that are difficult in every aspect of representation.** Clients don't own me. You hired me to represent you. You did not hire me to refrain from vacations, events for my kids, call you back three minutes after you call, or be available to every family member and friend that wants to know "what's up with the case?" I am also not your bank. You may be a client who needs some extra attention. I'm happy to give that to you. My job is to be available to you when it's necessary for me to be available. My job is not to convince you every minute of every day that your fee and your case is the only basis of my existence.

4. **I'm not in the referral fee business. Personal injury lawyers are a unique bunch.** They insist on paying referral fees. All of them. It's like arguing over a dinner check. What's the point? You want to pay, fine. Thanks. I don't pay referral fees. I don't take them either (save for the PI lawyers that insist). I'm not going to charge $5,000 to a client to handle their case, and pay you $1,250 because you made a phone call. Neither will I do that to you. If you don't want to refer me a case because I won't pay you, fine. I don't care, really. Go refer your friend, family member, or colleague to someone who will line your pocket. I won't tell them your real interest.

5. **I will communicate with lawyers informally (via phone, hallway conversations) until I am given a reason not to do so.** Not the reverse.

6. **I will not judge you as a lawyer based on what others say, until you prove to me you are the jerk, liar, and scumbag everyone says you are.** This I learned as time went on. I've dealt with prosecutors, civil lawyers, and judges that everyone hates. I've had respectful,

professional conversations and litigation with some of them. Even if you are that prosecutor that everyone talks about, I'm giving you the benefit of the doubt on our first encounter.

7. **I'm not handling your legal matter if it's not something I do.** I don't care if it's a phone call. The answer is no.

8. **I will not lie to get a case.** If I've never handled a case like yours, I'll tell you. If I know you are eligible for a dismissal just by showing up by yourself to the arraignment, I'll tell you. If the other lawyer you are talking to is a good lawyer, I'll tell you. If you tell me you think this is a simple case, I will tell you I don't handle simple cases and send you on your way.

9. **I will not reschedule a missed appointment with a new client unless there is a good reason.** If this isn't that important to you, it's not that important to me.

10. **I will not be the second lawyer in your case unless your first lawyer has done you an obvious disservice.** If you're not happy with your first lawyer, most likely you will not be happy with your second or third lawyer. Yes, there are exceptions, but they are rare.

11. **Unless I, not you, determine the case will be handled pro bono, I will not make a phone call, file a pleading, or do anything for you on the promise that you will pay me.** It is never the client's fault that the lawyer was not paid. It is always the fault of the lawyer.

12. **No one will ever give you legal advice in your case besides me, or a lawyer designated by me.** You hired me, not my assistant. So stop asking her.

13. **On that note, I will not allow you to be disrespectful to my staff.** I see this occasionally. You yell at my assistant because you haven't heard from me in an hour. I get on the phone, and you deny you were rude. I never buy it, and make sure you understand it's not to happen again.

14. **I will never support a judge for re-election that I believe does not belong on the bench.** Lawyers who support the incumbent are part of the problem. We are built to effect change, not fall in line like sheep.

15. **I will never outsource my marketing, and if you do, I will never refer you anything.** I know—those who outsource their marketing don't care where they get their cases from.

DO YOU WANT TO BE A TOP LAWYER OR JUST A GOOD LAWYER?

When I was in college I attended a political event at the invitation of a lawyer. He introduced me to another lawyer who shook my hand and said about my lawyer friend: "He's a good lawyer." At the time I thought that was the best compliment a lawyer could get—another lawyer saying a colleague was a "good lawyer." That's still a great compliment, but we've got many more lawyers than we had in 1989 and just being a "good" lawyer may not be enough.

A piece on law.com[2] regarding top lawyers begins with this premise: "Young attorneys are often led to the field of law because of a seductive proposition: You can do anything with a law degree." The next and absolutely true statement: "Unfortunately, a law degree does not even guarantee an opportunity in law, let alone an entree into a different field." Then the appropriate dig to Biglaw associates (I give this an 8 on a scale of 1–10): "A multitude of smart folks pass the bar, only to find themselves stuck behind prefabricated desks without much interest in the subject matter that fills their days. Their brains overloaded with statutes and data, many wonder why opportunities fail to abound."

Here is the crux: although you may be able to do anything with a law degree, a law degree and solid experience alone will not do it for you. For those young attorneys who dream of becoming top lawyers, the key is to be three parts lawyer and one part marketing agent.

Author Shai Littlejohn doesn't think of marketing as advertising or direct mail pieces, but more like "the total sum and breadth of your work history, reputation, involvement, initiative and personal values. Brand you is riding on whether people think you are competent, committed, available and willing to offer counsel. Sometimes for free. And often after hours."

This is my favorite part of this must-read article:

Top lawyers know that, while most of their colleagues look forward to relaxing at home at the end of the day, the highest-achieving ones do not focus on when one day ends and another begins. They look forward to the firm reception or foundation meeting at night because they are acutely aware that a little extra involvement is what moves the ordinarily competent attorney into the extraordinary, top attorney column. Even when not working, the top attorneys remain available and on call, considering the interests of their employers and communities at all times.

"I DON'T DO THAT WORK"

With a struggling legal economy, lawyers are doing everything they can do to stay afloat. It's understandable—homes have been bought, cars you can't afford have been leased, and Taco Bell doesn't taste as good as it did in school at 3 a.m. I've met with lawyers over the past few years who have told me to send them anything that comes my way that I don't want. These are real estate lawyers that will now draft employment contracts and civil litigators who are ready to draft a will. I see criminal defense lawyers taking on matters so far out of their practice area that I fear for the clients. Actually, I fear for all these clients.

Back in the day, the so called "country" or "neighborhood" lawyer did what today we pejoratively call "door law" (whatever walks in the door). There is a difference between a lawyer who handles several types of practice areas and a lawyer who doesn't, but will in order to make rent. The latter is dangerous. This is not to say that a lawyer who specializes in one area can't become competent in another, but what I'm seeing are lawyers just taking fees first, and then worrying about whether they can do the work. You see it—it's that lawyer on your listserv who handles wage and hour cases who is asking, "Does anyone have a sample complaint for a construction defect case?" You, well, maybe not you, just shake your head.

This problem is not getting any better, mainly because of the "everyone's got to make a living" mentality that has permeated our profession. Why shouldn't you take on a case you know nothing about when you can just send e-mails to lawyers, some who will laugh at you, others who will ignore you, but one who will help you? Those doing this type of "I'll take anything" practice don't realize, and don't care, that their public pronouncements of incompetence are the talk of their colleagues.

I've often joked about doing a continuing legal education (CLE) seminar titled "I Don't Do That Work." What is so terrible about telling a prospective client you don't handle their type of legal issue? Are you afraid of losing the client? That will be the least of your problems if you take on something you don't do and don't seek competent assistance.

I was asked about amending corporate documents. Do I know how to do that? Yeah, it's easy. Is there anything that could happen as a result of amending corporate documents? Are there tax or other issues? I have no idea. That's why I sent it to a corporate lawyer. He took care of it in a couple of hours, made the client happy, which in turn . . . well, I don't need to explain it. Could I have charged the client and done the work and taken the chance that what I did was OK? Sure. But I would never do that. I'd rather lose the money than wind up having an unhappy client, even if it was not because of malpractice or ethical issues.

There are a couple of things I want to highlight on this topic. One is obvious: don't take on work for the money. I know, easy for me to say, but that few grand you take for some "small" matter where you read how to handle it on the Internet or got a copy of a pleading from your listserv, will haunt you forever if you screw it up. Two is something I see few lawyers do: tell your referral sources what you don't do. I do this all the time. When you concentrate in a certain area, referral sources, even if they are other lawyers, may not know exactly what you do. They may think that because you're a tax lawyer, you handle international tax issues, audits, criminal tax investigations and prosecutions, and negotiations with the IRS on tax debt.

Finally, for those of you still in the dark ages of building relationships to build your practice, never forget that the work you don't do is a path to getting work that you do handle. That tax lawyer that only handles offers in compromise definitely has a network of tax lawyers that handle other types of matters. Can he handle the others? Maybe. But he's in a better place being "the guy" for what he does and having a circle of those that do similar things, as those lawyers get calls for what they don't do as well.

I know when you're young or just starting out in private practice you are hoping to keep the lights on, or the tall double-shot lattes flowing, but short-term thinking is for losers. Pick one or two practice areas, learn everything about them, and even when things are slow, consider that "I don't do that work" is the best thing you can say to a client if you're in this for the long term.

STRENGTHENING THE ATTORNEY/CLIENT RELATIONSHIP

Lawyers like to say, "I'm a lawyer, not a psychiatrist."

If you're dealing with people's problems, you're a lawyer *and* a psychiatrist. While clients understand you are the person hired to try and resolve their legal issues, the not-so-subtle secret of a successful practice is a slew of clients who believe their lawyer actually gives a crap about how their legal issues are affecting their personal life.

In a small-firm practice, you may be dealing with someone who just got served, or who is going through the anxiety of deciding whether to initiate litigation. Your client may be going through the stress of trying to buy a business, or asking you to split up his family. Someone else may be trying to get her spouse out of jail, while the person in jail is wondering about his future. The type of legal issues that we deal with in small law firms aren't whether a corporation will have to pay a million dollar fine or whether the bank will have to write off a loan—they're issues that cause people to lose sleep and sometimes just freak out.

And I know, I get the calls too. Clients want to talk about things that have nothing to do with the legal work I have to do. They ask the same questions that you can't answer: "When will this be over?" or "Do you think (this) will happen?" You're tired of telling the client, "I don't know, but just be patient." The client calls and says he "read" this, or "heard" this, or worse, "My friend had a case like this and . . . "

Sometimes I can't make the time to address these questions or concerns, and sometimes I'm dismissive. It's unavoidable. It's the middle of the day, the call comes in, you're busy, and playing psychiatrist isn't possible. However, I've learned that discussing the client's "feelings" and "thoughts" about the case or legal matter and how it's affecting their life, is required. Yes, you were paid to do a job; you weren't paid to hug your client or hold their hand, but that's why it's important for you to do just that—pay attention to the nonlegal issues facing your client.

The best way to deal with this is to make the time for it. At the initial consultation, after you've laid out all the non-legal issues, ask the client, "So how is all of this affecting you?" They'll talk about their spouse or their girlfriend, or their job, or their recent stint in rehab. More importantly, you'll establish that you're concerned with the full picture of the legal matter, not just what pleadings you have to file or what arguments you need to make. You can't control what happens in court or what the other side will do, but you can control how you relate to your client.

Make the time for it again. A few weeks into the attorney/client relationship, call the client in for a meeting to update them on the case and again ask a few personal questions. "How's your family dealing with this? Everything going well at work?" And hey, you Starbucks-dwelling virtual lawyers, you can do this too, right? Just e-mail your concerns, or better yet, Skype that concern right from your living room.

Some clients initially don't feel comfortable with these types of questions. They came to you for a legal issue, not to discuss their personal life. I've gotten responses like, "Why are you asking me this?" Push. As time goes on, the relationship will become more natural and the client will begin to bring things up without you asking. The attorney/client relationship goes beyond practicing law, and you need to let your clients know you understand that legal issues are more than just going to court or signing documents. Clients expect you to do your job, not to give a crap about them. So give a crap about them—*them*, not just their money or their legal issue.

DOES ANYONE WANT A MENTOR ANYMORE?

The ugly truth about the generational gap between those who claim the moniker of "Gen Y lawyer" and, well, everyone else, has been raging. While younger generations have always looked at their elders as stupid and not worth listening to, it has never been as much a part of the legal profession as it is now. The Gen Y cheerleading squad of lawyers and their marketers believe there actually is a revolution in the legal profession and that if those who have come before don't get with it and move their practices to the iPad, they (we) will go the way of the dinosaur.

They also think their elders want them to fail and are scared of them stealing our clients. I hate to break it to you kids, but I want you to succeed, and my clients aren't hiring you. They're not hiring your website or your Facebook fan page. Really, they're not.

While many Gen Y lawyers see the use for mentors, for the worst of Gen Y there is little room for the thought that they could learn something over a cup of coffee or an intelligent e-mail discourse with someone who's been practicing law longer than four minutes (and still practices). And so they continue to wonder why the few clients that call them for legal representation after seeing them on the first page of Google don't seem to have any money but "really like your website." Still, they hang on to the claims of their mentors, sorry, marketers, who tell them they are getting a lot of hits, and they hold out for the influx of great clients and great cases.

I believe their mentors, those they turn to for advice, those they respect, are the webmasters, the SEO hacks, the marketers—not lawyers, not those who came before them. When your practice is a website, an iPad, some videos, and a price list, why would you want to listen to someone with a bad website, no iPad, no videos, who still markets organically, through doing good work and developing relationships with real people? Those you listen to are telling you this is the future, and anyone that disagrees just needs to get on board. It's all a sham, created by those looking to sell you a future.

Futures are built, they are earned, and they are created through hard work. I don't care what year it is or what new technology or social media site is out, your future will never be something you can purchase from someone else. But I know, you analogize what I'm saying to asking for advice about managing money from your dad (who retired debt-free) instead of reading a few blog posts by a bunch of broke people who will thank you for retweeting their article.

I have mentors. They're mostly lawyers. One is in his 90s. The others have been practicing twice as long as me. They're never really nice to me, never that congratulatory. But they're always there to tell me they think my theory of a case is the dumbest thing they've ever heard or to shut up. They give advice like "you're dead wrong," and "is that a real question?" and "are you %&* kidding me?" Hugs and tissues are not part of the relationship. It's all about hearing about where they've been, where they've failed, and listening to how they became who they are. They know everything I'm doing, everything I've accomplished, but rarely say anything nice about any of it.

How did I meet them? In the courthouse. How did they become my mentors? Stalking.

I watched them work. I called them and said, "I'm a young lawyer in town and have a question." I went to places they went outside the courthouse. Initially, lunch wasn't attractive to them, but they returned calls and always said yes to "got a minute?" Of my five or so mentors, a couple of them routinely now call me for advice or thoughts, or to make sure I'm going to be at some event. Why? Because one, they're too smart to think they know everything (and they want to know if I've really been listening to them), and two, they're now a part of my life.

And I know, you have no courthouse to go to, you're a lawyer that works from a computer not far from your kitchen or barista. So what? You're telling me you don't know good lawyers in your community (your *offline* community) who could be mentors to you? You can't figure out where they hang out, where you can meet them, and how to attempt a relationship? Or is this just not your thing? Is it beyond you to contemplate that someone other than your brander, your webmaster, or your online coach could help you become the lawyer you want to be?

Maybe you should think about what kind of lawyer you want to be—whether you want to be like the well-respected ones in your community, or the ones with the great online presence. Maybe that answers your question.

BILL HODES SENDS AN E-MAIL ABOUT LAWYER ETHICS

Bill Hodes, former clerk to Justice Ruth Bader Ginsburg, a co-author of *The Law of Lawyering*, and a colleague of mine in the Association of Professional Responsibility Lawyers (APRL), gave me permission to post this slightly revised e-mail, which he posted to the APRL listserv:

Is our concern about the conduct of lawyers more properly thought of as a matter of ethics or a matter of morals?

I have always thought that many commentators have it exactly backwards as concerns the terminology to be used—while agreeing that terminology matters. Consider these four sentences, each of which I believe to be correct.

1. In the 1950s and 60s, before the Supreme Court decided the *Bates* case, it was almost universally accepted that lawyer advertising was unethical.
2. In the 1950s and 60s, before the Supreme Court decided the *Bates* case, virtually no one thought that lawyer advertising was immoral.
3. Virtually all lawyers agree that it is perfectly ethical to secure the acquittal of a defendant who is known (to the lawyer) to be factually guilty, by employing technical and tactical moves that do not involve lying.
4. Many lawyers have moral qualms about securing the acquittal of a defendant under the above circumstances.

To me, this means that the term "ethical" is best understood as "comporting with professional ethics norms," whether in law or journalism or the profession of arms. The term "moral," on the other hand, applies to human conduct generally, and asks whether the conduct is "right" or "wrong," according to some coherent system of distinguishing between the two. (And I am not a moral relativist; some moral schemes are so deeply flawed as to be immoral themselves.)

It wouldn't bother me to add the reminder—often or even always—that when we are speaking of "ethics," we are speaking of "professional" ethics. And I do not tarry long on the enforceability issue either. In my view, the ABA Model Rules are not "law," and not enforceable as such, but when the highest court in a jurisdiction adopts a Code or a set of Rules along the same lines, those are the law of the jurisdiction, and they are enforceable if the REQUISITE "shall or shall not" language is present. Rules of morality, on the other hand, are enforced only by peer pressure, community shaming, and—most of all, I hope—by the drive for self-respect. (Along the same lines, the Restatement of the Law Governing Lawyers is not "the law" either, but many of its tenets are adopted as the common law of many jurisdictions, in which case they become enforceable in the courts of those jurisdictions.)

I think we can and must teach the content of the rules of professional ethics to young lawyers, and also the common law and fiduciary principles that will govern their lives as lawyers. Moral values can be inculcated, perhaps, but not taught, other than by example and seriousness of purpose. But I agree most of all that all lawyers should conduct themselves in accord with the ethics of our profession, because that is the right thing to do!

WHEN IT COSTS YOU TO BE HONEST

He came to the office wanting only one thing: to clear his name by fighting the accusations. They were accusations that were currently civil (and very public) in nature, but could become criminal and administrative. He got my name, and he brought his file and his checkbook. He had his assignment for me, and just wanted a pen.

There was nothing I needed to do. No selling of my qualifications, no answering questions about what I think about other lawyers, no Internet marketer to thank. He checked me out, was told the possible amount of fees, and made his decision before walking in the door.

I read his documents, asked a few questions, noted a few things I saw, and then told him he was going to get destroyed in this case. I explained not only the legal aspects of his case, but the consequences of fighting and losing. I also explained his other options based on things he wanted to do, and why I thought there was another way to go that would put him in a better position to avoid other issues that would surely arise.

He wanted to continue talking.

You may be thinking this is pretty obvious. This is what lawyers do— they give advice to potential clients on the risks and possibilities and let the client make the decision. But we know that's not true.

When a client comes in, especially with money, we want the case. Just admit it. If not you, the client is going to hire someone else, so why not just passively nod your head, agree with the client on everything, and say all the right things? You're here to make a living, and the client wants a lawyer.

But our best work is in being honest with potential clients, even against our financial interest. We live in a world where we have to earn any bit of respect we get from the public. They expect us to be manipulative, lying, greedy people. When we resist taking their money, or suggest options that are the right ones to take (and at serious cost savings) they are shocked. By telling them their perception of how things work is wrong, and using any experience we have to provide other options—especially when it's not in our financial interest—we gain a trust that can only serve as a benefit in the long term.

We finally got to the fee discussion. I told him the estimated fee to fight and the one to resolve the matter. The fee to resolve the case would be about 70 percent less. After the meeting, the potential client called the referral source, not just to say thank you, but to tell the story.

In the end, this client could do what he wanted. He knew what he wanted to do, and what he was advised to do. What he realized is that what he really wanted was a lawyer who would give him good advice, even at the lawyer's expense.

I sense I'll make up that 70 percent somewhere.

CREATING TIME

The ethics rules make us lawyers 24 hours a day. Lawyers are not only disciplined for what they do with clients, but what they do in business, at restaurants, or while driving cars. Knowing that we have to behave at all times doesn't mean we can never take a break from practicing law. There is time for everything.

There is nothing more important to lawyers than time. Time spent on cases (especially if you're trying to win the most billable hours contest award at your funeral), time in the day to do everything, time to enjoy the fruits of your labor. Everything comes down to time. The reason you don't do certain things is because you claim to have no time.

Lawyers base their entire lives on time. Many try to figure out the latest time they can roll out of bed to be on time to the office or court. We live on deadlines. We appear in court when told, file documents on certain dates (or fax them on certain dates at 4:59), and we set appointments for things. There are other things we want to do, other things we need to do, but we use the excuse of "no time" as a crutch.

The truth is, we have plenty of time, we just don't use it well. We let our practices control us, instead of trying to control our practices. Clients and cases will run your life, if you let them. Some lawyers believe the essence of being a lawyer is letting clients run their lives, that we must let clients know we are available 24/7. You can call me 24/7, but I'm no longer answering the phone when I'm doing something I consider more important than making money. Things I consider more important than making more money include sleeping, being with my family, and about 400 other things.

I know, I may miss the big case or piss off a client. I don't care. I have a life, you should get one too. Sometimes getting a life as a small-law lawyer takes time, because when you're young, building a practice requires your constant availability. After a while, if the client is going to go down the street because you didn't call him back in 23 seconds, you learn to appreciate that this type of client would suck anyway. If you work for someone who believes you should have no life, you should get a new one—a new boss that is.

You need to take control of your time. As time goes on, you either want to or are asked to do other things: network, join bar associations, fire the marketer and actually write your own crap on the Internet, play with your kids (those little people tugging at your dress shirt), or spend less time anonymously commenting on blogs about your misery and actually talk to your significant other. But you use the "have no time" excuse every time.

This is my advice for those who think they have no time. It may work for you, it may not. Your life may not be as wonderful and fulfilling as mine, your spouse and family may not want you around more because you're such a miserable human being, and maybe all you want to do is play civil discovery all your life. I can only tell you what works for me.

LOSERS WAKE UP AT THE SOUND OF THE BEGINNING OF *THE TODAY SHOW*

There is nothing like 5:30 a.m., especially if you're married with kids. The dog even gives you the half-nod and goes back to sleep. You want to write, read, think, prepare, I give you those precious moments before "Mommy, where's my pink bow?" starts. (I have daughters.) Even if you're single or don't have kids, you know as a lawyer that waking up well before the start of e-mails and phone calls is the best way to beat the man. It also gives you an extra hour or so that you can have later in the day to do something you want to do. Working without e-mail dings or phone calls makes an hour seem like three (and that's awesome for those who like to fraudulently bill).

TV MAKES YOU STUPID

I don't watch much TV. I'll catch some sports and news, an occasional documentary, and sometimes an episode of *Pawn Stars* (I think I relate to the old man). But I've never watched *The Sopranos*, or the other 45 HBO series. I couldn't tell you what's on at 9 p.m. on Wednesdays, and I'm the guy who walks away from the staff chat in the kitchen when the "Did you see _____ last night?" conversation starts. Apparently I'm missing out on life by not watching *Mad Men*.

You all are addicted to mindless television. You are wasting your time watching this crap. Some of you could retire if you could bill for the TV shows you watch routinely every week. Maybe spend that time working, or going to a networking event or bar association committee meeting, or have a conversation with a real person. When you get old you can sit around and watch TV and not talk to anyone. If you can't get away from this garbage, DVR it. That will guarantee you'll never watch it.

TAKE A BREAK (A REAL ONE) FROM WORK, EVERY WEEK

I take Friday nights off to be with my family. I started doing this a couple years ago. Yeah, it's the Sabbath, but that's not the reason (sorry fellow Jews). It's the end of the week. I'm done. I don't go to any events unless they are essential, like a good friend getting an award, or some other obligatory event, and I don't make plans that don't involve my family. Phone calls and e-mails get returned Saturday.

Maybe Friday night doesn't work for you. It's OK, there are six other choices. Pick one. You lawyers that think there is a badge of honor for working every night and on the weekends probably also know which episode of *Game of Thrones* you've missed.

Be efficient, take control, and you'll have the time to do the things you want and need to do. I understand to many of you this sounds impossible because you work for miserable, lifeless people, and accept every bad client that walks in the door because they have a few bucks, but hey, I can't fix stupid.

WHAT (SOME) CLIENTS WANT IN A LAWYER

The question of what makes a good lawyer is answered much like asking "What is art?"—it's in the eyes of the beholder. Is a good lawyer one who wins a case? One who takes the time to explain the most mundane legal proceedings? One who spends years fighting for one client's innocence? One who handles traffic tickets on a daily basis and gets most of them dismissed? The answer is yes, to all of them. Conversely, one can say that a lawyer who wins a case but is abusive to opposing counsel or fails to be "nice" to the client is not a good lawyer. Plenty of good lawyers are those who the client would never recommend.

My friend Lee Rosen asked in a post why some crappy lawyers have happy clients?[3] Lee says he knows one personally:

> She's a terrible lawyer. She can't read and understand a court opinion. She misreads statutes. She's an embarrassment in court. Her pleadings are poorly drafted. Her correspondence is filled with errors. She says things in chambers that make her look like an idiot. Her objections are overruled. Her court appearances are dominated by illogical arguments.
>
> Her clients, however, love her. They refer business to her like crazy. She spends nearly nothing on marketing and is making a freaking fortune. She can't see a new client for weeks because she is solidly booked.

He wants to know how it is that she's so crappy, yet seemingly so successful?

I know lawyers like this. We all do. One lawyer I know has been sanctioned by the bar several times. Judges don't like this lawyer. Lawyers don't like this lawyer. This lawyer's name is used to describe bad behavior.

He's got tons of clients. They love him.

Here is Lee's correct analysis:

Here's the deal. She does things that make it clear that she cares about her clients. She rants and raves in court, like a maniac, on behalf of her clients. She crosses over every line and gets personally involved with her clients. She laughs with her clients, she cries with her clients. She returns calls, she calls at night, she stays on the phone forever. She loves her clients and it shows. She knows it and her clients know it. She'd do anything to help them. They are her friends.

Her clients love her. They love her when she wins, they love her when she loses. They know she's committed to their cause. They know she did her best, even when her best isn't good enough.

Recently a client called to say he was hiring another lawyer. I asked why. "The other lawyer we met with (practicing less than half as long as me) told us about all his results including that he recently won a case involving a friend of ours."

Oh well. Hope he's on one of those rare winning streaks.

We all know that clients hire lawyers for the strangest reasons. One thing the lawyer says or does can determine the client's happiness with the lawyer. In criminal practice, we experience the difference between the client who barely shakes your hand when you win his case, and the client who hugs you after you lose his case and before he's shipped off to jail.

The definition of a crappy lawyer from a client's perspective is completely different from that within the profession. Lee asks the important question:

It all makes me wonder whether she's really a crappy lawyer or whether I have ideas about what's important that might be irrelevant. Who sets the standard for crappy? Lawyers or clients? Maybe my idea of crappy doesn't really matter?

Maybe.

LAWYERS: IN THIS ECONOMY, BE AS SMART AS YOU THINK YOU ARE

Every once in a while it's time to go back to basics. Update your website all you want, refine your retainer agreements, firm up your initial consultation speech to potential clients, make sure you have collar stays (I'm big on collar stays). But remember, the basics will always matter.

In this economy there are some things that lawyers need to consider. I say what I am about to say from recent experience:

1. **Please don't take on matters in areas in which you have no working knowledge of the law.** Lines of credit are for paying rent in slow times, not taking cases in areas you have no idea how to practice.
2. **That money in the trust account is not yours.** There is no "borrowing" the money for a little while.
3. **That settlement you received is not totally yours, no matter what you consider "costs."** This is not a time to get creative with documents you send to your clients.
4. **The flat-fee retainer agreement you signed is a contract.** Honor your contract. You may not have as much money right now, but you do have your reputation. You'll have money again, but that won't buy your reputation back.

Just some thoughts from some conversations I've had recently.

THE DANGER AND PLEASURE OF A NICHE PRACTICE

If there is one theory I've developed as a lawyer, it's that there is no greater road to success than a niche practice. This should be obvious, but I still see so many lawyers who claim to have seven different practice areas and wonder why they're always broke. The legal profession is much like the medical profession. Being a general practitioner will bring in a nice flow of clients with different problems. Being a doctor who only handles pediatric heart issues creates a high demand for specialized services, higher rates, and allows that doctor to concentrate on one area of medicine. Sure, it takes time to become proficient in that one area, but the rewards are much greater.

A few years ago I was introduced to an intellectual property (IP) lawyer. Yawn. Another IP lawyer churning out trademark and copyright applications. Meeting one of them these days is no different than going to a lawyer cocktail hour and meeting yet another commercial litigator. But I quickly saw in his e-mail that this wasn't just another IP lawyer:

> My area of practice is intellectual property, but with a twist: I represent technology companies in transactions involving the licensure, commercial exploitation and/or research & development of technologies—that is about 50% of my practice. The other 50% is representing digital marketing agencies, digital production companies, and related businesses in all of their IP and corporate needs. I handle a great deal of work in the area of data privacy rules & regulations, compliance with FTC rules for digital advertising, and matters involving outsourced technology transactions.

Interesting. The next step was to meet this guy face to face, mainly so I could understand what that e-mail said. I realize he doesn't want referrals from every guy in a garage with the next great invention, but although I think I know, I want to learn how and from where he gets his referrals, and how he built his practice.

There has been a lot written about niche practices. A lot of it has been written by nonpracticing lawyers, or those with a niche that they've had for five minutes. Although today's kids would rather hear from those idiots than someone who has been doing it themselves for a while, I'll do what I do every week, and offer some advice that may make you less miserable, and cause you to think differently about your practice.

So you're out there scrapping along as just another lawyer practicing commercial lit, or real estate, or another general area of law. It seemed like a good idea at the time, but like the medical profession, it's the specialists, those who do what most others don't do, that can find themselves in demand, enjoying the practice more, and becoming a good referral source for the masses.

A *niche* is two different things. It's either a type of practice that most lawyers don't do, or a reputation in a typical practice area that makes you "the man" (no sexism intended) in that discipline. Examples? I know two lawyers that handle liquor licenses. I know one lawyer that represents pharmacists. I know one lawyer who represents doctors in the sale and purchase of medical practices and facilities. I know one lawyer who represents gays and lesbians in domestic matters.

If you're out there trying to build a practice as a generalist, the only way you will do that is by undercutting your competition (unless you want to do one of those old-school, non-Internet things and try to build a practice by doing outstanding work that gets noticed). As a niche practitioner, you can charge more, know more about a particular area of practice, and watch your generalist friends try unsuccessfully to differentiate themselves with the same marketing buzzwords everyone else uses.

To do this, you must give back.

I wound up having lunch with my new IP lawyer friend, who told me that he gets calls for all kinds of IP work, but he refers even matters he can handle out to other IP lawyers so that he can receive referrals from them for the areas in which he concentrates. If you want to build a niche in your general practice area, be prepared to give business away. (Yes, I just said that.) But don't think having a niche practice will cause you to always be in demand. One of the dangers is if no one knows or understands what you do. I've read that marketing in a niche practice is easier. I disagree. It's harder. You must constantly be reminding other lawyers what you do—through advertising, speaking, writing, and networking. Otherwise, you'll be receiving apology after apology for that case that went elsewhere because "I didn't know you did that type of work."

The perfect niche practice combination is having that narrow practice area where you become "the man." That's when it all comes together, and you can stop doing stupid things like giving free consultations and negotiating fees. But it takes time. It doesn't happen overnight, and it requires your willingness to spread the wealth.

Sorry to disappoint.

WHERE HAVE ALL THE LAWYERS GONE?

I once wrote about a lawyer who wanted to create a civil practice partly by gaining experience with criminal defendants. Of course, I wasn't nice about it. The comments were mostly that I was "mean." The thank you came from the young lawyer to whom the post was directed.

He had sent his e-mail requesting criminal cases to 4,000 people. I was supposed to be sensitive to this generation's goal of coddling, being nice, not ruffling feathers, giving hugs, and making sure everyone is happy. The desire for mentors—real mentors who will tell it like it is—is almost gone. The 50 or so comments convinced me of this. Few of today's young lawyers want mentors; they are more concerned about whether someone is being "mean" than whether they are being honest, although there are still some young lawyers who don't mind being told they are not as cute as everyone on their listserv is telling them.

Here is a sampling of what lawyers, yes, lawyers, had to say to me:

Are you just looking for content for your blog?

Unfortunately, many people on the list spent far more time taking this lawyer to task for seeking advice than actually trying to help him out.

You posted a highly critical and demeaning attack on another lawyer, and you didn't bother to contact that lawyer to get his perspective. That's not fair. In fact, it's just plain wrong.

I think you have done the profession a disservice in this post.

And from the lawyer who was the subject of the post?

Brian, and everyone else, I will take your advice. It is not lost on deaf ears . . . I do not agree with everything that has been said, but I wanted you all to understand that I am listening instead of tuning you out. My defensiveness was instinctual, but it's not the end all be all of my personality. I will learn, because I must. I'm not a fan of hard knocks, but sometimes they are necessary.

I became a lawyer to be an advocate. When I graduated, I started advocating. After a few years of learning, I thought I'd try to earn a living from what I learned, all the while continuing to learn. The Internet was nothing. It was all about the yellow pages. We were told that to get business you had to meet people, do a good job, and build a reputation. Some decided to avoid all that by renting billboards, buying the back cover of the yellow pages, sending mailers, and anything else that would yell "HIRE ME." And hire they did. Most prospective clients are looking for a lawyer, any lawyer. The key for me was to be a lawyer for those clients looking for a certain type of lawyer. It was hard. I didn't have 12 people in my lobby waiting to write me $500 checks. I was looking for that one client a week.

Today the path is graduate, open a Twitter account and Facebook fan page, buy an iPad, buy a newer iPad, stand in line for yet a newer iPad, hire an SEO guy to get you to the first page of Google, and fake it 'til you make it. The marketers will say that they will only market for competent lawyers, but the truth is that with few exceptions, most of them will market for anyone with a dollar. And it's not confined to young lawyers. Biglaw is so desperate to market themselves that they'll talk to a six-month, no-longer-practicing lawyer because he claims to be able to teach them how to be rainmakers by using social media. He never made rain as a lawyer, but no one seems to care. It's all about the sales job. This is why lawyers are the number one group of people scammed by these Nigerian e-mails. We're so desperate for money we'll listen to anyone who mentions the word.

The rush to the marketing table is like the running of the bulls. Run fast or die, they say.

I don't run very fast, and I don't see any bulls behind me. I've taken some great advice over the years, and kept my eye on the goal of building a practice of which I could be proud, regardless of what others think. Today, though, building a practice is nothing more than collecting dollars. Sure, there are those who want to become respected advocates of the bar. But so many are merely running in the direction of anyone who will tell them how to game the Internet, and nowhere else. When I tell young lawyers to join their local Rotary, sponsor charity events, go out and meet people, I hear "How will that make me money?" or "How will that affect my Internet presence?"

Where have all the lawyers gone? Where are the new, up-and-coming lawyers who laugh at the social media consultants, envision a practice of clients and cases and research and advocacy, desire the respect of their peers, author articles on key legal issues, and have speaking engagements at real legal conferences? Where have all the lawyers gone who are less interested in collecting those clients looking for lawyers on the Internet, and more interested in collecting clients looking for good lawyers through referrals? Are they on listservs speaking their minds about the state of the profession, or are they more concerned about whether some other lawyer may call them a "meanie"?

CHAPTER 2

WHAT IS THE FUTURE OF LAW?

THE FUTURE OF LAW IS OFFICIALLY A JOKE

One thing that has irked me over the past few years is this notion of "the future of law." We are all told we're doing it wrong and that if we don't "get on board" with what the future will bring, we will die as lawyers. The problem is that when you look behind the advice and fearmongering, the "law futurists" are mostly unemployed and failed lawyers who want to convince us that they know how it will be, soon.

I don't care how things will be in the future. I care how they are now. If there is a new shiny toy that comes out that I need to have, I'll take a look at it. If there is a better way to do something I'm doing, I'll look into it. I still believe though, that relationships drive business, and that there will always be clients looking for lawyers. To those that think the future of the profession is solely based on a computer and buying legal forms, I wish you the best of luck.

There is a notion (held mostly by the unemployed and unhappy people) that I may be the only person writing about the possibility that the Internet and those that "sell" the Internet to lawyers, as well as this notion of "branding" and spending your day reading self-fulfilling predictions on "the future of law" from the losers of our profession is, well, maybe not the be-all and end-all in the practice of law.

Sometimes I think maybe I'm wrong (no I don't). Maybe the goal of all lawyers should be to be first on Google; maybe these LinkedIn endorsements will result in something, anything. Maybe I do need to pay some 28-year-old former lawyer to teach me how to use the Internet. Maybe I'm not using Facebook in a way that will get high-net-worth clients calling my office every day. Maybe instead of building a practice by doing well for clients, I need to be a brand like Coca-Cola or Amazon.com. There is a reason all these future-of-law people have an effect on lawyers: Lawyers want to make money. Lawyers want to believe. We want to continue to hope that what we convinced ourselves of is true—that a law degree is a ticket to wealth and fame. If it's not happening for us, we will seek out those that say we're doing it wrong, and for a fee, they can make everything peachy.

It's no different from the late-night infomercials from the 1980s promising a real estate empire with no money down. We like to listen to, and pay, those that make us believe they can make our lives better. And we don't even ask questions like "How long did you practice law?" or "Can I have five references?" This is from the horse's mouth: a marketer told me once that there are no easier clients to obtain than lawyers—they don't ask questions.

In fact, there was a webinar for lawyers about how to make oodles of money. It was hosted by a former practicing lawyer whose efforts to make money teaching lawyers how to make money resulted in bankruptcy and financial disaster.

Dozens signed up.

Because of this, I'm considering a webinar on how to be tall and Catholic, just to see the numbers of registered lawyers.

Shame on our profession.

But all is not lost. Others have noted the joke that we have made of our profession. This silly notion that success in the law doesn't come from good legal work, but from being able to obtain a volume of calls from a fake presence, a creation of a "brand," and trying very, very hard to get our hand to the top of the baseball bat of the Internet. Sure, the Internet is a great resource for connections and information, but those that sit at their kitchen table and try to sell to lawyers can only do so through the Internet. They have no other way to communicate, get business, and work—and their goal is to convince you of the same.

And so here it is. The Internet, the place I often write about, has taken note of the same idiots you pray to as shepherds of numerous and high-paying clients. All this stuff made me laugh, as good jokes do. What makes me laugh harder, almost to the point of tears, is when I get an e-mail from a young lawyer sheepishly admitting they've wasted their money on all this crap—and it has resulted in nothing but a dwindling bank account.

At least now you can laugh about it, and I won't be the only one.

WHAT MAKES YOU MORE MONEY, THE PAST OR THE FUTURE?

Two factions of the legal profession seem louder than the others: those wallowing in the past, the ones spending their days blaming their law schools for forcing them to attend based on the promises of wealth and happiness, and those predicting the future of law, who want you to believe that if you know now how the practice will be 10 or 20 or 500 years from now, it will help you today. So tell me, which one has helped build your practice: whining about the past, or thinking about how things may be in the future?

I like to live in the present, while remembering the mistakes of my past and knowing that the future will eventually be here, and I may not. But when I talk about the present, how I do things, and how people I respect do things, I often hear that those things don't work anymore. You haven't tried those things, but because someone you don't know seems to have the best crystal ball (at a reasonable price), they know better. Most of you are looking to make money now, not in "the future of law," and knowing that in reality, bitching about the past does nothing—even if you are delusional enough to think anyone cares.

I don't have the ability to tell you how you will make money when "the future of law" is here. I can predict that on that day, other people will be right there to tell you about the "new" future of law. I know that in the future there will be more things and more other things and new and cool things. If you want to make money now, and you're too stupid to realize that there are plenty of ways to make money outside the law, the first thing I'd do is learn something.

I know, you're thinking, "But I have allowed the world to convince me that all I need is a law degree from my awesome school, stellar grades, and bar admission." Right, and where has this gotten you? Learn how to do something people need. No, don't wait for someone to pay you what you think you deserve to do legal work—learn how to take a matter from start to finish. People need wills, they need counsel in simple divorces, they get traffic tickets. I know that all of this is beneath you, but for those of you whose egos aren't in the stratosphere and understand that doing small things for people leads to big matters, I offer this advice.

Maybe if you learn something, then when you're on that interview you finally got after sending out 300 résumés, you can tell the hiring partner that you've actually done something relevant other than try to convince others not to go to law school because yours lied to you.

Now I understand Biglaw won't be impressed, and they'll actually be petrified that you've had client contact. This advice is more for the people looking to actually practice law, not those looking for a closet to sit in while "earning" their $100K. Small firms and solos looking to hire will be more apt to take a second look at someone who has actually given legal advice, walked into a courtroom, drafted a document, taken a call from an angry client, and quoted a fee (even if it's $100 because the Starbucks card was out of cash).

So where do you learn? Your state bar has plenty of basic CLE seminars out there, and I know, they cost money you don't have. There is always an excuse. Start a fund, order the tapes instead of attending, see what's free out there. Maybe read the statutes and rules of procedure (I'm just kidding). Just please don't waste your money paying for some online snake oil.

If I were sitting across from a potential associate, I'd much rather hear that they were doing something, than nothing. "Well, Mr. Tannebaum, I'm still pretty angry at my law school, so I spend most of my day anonymously commenting on blogs hoping to convince people not to go to law school, and I also hear that in 25 years I can practice from my toilet, so I'm waiting for that as well."

If you're going to take my advice and learn something, remember, the key is to be competent. If you don't feel comfortable doing the legal work, get someone to help you. The estate planning lawyer you call to help you with a simple will may be looking for an associate or at least someone to send business she doesn't want. No reason to be telling the state bar at 26 years old why you screwed up the client's case so badly.

This notion that the past and the future are things we should be spending a lot of time reading and thinking about is just garbage. No new advancement in tech or the way people hire lawyers is going to change the fact that people will always be looking for good lawyers to do needed legal work. Neither your horrible, mean, lying law school nor what may happen in the future is going to put money in your pocket now. Knowing how to help a client will.

Or you can sit around and complain and wait for the future. You probably know what's best for you.

RIP: THE END OF THE LAW FUTURIST

There is that old adage that if you say something enough times, you actually believe it to be true, even if it isn't true. This is part of my issue with the law futurists. The mostly no-longer-practicing or never-practiced, pound their keyboards daily trying to convince those of us that actually do have clients that we need to be scared, very scared. Everything around us is seemingly changing, and as the phrase goes that inspired my bio on *Above the Law*, if we don't get on board immediately, it's all over and we may tragically end up also pounding keyboards telling practicing lawyers that the future is coming tomorrow and they better be prepared.

Canadian Jordan Furlong writes at Law21[4] and is someone I call a law futurist. His bio says the same thing, just in more words:

> Jordan Furlong delivers dynamic and thought-provoking pre-
> sentations to law firms and legal organizations throughout North
> America on how to survive and profit from the extraordinary changes
> underway in the legal services marketplace. He is a partner with
> Edge International and a senior consultant with Stem Legal Web
> Enterprises.

Jordan is also a lawyer, although his bio reflects no actual current law practice.

I've never spoken with Jordan because I'm one of those people who doesn't have good, happy conversations with the cheerleading world of law futurists. I'm a mean troll, bully, buzzkill. I'm sure Jordan is a great guy, and I see people on the Internet smiling at many of his thoughts, but I'm a bit of a skeptic when nonpracticing lawyers try to convince those that do, that we are doing it wrong and, for a fee, the answers are nearby.

Jordan took a survey. Only 73 people responded, but the results were . . . well . . . probably not what the law futurist world wanted to hear, and probably why I didn't see much about it on the Internet. The law futurist world scatters when dissension appears—it's not good for business, and it makes the futurists sad. Still, I credit Jordan. Even though what people actually think about the nonexistent "future of law" that I've written about is not the same as the nonpracticing futurists want it to be, Jordan published the results.

Jordan's survey[5] asked people to prioritize a "future legal survival kit." Note, the question is related not to what lawyers need now, but in the future. You know, the big, scary lawyer future train we all need to get on board.

The results?

1. Strategic placement online including mobile apps, websites, and social media.
2. Tablet devices.
3. The cloud.

No, wait, sorry. The real results, in order of priority:

1. Emotional intelligence that fosters *great relationships*, especially with clients.
2. *Connections*: Strong and productive relationships with clients in your chosen field.
3. Moral fibre: You're renowned for *strength of character* and high levels of *integrity*.
4. Legal knowledge: Good old-fashioned *legal know-how*.

Wow. Bummer.

By the way, before you unemployed top 10 percent folks start telling me that "fibre" is spelled "fiber," in deference to Jordan and all my close personal Canadian friends, the word is spelled "fiber" in America and "fibre" in Canada. It will remain as written in the original post to avoid any international incidents.

Anyway.

"Old-fashioned"? Future?

I know you're thinking, "In what aisle at Best Buy can I find these?" and "Which SEO spam specialist offers these services?" I actually feel bad. It's much easier for law futurists to scream about how "you must use the cloud," or "it's your website that's the problem," or "having an office is a bad thing," than to say that "you must be able to connect with your clients on an emotional level, have strong and productive relationships with those clients, have a reputation for strength of character and high levels of integrity, and know the law."

Kind of boring, huh? The future sounds suspiciously just like the past, and the present. Sounds like what that dinosaur Tannebaum is always bitching about. Wait 'til the futurists convince him otherwise.

Where was tech knowledge? Must have been right below these, right?

10th.

Branding?

Last.

Jordan acknowledges the issue: "I can't help but observe that if I had asked for the top five features of a traditional law practice in the halcyon bygone days of the profession, I would have wound up with a very similar list."

I know Jordan, but that's not what you asked. You wanted to know what was thought to be the most important priorities in a "survival kit," for lawyers to survive in the future. That's what you asked. So what does a law futurist do when the answers reflect that this whole "future of law" consulting gig may not be the future? Explain away the results by questioning the readers and assuming their motives:

> This isn't to say that Law21 readers are reactionary conservatives, which I'm pretty sure you're not. More likely, it represents a yearning for the future profession to return to the fundamental bedrock values that we perceive underlay the successful law practices of our parents' and even grandparents' generations.

Um, Jordan, these are bedrock values that lawyers believe underlay the successful law practices not only of our parents and grandparents, but of today, and the future. The problem with the survey results is that they absolutely kill the entire law futurist industry. The law futurist industry just got told that the future looks much like today and that the sales job isn't working.

Things are changing. We have cell phones and can access the Internet anywhere. We can advertise on hundreds of different mediums. We can read a document without actually having the document. When we look at the top four survival kit items, none of that matters. I think the law futurists should just accept this and go get a real job. But Jordan continues to pretend that this survey is simply a misunderstanding of the absolute all-important necessity of the law futurist:

> However much we may wish for a return to the old days (and they weren't wholly fabulous, let's keep in mind), they're not coming back. We can't simply revisit the past to build the future: the architecture of legal practice has to adapt.

I understand, the law futurists were wounded by the survey. The results weren't what they were supposed to be, and the lawyers obviously don't get it. Law futurists have no clue how to sell to lawyers the items of integrity or legal knowledge or the ability to connect with a client. If the law futurists can't sell it, then it's not something lawyers should prioritize.

While Jordan expresses his approval that emotional intelligence and moral fibre were rated so high, he thinks we're just wrong about connections, and gives it his own rating—zero:

> I can see the desirability of having strong relationships in place to help jump-start a future law practice. But to my way of thinking, this is a secondary characteristic, one that I can develop if I have many of the other listed skills and assets. My zero doesn't suggest that I think this trait is worthless; it's simply that I value other things more.

I know Jordan, but your way of thinking apparently is in the minority. Apparently, real actual live lawyers think differently. That's your customer base—something to consider when trying to convince others what the future holds.

And here is where you should realize that the law futurists' view of our profession is pretty scary.

Jordan gives legal knowledge a zero. His reasons?

Again, it's not that I believe legal know-how has no value in a law practice; obviously it does. But I don't need to personally possess this feature or have it in place, in-house, in my practice. Legal knowledge is now widespread and easily accessible, and its price keeps dropping. I can outsource this asset, retrieve it when and from whom I need it, and build up other resources instead.

Yeah, he said that.

I assume Jordan is referring to case law and statutes, which have been available online for a while now. Before that, you could buy books or go to a library. I assume he means that I just need a Westlaw or Lexis account. I assume he means that I as the lawyer don't really need to know the law as I can just look it up . . . as I always could.

But "I don't need to personally possess this feature or have it in place, in-house, in my practice?" What the hell are you talking about? Now I understand this comes from someone that doesn't practice law, but what benefit is it to the client to ask a lawyer a legal question if the lawyer says 100 percent of the time, "I don't know, but I know where I can find out"? When so-called consultants to the profession start saying that knowledge of the law is not important, all of us who actually believe this is a profession should stop listening.

That is, if you ever actually did listen to any of it.

I'm encouraged by the survey results, and not at all surprised that they are not what the futurists need to keep the lights on. So rest in peace law futurists. Unfortunately, those that belong in the legal profession appear to be ready.

THE TECHNOLOGY CURMUDGEON GIVES HIS TECHNOLOGY SECRETS

I remember when the iPad was released. It's this generation's version of remembering when Kennedy was assassinated, or the *Challenger* explosion. This was Apple's equivalent of Sony releasing a 52-inch TV when the only one available was 20 inches. The iPad is nothing more than a big iPhone with a few more features, will not cure cancer, clean the house, or get lawyers clients, but man did it make a splash. I remember seeing people online live-tweeting the wait for the UPS guy to deliver their dream toy.

Tech geeks everywhere were hysterical. Prior to the release, bloggers were bold enough, as they always are whenever Apple farts, to say that the iPad would change the world. After it was released, techys on Twitter went bonkers. It was, in a word, pathetic. All of this inspired me to finally disclose how technology works in my practice. See, there are folks out there who want to convince you that technology is what makes you a better lawyer.

It isn't. It never will be.

It may make your life easier, but it will never make you a better lawyer. Sorry to blow the fallacy and bullshit that gives tech-for-lawyer folks credibility. Now back to me, and how technology works in my practice.

First, I have an office. A real office where I pay rent, have a reception area, a receptionist, a secretary, a conference room, and yes, even a kitchen. The tech-for-lawyers crowd is mostly geared toward lawyers who have no office, save for an available seat at a local Starbucks with free Wi-Fi.

In my office is a telephone. My receptionist also has one. So do the other lawyers in my office and the other support staff. This is how clients normally reach me. In a very non-techy way, my clients, mostly lawyers, law students, and alleged criminals, like to be pretty traditional and come to my office and meet with me. They're not real big on video conferencing, e-mail, or Starbucks.

The phone has voice mail for after-hours calls. If the client wants to press "9," the call will transfer to my cell phone. All messages left on my cell phone are transcribed to text and e-mailed to me. In turn, when I am in court, a meeting, a deposition, or otherwise cannot listen to a voice mail or return a call, I can reply to the message via e-mail or text.

My cell phone. It was a Blackberry, now it's an Android. When a new one is released, I get it immediately. I don't blog about it, tweet hysterically about it, nor will I ever wait in line for one. I call AT&T and have it sent to me. It's all very quiet. My Android has a personal enterprise server for which I pay an additional $30 a month. This allows all e-mails, contacts, and calendar items to wirelessly sync with my office. It allows my receptionist and secretary to input and delete calendar items, and for me to do the same, and have it appear instantaneously on everyone's desktop and my Android.

My office desktop is my laptop, and it is connected to a docking station. In the office I have two monitors: one for documents and one for the Internet. Most "real" lawyers walk in my office and think that having two monitors is the most advanced thing they've ever seen.

All documents received in my office relating to client files are scanned into a client directory. Most other mail is thrown out, as it is largely from others who believe they can make me a better lawyer by selling me something. When I am not in the office, I can sign in to my office server from my laptop and access all of my client's documents.

In watching the release of the iPad, I've heard tons about what games it has, how you can read Kindle books, and how it can download Netflix movies. I'm sure the iPad has uses for real lawyers in real situations, but the hysterics over its release have nothing to do with the practice of law. It's all about the new toy, and the kids who are enamored with something new to play with. So here's a challenge: read this post, envision my practice, and tell me how the iPad will significantly change how I practice law.

I'm waiting.

A NOTE ABOUT THE IPAD

When the iPad came out, legal technologists did what they always do to try and appear relevant—they went crazy. If you don't read anything written by legal technologists, let me summarize: (1) New shiny toy or software or app comes out. (2) Legal technologist feverishly writes that it's a "game changer" for lawyers. Although anytime a new Apple product comes out it creates a feverish vibe, bringing unemployed lawyers and other mommy's-basement-dwellers and their lawn chairs and tents to Apple stores everywhere, the iPad, nothing more than a big iPhone, was different. Books would be written and CLE seminars for which no state bar would ever consider giving CLE credits—"iPad for Lawyers," or "How Lawyers Can Use an iPad," or "Using the iPad, for Lawyers"—sprouted up all over the country. We were all told we had to have one because . . . because.

I, hoping it wasn't true that the legal technologists trying hard to find a way to make a living telling everyone that law practices would "die" without one, ignored the hype and continued to try and get by with a laptop. I first saw an iPad in court when a lawyer showed me his and said, "Look, you can watch movies on it." Having never had the thought of watching a movie in court, I didn't see the urgency to get one. Plus, of course, I hate technology. Hate it.

Three years and a couple hundred clients later, I asked my daughter if the iPad 2 sitting in her room collecting dust was available for daddy to use. It was time to see the miracles that would come my way by carrying around a big iPhone with a pink cover. I first deleted about 100 game apps. Then I added a PDF reader app, another app to sign PDFs that I have on my Android, and . . . yeah, I think that's about it. I see it has an e-mail app and an Internet app. Amazing. Mine also has 3G because although I know it's blasphemy, I don't spend my days in coffee shops scarfing free Wi-Fi pretending I'm living the life of a lawyer.

Here is how the iPad has changed my life:

In the month I had it, I never took it to the office because, well, I have an office with a computer. I took it on a trip where I had a hearing and a meeting and it sat in my bag. If there is a way to use track changes in Word documents, I don't know about it. It's a lot easier to type long e-mails and documents on a laptop, so if you're a lawyer that actually writes things instead of playing games or watching videos, I don't see the use unless you want to get a keyboard which, well, just turns it into a modified laptop. I had to travel to a meeting for a day where I just needed some documents, so I brought it and not the laptop. It was fine, easier to carry around than the laptop. Had I wanted to do other work, I would have wanted the laptop. I do like that cover thing though, the one that keeps it off when covered? It keeps the battery charged when not in use. Oh, and I updated the operating system, so now it looks different.

So I'm sorry to be the buzzkill to the "iPad for lawyers" crew. I hope this doesn't keep them from putting food on the table by convincing naive lawyers that having one of these things means you will be a better lawyer, and that there are all kinds of secrets. There is no iPad for lawyers. I trust, though, that I'll be receiving e-mails telling me that I'm missing out on an app that will change my life or law practice or both, or that I "just don't understand."

I'm going to keep the iPad. If I remember where I put it, I may open it from time to time to read something or sign something or check out a website. I've always seen tech for what it is though: something that adds convenience to life. It does nothing more, regardless of what anyone charges you money to hear or read. It's nothing to hate or love, it's just something with a battery and an on/off switch. Really.

Now where is my laptop cord . . . I need to charge this thing.

CHAPTER 3

GETTING THAT FIRST JOB, OR A NEW ONE

JOBLESS? OMG, MAYBE IT'S YOU

Living in a post-*Oprah* show world is tough for people like me. Oprah was the one who convinced many people that no matter what happens in your life, it's not your fault. There is always how your mother treated you, how you were bullied in third grade, your bad relationships, and, of course, the law school that held a gun to your head while showing you fake statistics and promising a job handed to you at the same time you shake the dean's hand and receive your degree.

While I believe that anyone stupid enough to choose a law school based on its job placement statistics should never, ever, ever, be a practicing lawyer, there are many of you out there. Even though you should run as fast as you can to another profession or career, I want to help you at least try to find a legal job, so in a year you can realize that the real problem is that you never wanted to be a lawyer anyway—you were just looking for some easy cash, like everyone promised.

I realize one of the problems that causes seemingly intelligent people with law degrees to respond with unintelligible rants about how I don't understand, is that I am actually working as a lawyer. Misery loves company, so there is a notion that because I'm not sitting in my parents' basement lashing out at the computer screen in an effort to convince people not to go to law school, I am just wrong. Before you throw in the towel and go to that world of becoming a social media rock star, I want you to know that I'm not the only one out there giving you advice that does nothing but anger you. There is also Anna Ivey.

Ms. Ivey is a former lawyer and former admissions dean at the University of Chicago Law School, and is now an admissions consultant for college, law school, and MBA applicants. Of course, to you this means she has no idea what she is talking about because she has actually been employed, is still working, and doesn't understand, well, anything. Ms. Ivey has Six Skills Every Law Student Needs to Master,[6] or as you may call it, "Six things that make me want to rip her face off and throw something through my parents' window." I'd like to highlight several of her suggestions. You may have heard things like this before from someone else, somewhere, maybe. Ms. Ivey begins:

> Don't get complacent just because you're at a top law school and making good grades, or you just landed a coveted law firm or public interest job for the summer. To move up in the long run, you'll need something extra. Smarts and a fancy credential aren't enough anymore.

Yeah, we know that. The Association of "Wait, I Went to a Top Law School and Graduated with Honors, but No One Thinks I Am as Awesome as I Do" tells us that daily. As per the title of her post, Ms. Ivey lays out the issue:

> You cannot afford to wait to work on the skills you need to succeed once you're in a job. There are some skills you need to acquire now.

Skills? What?
Yes.

IMPROVE YOUR WRITING

Ms. Ivey says, "Work on a journal; take classes that require longer papers; do moot court (for the oral argument and the extra practice in brief writing). And take those contract drafting classes." She also wants you to get feedback. If the only feedback you've received up to now is that you are very special, it's probably not the feedback you're going to get. If that scares you, maybe you should just skip this tip.

I would also add to cease the LOL, OMG, "preso" for presentation, "convo" for conversation, "vacay" for vacation, and all those cool ways you shorten every word you type online, K?

TALK LIKE AN ADULT

That means learning how to write a decent cover letter and sounding professional on the phone. It also means using grown-up speech patterns. Many law school students don't and won't, and it puts them at a disadvantage.

So, like, I read this, and I'm like, oh-my-God! What-ev-er. Like who does she think she's talking about?

Then she's just a mean, mean bully:

The client, boss, hiring partner, judge, etc., will be less inclined to listen to you if you sound like a high school babysitter.

(Face of shock, jaw dropped.)
Of course, I just laughed.

ALWAYS NETWORK IN PERSON

Blasting out e-mails to people you've never met, hoping that they'll give you something (time, money, advice, a job, a favor), is a horribly inefficient way to get ahead. E-mail is fine if you already have a preexisting connection, but in many cases, establishing relationship capital means getting off your laptop, heading out the front door, and talking to people in person.

Who is this wretched old woman? Get off my laptop? The couch too? What's next, put on professional clothes and go meet lawyers at a seminar or networking event? Can I bring my iPad?

This one is classic. She wants you to "think like a creative problem solver and a businessperson":

You may have defaulted into law school because you are not attracted to the "business world" (law students have a fuzzy notion of what that means). But you need to start thinking like a business-person—which is what many of you will turn out to be . . .

She advises those who are working at summer jobs while in law school to watch the senior people and "notice how they don't just issue-spot and identify problems (lawyers are great at this part), but also how they solve those problems creatively and cost-effectively (lawyers can be terrible at that part)."

This is where my usual tech rant comes in. We are raising a generation of lawyers who are being convinced that tech is the answer to all their problems, concerns, and client representation. It's not. Tech is great, it can save time, help you work while out of the office (if you're one of those dinosaurs who has an office), and keep you connected to the world. It cannot think for you. It cannot mentor you. It cannot fully analyze a complex issue for a client. We need lawyers who can think, not just those who can point and click.

So there it is, tips from someone who practiced law, admitted law students, and now counsels them. Hurry, go tell her she's mean and wrong.

She's not.

EIGHT WAYS LAW STUDENTS GET THEIR COVER LETTER AND RESUME IN MY GARBAGE

1. Spell my name or the name of my firm wrong.
2. Immediately advise that you are irrelevant to my practice. I do criminal defense and Bar discipline work. I don't care if your experience is working in a personal injury firm.
3. Send a letter from another state and don't specify why you're moving to my town or when.
4. Say nothing that indicates you've even taken the time to look at my firm's website.
5. Say nothing about what type of lawyer you want to be. More specifically, make it clear you're looking for a job, any job.
6. Say nothing interesting. You've been on this planet at least 20 years. You must have *something* interesting to say.
7. Address the letter "Dear managing partner."
8. Lack creativity. I know you're a law student with a grade point average. Begin with something else.

FIVE THOUGHTS ON GOING SOLO

1. **Decide what type of lawyer you want to be.** If you are going to do "door law" (whatever walks in the door), you will be a failure. You will be running around town doing mildly competent work for little money. Be a master of a practice area, or two at the most.

2. **Keep your mouth shut.** If you now work for a firm and you're going to leave for solo practice, don't talk to anyone at the firm. Not even that guy. Find your advice outside the firm. Far outside the firm.

3. **Don't buy shit.** "Shit" meaning garbage. There are plenty of resources out there that appear to be important. I recommend a shared office space arrangement for low or work-for rent rates, a computer, and business cards to start. Most other stuff turns out to be shit.

4. **Read everything you can.** There are so many resources online. Google "lawyer going solo." You're welcome.

5. **Stay out of the office.** This refers to your marketing. If you want to do the mass mailing thing, great. Then you can stay in your office and take calls. If you are building a referral-based business, every lunch you eat at your desk costs you money. If you don't understand that, I can't help you.

LEAVING BIGLAW TO BECOME A RELEVANT REAL-WORLD LAWYER

A term that Biglaw lawyers use to refer to lawyers like me (otherwise called "consumer lawyers," meaning we represent consumers in need of typical legal services like personal injury, divorce, and criminal defense) is "shit law."

I am a shit law lawyer. I represent real people with real problems. They need legal services. They need arguments made on their behalf. They need advice. They need something other than an edited pre-bill in the mail once a month. I love shit law, and I love talking to Biglaw lawyers about their desire to join shit law. And while I always thought lawyers were smart enough to leave the confines of ".2 receive and review correspondence" law to strike out on their own practicing real law, I realize now that the Biglaw lawyers who tell me they hate their jobs, hate that they can't bring in clients because they can only pony up $10,000 for a retainer, and want to have their own practice, are apparently all lying.

So this advice is for those of you who haven't been brainwashed into thinking that the practice of law is on the 46th floor in a small office trying to meet the important goal of having the divorced-three-times 53-year-old partner walk by at 8 p.m. and see you there in the thick of it, preparing irrelevant motions to compel discovery for cases that will never go to trial. This is for those who can't wait to leave, those who realize that no one can name the best Biglaw commercial litigator in their town, but can name the best of various types of shit law lawyers. This advice is for those that want to practice law, and not feed the billable hour factory that is Biglaw.

DO NOT LEAVE UNLESS YOU ARE EXCEEDINGLY MISERABLE

Being unhappy, dissatisfied, or overworked are not reasons to leave. Not now. The economy sucks. This is no time to be stupid and give up that six-figure salary you don't deserve for the hopes of starting your own firm, especially if you have done nothing but take orders and worked on pieces of cases without ever meeting a client. Unless you have family money or have saved $50,000, you must be on the verge of wanting to leave the practice of law, or have some ability to bring in business, before you make the jump to shit law.

DO NOT CALCULATE WHETHER YOU CAN MAKE WHAT YOU ARE MAKING NOW

Calculate what you need to pay your bills. Bills are things like rent, the BMW you can't afford, and anything else needed to sustain your life. Happy hour, a new game for the Xbox, and the new iPad that some idiot tech hack said would be essential to your law practice, are not needed to sustain your life. Remember, the bad news is that in your small or solo practice, no one will just hand you money every two weeks. I know, hard to imagine.

DO NOT RENT AN OFFICE, FURNISH IT, AND LEASE OFFICE EQUIPMENT

You can't afford it. Find a lawyer or small firm with space (preferably lawyers who don't do what you do) and make a deal. See if they need work in exchange for rent. If you want to do a Regus-type thing, fine, but it can become less cost-effective if you get busy. One more thing: an office is not an iPad or laptop and a seat at Starbucks.

DO NOT SPEND A DIME ON . . .

SEO, Internet marketing, learning social media, or tips from a failed lawyer who says he knows how to start a firm. Take that money and sponsor a golf tournament, charity event, or bar association event; take some people out for a meal; or burn it. Call a lawyer who is actually smarter than you thought you were at Biglaw and see if they have any crap cases they don't want or will consider referring you what they turn down.

SPEAKING OF LUNCH . . .

Eating tuna sandwiches at your desk is a quick road to nothing. Lawyers who pride themselves on never going out to lunch are the same insufferable bastards that never go on vacation, but need to. (Did you law-review types just see I ended a sentence with a preposition?) Go out to lunch. Meet someone. Develop a relationship outside your online world. There is no one to impress in the office.

IF YOU DON'T HANDLE THE TYPE OF CASE THAT WALKS IN THE DOOR . . .

Don't take the case. Refer it to a lawyer that handles that type of case, and ask to co-counsel. Do not ask for a referral fee. Referral fees are for small, cheap, greedy, annoying lawyers. This is a practice based on relationships, not transactions.

TWO MORE THINGS

Do not tell anyone you are leaving until you have made the decision to leave—not even that guy—and read the ethics rules on lawyers leaving law firms. Read them twice.

THE STUPIDITY OF ASSOCIATES WITH GOLDEN HANDCUFFS

There are two types of law firm associates: those expected to lock themselves in an office and stay there seven days a week, and those who are expected to bring in business. I'm speaking to the latter.

Why are you so stupid?

Specifically, if your firm wants you to develop business, but won't help you learn how to develop business, why are you still working there? I know the answer—you're there for the paycheck. You're there because you have little self-worth.

Let me break this down. You are expected to bring in business, or you realize you won't be at the firm forever and want to learn how to bring in business and your firm is indifferent. By "learning," I mean attending a seminar about business development, or attending a CLE conference. One is coming up. You want to go, but you won't unless your firm will pay for it. You are interested in personal development that will lead to business development, but have other priorities when it comes to money, like going out to dinner and paying the lease on your car that you can't afford. So you won't pay for it, and then you learn your firm won't pay for it. You get mad. You don't go. Rinse and repeat.

If you want to be a lawyer who can run your own practice, or pay for yourself at a firm and share in the profits, it's important to hone these skills. To some, it's natural, although there are always things to learn. To others, the concept of "rainmaking" or "business development" is completely foreign.

I am tired of hearing from associates who want to learn about business development, but won't take a dollar out of their pocket to further their career. If your firm won't give you a day off or write a check for a few hundred dollars, they do not support your efforts to develop business. If you stay there, you're a moron.

To go to work every day annoyed that your law firm is holding you back from learning the business side of your profession is a complete waste of a law degree. To fail to make a personal investment in learning the business side of law, if that's what you want to do, is shameful. Nothing is free. To expect others to invest in your continuing legal education, and then when they don't, avoiding the concept of sticking your hand in your own pocket, is the best way to never be more than you are today.

A WORD TO GOVERNMENT LAWYERS TAKING THE PLUNGE

For those AUSAs (assistant U.S. attorneys) taking the plunge into Biglaw because Biglaw orgasms over having a former federal prosecutor handling their white-collar work, my advice is to call me when you realize you're merely reading compliance documents and walking corporate executives over to your old office to give proffers. For now, you can stop reading here.

Leaving government work to open your own shop is a unique proposition. If you're leaving Biglaw, your main concern is that you won't make what you're making now. If you're going solo right out of law school, you're worried about making any money at all. Leaving government service is leaving a guaranteed salary, precious benefits, and if you've been there for a good amount of years, a level of comfort not found in small law firms (with the exception of federal public defenders who have fallen victim to the sequester and deserve better). The main reason people leave government is the perception that there is more money in the private sector. That was mostly true before the economy tanked. Now it's not so certain, and it's something you need to consider before cashing out on your accrued vacation and sick time.

The informal rule used to be that you should leave government work in three to five years, and I think that's still correct. Contrary to what you read on the Internet, you actually need a few years to learn how to practice law, and then a little more time to become proficient and figure out where you're going next. If you stay longer than five years, it's harder to leave, and if you're looking for a boss, they may not appreciate that you've spent nine years not worrying about bringing in any business or billing hours.

The majority of government lawyers I speak to about leaving who have been there more than five years are more concerned about benefits than salary. Small law firms often don't have the same benefits that the government provides, nor do small law firms appreciate your laser focus on the benefits. If being comfortable is the most important thing to you, which normally includes the all-important health insurance, don't leave.

It is easier to leave if you know a few people. If you're just starting out or are early in your government career, make sure you network. Prosecutor, county attorney, I don't care—go to bar events, join a committee, do something with other lawyers or community leaders. Obviously, you have to make sure there are no conflicts and that your office allows this, but too many good government lawyers go into the private sector and then try to develop relationships. It doesn't work as well.

Speaking of good government lawyers, some of the best tacticians, strategists, and legal minds couldn't make a buck with some ink and a counterfeit bill maker. There are lawyers out there who are great at lawyering and terrible at business, and vice versa. Make sure that leaving government service is not a suicide mission. Being a great lawyer is meaningless if asking for money scares the crap out of you or your personality is one that scares children.

The most important things to remember for a government lawyer heading to solo or small law practice are that it's not a nine-to-five proposition and that there are no guarantees. And I know, government lawyers get defensive and say, "I work eight to seven." My point is that in a solo practice or small law firm, there are not as many people doing your work for you (preparing documents, scheduling hearings and depositions, making sure there is paper in the copy machine, making sure rent is paid, making sure your computer works, and about 400 other things). You can't just leave the office and not worry about the practice.

So it's simple, government lawyer. You love your job? The only pressure to leave is your own? Don't be so quick to leave. These days, there are experienced and reputable solo and small law firm practitioners out there making less than young government lawyers. Make sure you understand what it's going to cost you to maintain your life as it is now, or at least at an acceptable level. That insurance policy you pay $100 a month for is now $1,500. We can start there.

People always ask me if I miss the public defender's office. Yes, every day. I tell them if I were a trust fund baby, I would go back there. I love my practice, but the days of just going to court every day and not working on the business aspect of the practice were my favorite. It was the best job I ever had.

CHAPTER 4

THE GREAT OFFICE DEBATE

THE GREAT (STUPID) OFFICE DEBATE

When you went to law school or started thinking about starting your own practice, did you have dreams of waking up in the morning, walking down the hall to another room in your house and sitting down to do legal work? Did you hope to bounce ideas off of the dog, or plan strategy watching *Matlock* reruns at 2 p.m.?

I'm sorry, I just don't get this "Do I need an office?" back and forth. My "future of law" friends are quick to say, "You don't need an office."

No, you don't need an office. They're right. You also don't *need* to wear clothes that make you look respectable. You don't even have to have any idea what you're doing. You can work from your computer in your dining room, in shorts, and find answers (some of which are correct) to questions like "how to draft a will" on the Internet. Some client, somewhere, will hire you. Maybe a few.

As you build your practice, you can do everything small, cheap, and sloppy. Forget about being downtown or by the courthouse. Forget about having to dress like you want to be hired for important legal work. Forget about building anything of significance. Just stay home and be happy that you're saving money every month on an office. Way to go. Hopefully you won't take advice from business owners who know that building a business takes investment.

I'll go back to divorce lawyer Lee Rosen, who continues to write some great stuff about the practice of law (and won't be mean to you), and has a few posts on this topic. More than 20 years ago, he quit his law firm job and, as he puts it:[7]

> I rented a room in someone else's office and bought some furniture. I was up and running in 48 hours and off to the races. I worked like crazy chasing after new clients, scrambling to get the work done while figuring out how to deal with the mundane issues of setting up a law practice. It was crazy, exhausting, and exhilarating.

The first year he made $700.

Lee's not a fan of the virtual law office, where the entire practice is online, but he has created a modified version of a virtual practice, where his firm uses conference space and has no offices.

Before you dive in on the hypocrisy here, understand that Lee started out with a cheap office, built relationships and thus his practice, opened more offices, and then determined that he could be more efficient with physical conference space and no offices. He built something before he made the decision to go without an office.

For those of you who went to a college where you lived on campus the first year, think about how different your experience would be if you didn't. You built relationships, got to know people, and then moved off campus. If you've got a few years under your belt and a somewhat established practice, fine, move "off campus." But to start out without an office is robbing yourself of opportunities to become a part of the greater profession. With an office, every day you're around others, you're developing relationships, you're saying hello to other lawyers, other business owners, and the public. At some point in your practice, moving away from a business district may be OK, but why start out that way? There are advantages to leaving your house for a few hours a day and being around like-minded people (other than that place where you order complicated coffee and type away with college students).

An office is a small investment in putting yourself in the middle of the business world, instead of 10 feet from your bedroom. You can't afford an office? You're a lawyer, negotiate something. Especially when you're young or building a new practice, do what you can to be around people—real people, not the ones on your computer screen.

Then again, maybe the mailman needs a lawyer.

MOVING OFFICES

The thing that gets me yelled at almost as much as when I rail on SEO and tech hacks is when I dare to mention that practicing lawyers looking to build their practice should have an office. Your practice may be built. You may be getting more calls than you can handle. You may be a low-volume lawyer who only needs or wants a couple of cases a month, and your referral sources take care of that for you.

I'm talking about the rest of the profession. The debt-laden, the hungry, the ones still trying to get to that place where they have the types of clients and cases they want.

This is not a post about the merits of having an office; it's about when it's time to move—to something nicer, closer to the business center of town, or closer to the courthouse you are in three days a week. If you've already decided that having an office is the worst thing you could ever imagine because "no one has an office anymore," stop reading here.

A while back, I had the opportunity to talk to a few lawyers about moving offices. Some space opened in my office due to a lawyer needing more space than I could offer. In speaking to these lawyers, I discovered some issues that caused me to wonder what lawyers are thinking when they decide to make a move.

If you have an office, you spend a lot of time there. People visit, whether potential clients, actual clients, vendors, or solicitors. You may be a great estate planning lawyer in your city, but for those who don't know that, when they see your crappy office that's a mess and in a part of town that makes them hope their car will be there when they leave, that's their first impression. But maybe it isn't that you have a crappy office in a bad part of town that causes you to want to move. It may be that you need more space, or you are in a location where there aren't many other lawyers, or your landlord is a jerk.

One thing I keep hearing is, "I want to move to a better place, but do not want to pay more than I do now." Great idea. Just like when you want to move to a new house, in a neighborhood with better schools and parks, but keep the rent the same. That works. I know, you can't afford another

$300 a month because then you have to cut back on some of your spending, or take home a little less for a while, or God forbid, reduce what you spend on Internet marketing.

Try thinking of the office space as marketing space. Understand that being around different lawyers, in a different part of town, or having to spend less time in the car getting to the courthouse, are all things that can make you money. The increased rent is an investment, not an expense. It's not just that the aesthetics are better—that clients will be impressed with better floors, nicer elevators, or a bigger office—it's that if you are in a better location, you have a better opportunity to build your practice because you are in an environment of like-minded people. Having your office downtown and being able to walk down the street and say hello to two lawyers on your walk to lunch may get you a phone call with someone wanting to make you their lawyer. Waiting in line at the drive-thru for some heart-attack-causing tacos down the street from your suburban office can save you a few bucks a month.

If your goal is to build your practice, then your efforts must be geared toward things that will help you build your practice. Trying to save money on the places you spend the most time, and where your clients make decisions, will only save you money. It will never make you money.

THE FUTURE OF THE LEGAL PROFESSION: HOW TO ETHICALLY LIE ABOUT YOUR FAKE OFFICE

So much discussion about the future of the legal profession is going around the Internet these days that you may begin to think that the people talking about it actually know what they are talking about. Look a bit closer and you will see that the so-called future is being described by those who are tired of practicing, addicted to tech, have no real substantive practice to speak of, and generally make things up to bolster their self-fulfilling prophecies. In essence, those that talk about the future of the legal profession these days are mainly spewing their own vision of the profession—a vision that many "real" lawyers don't share.

One vision I do share with these "future of the legal profession" idiots is that the future includes more acceptable lying. You know, pretending you have a certain amount of experience, or credentials, or yes, even a certain type of office. Which brings me to the topic at hand.

Why do some lawyers put photos of their office building on their website? I don't have a picture of my office building on my website. Maybe I should. Maybe one day I will. But when I do, it will be a picture of the office building where I have an office, with a desk, and people working for me and with me. It will not be a picture of the building in which some time-share company owns a floor and of the address I own for the $100 a month I pay the virtual office company.

Which leads me to the answer to my own question. There are lawyers who put a picture of the building in which their "office" is located in order to create an impression that they in fact, have an office there. In fact, I, as well as many other lawyers (not potential clients though), know that in every city there are class A office buildings that have a floor rented by a virtual office company that in turn provides fee-for-service office solutions for lawyers and other businesses. A lawyer can merely have the address to receive mail, or someone answering a dedicated phone line, or conference room time, office time, and yes, lawyers can actually rent offices and work there like in any other place. But for the most part, in this future of the legal profession, lawyers buy the address and pretend (lie) that this is actually where they practice. Cool, huh?

Welcome to the future.

DRY CLEANERS, RENTAL CARS, AND THE PRACTICE OF LAW

Ten years ago I began using a dry cleaning company that comes to my house, picks up the week's wears, and drops them off at next week's pickup. It's more expensive then standing in line at the dry cleaners next to my local breakfast joint on a Saturday where moms in jogging suits and dads in T-shirts evidencing their last good trip sigh as they hold the pile of whites and blues of the week. As I walk past them on Saturdays on my way in to have Tania pour me some coffee and bring me a couple of eggs, I shake my head at how people can wait in line to have their clothes dry-cleaned. But they do. They do there and at the dozens that I pass every day as I travel through town. While pickup and delivery is more convenient, I don't see dry cleaners closing up store fronts and buying vans in their place.

Why?

Because there are still and will always be people who don't trust leaving their clothes on the front porch. Maybe they like saying hello to the angry Greek guy who runs the place. Maybe they like to explain exactly how they want their clothes cleaned. Maybe they can't afford the pickup and delivery service. Maybe they just like doing it the way they've done it for years and have no reason to change.

Then there are rental cars. I think Hertz was the first company to have a service where you got off the plane and went right to the car. No stopping at the counter. Plane, car, done. But I still see counters. I still see lines of people there.

There are guys like me who can't understand any of this. Why wouldn't you pay a little more for the convenience? Why would you do it the way you've been doing it for all these years?

The problem is that I'm not one of these new-fangled "evangelists" who spends their days trying to convince people that the way I do things is the way they are going to be done and therefore you must do them this way or you will die. Listen to the evangelists of the Internet today as it pertains to law practice, and you will think that in five years there will be no offices, no paper, no pens, no clients meeting lawyers face-to-face—nothing will be like it is today. But don't ever forget that those who are making these claims are doing so because they are doing things differently (or not doing them at all), and can't imagine doing it any other way.

See, I think there are many ways to practice law. I know very good lawyers with nice offices and computers that sit on a credenza behind their desk collecting dust. I also know very good lawyers who are hired by fax and credit card and have well-organized car trunks.

Don't tell me I have to get on board. Don't tell young lawyers looking to rent an office and hire a secretary that this spells disaster.

Just put your pajamas back on, sit at the dining room table, and shut up.

The people in line at the dry cleaners and rental car counters don't give a crap what you think.

CHAPTER 5
NETWORKING

ENOUGH WITH THE WORTHLESS NETWORKING

Being a small-firm lawyer usually means that you're not a cog in the wheel of some multinational corporation while enjoying a stream of business sent to your firm because of someone on another floor. Small-firm lawyers either have to blow their brains out on ads featuring their angry mugs (arms crossed in an aggressive, "fight-for-you" display), direct mail, or the art and science of talking to people and developing relationships, otherwise known as networking.

In this arena, there are two types of lawyers: those who "don't do networking," and those who do it because it is required to establish a word-of-mouth practice. I know you think there is a third—those who love networking—but those lawyers are to be avoided at all costs. Lawyers who love going out after work and eating bar food, drinking low-level vodka, and asking "So, where's your office?" are rejects. Ignore them. They just want to give you their business card the minute they lay eyes on you and tell you to "Call whenever you have a (usually PI or real estate) matter."

For those that want the word-of-mouth practice, and the reputation in the community as a go-to person (assuming you are a competent lawyer, and these days, that's a big assumption), here are some things to consider.

BUSINESS CARDS ARE YOUR ENEMY

I don't carry business cards anymore. What's the point? Yes, mine say "attorney at law" (so cool), and have my phone number and e-mail address, but who gives a crap? You know who says "always carry business cards"? People who take them and put you on their garbage newsletter e-mail lists and think it's OK to never talk to you again. I'll take your card and you can look me up on Google if you want to stalk me. Plus, cards don't equal relationships—hand me yours the minute we meet, and we're done. Let's talk, let's have a conversation; if there is a reason we should talk again, we'll find each other. Trust me, if I need to remember you, I will.

PEOPLE OTHER THAN LAWYERS NETWORK (REALLY!)

You're a lawyer, so of course you're only going to the bar association networking events and judicial receptions. That's nice, and very narrow-minded. Charities have networking events. You like charity? Go hang out with some doctors, accountants, business owners, moms, and people who actually don't spend their days talking to lawyers—people who won't immediately say, "I think we have a case together." Non-lawyers are actually more interested in speaking to lawyers at social events than lawyers. Even if you don't do criminal law, some flirtatious cutie (can I say that here?) will ask after three drinks, "So can I call you if I get a DUI?"

FOLLOW UP LIKE A NON-LAWYER

"Dear Tom, it was a pleasure . . . "

Oh, shut the hell up. Write like you actually want to talk to the guy again—and not everyone is worth a follow-up. Most people you meet have nothing to offer and there is nothing you can do for them, so save it for the real potential relationships. "Tom, I've attached an article, invitation to (whatever). I thought based on our conversation you may be interested . . . blah, blah, blah. If you can't make it, let me know so I can take you to lunch in the next couple of weeks. I'd like to learn more about your (business, practice, meth habit, whatever) as I think I may be able to send some business your way."

And for all those e-mail gurus who think the subject line has to be magical, the most magical subject line that causes me to open an e-mail is no subject. All the other e-mails have "guru magic" subjects, and I delete them.

BE A HOST

Yeah, I know, freeloading on someone else's liquor and those small quiches (which are always terrible), all in the name of getting some business, is attractive. But where does it put you in the networking world if every month, or quarter, or twice a year, you're the host of an event? Partner up with a bank, vendor (all those accounting firms that claim to do "litigation support"), or venue looking for a crowd on a Tuesday night. Invite lawyers, non-lawyers, and judges, and have no agenda. Yes, it may cost you some money, sorry to disappoint. No speeches, no name tags, just people talking and trying to converse without the use of a smartphone. And never, ever forget the most polite way to end a conversation at any networking event: "Where's the bar?" (Don't say you'll be right back, no one ever is.)

HOW NETWORKING REALLY WORKS

The news continues to be bad for the impatient "just get me on the Internet" types regarding the development of relationships. Regardless of how many times your name appears on the first page of Google, developing meaningful professional relationships still takes time, and it always will. Sorry.

I recently read of a lawyer who closed up shop, a prominent reason being that after dropping from the first page to fourth page of Google, "the phone stopped ringing." Google doesn't develop relationships that bring referrals. Some learn that the hard way.

I spoke at a local breakfast meeting. It was a kickoff of a new chapter of a monthly lawyers group. There were 20 lawyers. One guy was in his 70s and is now of counsel to a firm after a long career, while another just graduated law school and drove two hours to meet some lawyers. Not sure why he drove so far to meet lawyers instead of sitting at home and poking around on LinkedIn. Anyway, a few said they were with firms I knew, and there were a bunch of solo practitioners, some just a few years in, and others who had been at it for a while. I know, you're thinking, "Sounds like BNI." Kind of, but BNI (Business Network International[8]) is weekly, and not limited to lawyers.

Because this was the first meeting of the second local chapter, everyone was there to check it out, to decide whether they would attend a second meeting. After going around the room and introducing themselves to each other, and then ending the meeting by walking around and exchanging business cards and "do you know so and so," some will attend, while others will see getting up for a 7:30 a.m. breakfast once a month as the most awful thing they could think of and never come back.

The host of the meeting said something that may cause some not to return: "No one in this room is required to refer clients to each other."

Wait, what? You can't just sit there, eat eggs, and the cases will come?

No, you can't. Just like you can't attend a random lawyer's happy hour, hand out your next-stop-trash-can business card, tell the person receiving your card to "send me all your clients," and expect to profit.

During the introductions, a visiting 25-year criminal defense lawyer who is a member in the other chapter, spoke about his success in the group. "If you're going to just come to the breakfast once a month, save your money, you won't get anything out of it—it will be a waste of time." He spoke of the relationships he's developed, how he reaches out to members for lunch or coffee and gets to know them outside of the two hours a month they meet. When he gets calls for referrals for other practice areas, he's not just referring someone to a person he has breakfast with once a month, but to someone he knows personally, and who has a stake in making sure the client is well-served. He's also at the top of the list for those lawyers who need him.

I sat next to a young divorce lawyer. She told me, "I tried BNI but it didn't work." I asked her how long she was a member of BNI. "Couple of months." Unfortunately I'm not good with facial reactions, as you can imagine, which invited her next response of, "Maybe I didn't give it long enough." Twelve years ago, I myself joined a BNI chapter. It too was a new chapter. There were about 20 people, and three other lawyers. I sat there getting to know the people in the room for five months before someone referred me a case. Five months, 20 breakfasts at 7 a.m., one case. One really good case.

Something else though was happening during that time. I was not only getting to know the people in the room, but the people they knew. With what I call "structured networking," this is the essence. It's not who is in the room. Chances are those people will never need you. The goal is to get to know who they know. I once heard that the average person has 250 relationships. With 20 people in a room . . . well, you can do the math.

Although I became bored and dissatisfied and left for three years after a seven-year stint, I returned to the group, which now has 53 members, 13 being lawyers. In addition to a weekly meeting, the lawyers meet once a month for lunch. Why did I go back? I realized that while I was still attending events and developing relationships, I missed the structured networking. I had friends in that room who had done and would continue to do a lot for me, and being around them meant I could continue to expand my network.

I obviously believe in structured networking, and in giving it time. You also have to find the right group. I know, let me guess, you probably tried it and it didn't work, or you avoid it because you won't get up that early or have heard it's worthless. Yes, you're going to get garbage referrals, but that's mainly because people don't understand what you do and hence, it's your fault. There are only two reasons it won't work for you: you're a bozo, or you were in a group with a bunch of cheesy networking types that you would be embarrassed to introduce to anyone.

It does work, as long as you understand that relationships are not business cards and a weekly or monthly meal. The best referral you will ever get is likely to come from a group like this. The result, though, will never be a bunch of people calling you daily to say they found you on the Internet. It will be one or two people every so often looking to give you a really nice case.

GETTING INVOLVED IN THE (OFFLINE) COMMUNITY

I did a Google search for "lawyers getting involved in the community." The first result was some article about pro bono. Let's be honest: why would a lawyer trying to build a practice spend time doing free legal work for the needy instead of trying to figure out whether Pinterest can be monetized to bring in clients?

Being a lawyer who *is* involved in the community, I used to frequently be asked, "Hey, I want to get involved in the community, can you tell me how?" I don't get asked that much anymore. "Community" is considered the Twitter community or the blogosphere. While the tech hacks haven't yet declared community involvement dead, the fact that the result of becoming involved in the community is often organically developed, real relationships with other like-minded people that may lead to business, makes it unattractive to those who have bought into the notion that a collection of followers and friends online is a quicker path to lots of phone calls.

So if there are any lawyers left out there who are still contemplating community involvement, I offer the following.

COMMUNITY INVOLVEMENT WILL GET YOU BUSINESS

But stop asking if it will get you business. This is a question of the "I only do things that make me money" lawyers, the people who ask, "Does that get you cases?" or "Why do you do all these things in the community, you running for judge or something?" If you are involved enough, for long enough, someone is going to refer you business. Trust me, this is the way we lawyers way back in the '90s used to build our practices—we got to know people and developed real relationships. If your goal is to get business, you will be very unhappy, as it will take a while (more than a few keystrokes).

INVOLVEMENT IN A BAR ASSOCIATION IS NOT COMMUNITY INVOLVEMENT

I know, it's the young lawyers' organization or your niche bar association. Sure, join them, get involved, but "the community" is not a group of lawyers. Consider a charity, hospital, rotary, Kiwanis, chamber of commerce. Yes, this type of involvement will cost you money—some even have minimum financial commitments. Just lay off the Starbucks, dump the SEO kid, and postpone buying your third iPad. You'll be OK.

I know the thought of meeting non-lawyers who own businesses or work in industries other than law may be a foreign concept to you, but I assure you that if you put your mind to it, you can have a conversation that doesn't revolve around whether moving to the cloud is necessary, or whether you made the right decision to leave Biglaw.

INVOLVEMENT IS NOT A HAPPY HOUR

I know, you don't have time to get involved, you have kids. How unique.

Cut the crap, you have time. Stop using your kids or self-importance to avoid getting involved. You have time for one committee meeting a month (or so), and if you insist your time is just so precious and limited, take on a specific project that allows you to have meetings or conference calls around your schedule. If your idea of getting involved is showing up for a drink, get involved in a bar (small "b").

FIND YOUR PASSION

Yeah, I know it's a cliché, but I find the reason people refrain from community involvement is because they don't really give a crap about anything. No disease has touched them or their family, children's issues (other than their own) are not interesting, and of course, they don't see immediate cash filling their coffers. If you're one of these folks, my advice is to look for something off the beaten path. Stay away from the major charities and service organizations and look for something new, small, and under the radar that focuses on a need not served by other organizations. You'll have a better opportunity to make an impact.

Sorry to interrupt your online marketing efforts. You may now go back to entering good keywords on your website and increasing your Google AdWords budget. It's probably better to do that then go to a gala that you cosponsored for a local charity that helps foster children.

GET A HOBBY

From Wikipedia:[9]

A hobby is a regularly undertaken activity that is done for pleasure, typically, during one's leisure time. Hobbies can include the collection of themed items and objects, engaging in creative and artistic pursuits, tinkering, playing sports, along with many more examples. By continually participating in a particular hobby, one can acquire substantial skill and knowledge in that area.

Although unintentional, a hobby is one of the best marketing tools around.

Oh, now I have your attention?

Does anyone have hobbies anymore, or are we too busy complaining or figuring out our marketing strategy? I'm not talking about hookers and blow, I'm talking about those things people used to do before we decided that all our free time was best spent in front of a computer or smartphone.

Does anyone play golf, bike, coach youth sports, or collect ceramic elephants or rare books? Or is being a lawyer the sum total of your life?

As lawyers, we often make the mistake of thinking we are fascinating people because, well, we're lawyers. There is no time for hobbies; we're too busy going from lawyer networking event to lawyer networking event talking about how awesome our awesomeness is, or how miserable is our misery. We believe business development is limited to doing all the typical stuff—advertising, events, and following all the other lawyers around town to wherever they are going that day, handing out cards and saying, "Call me if . . . " Hobbies don't make us money.

But in this age where everyone is trying to outdo each other on the World Wide Web like little dogs trying to jump a fence, we are too busy trying to differentiate ourselves by, of course, doing the same thing everyone else is doing. Lawyers are hoping, and being sold on the lie, that if their name appears more on a computer screen than the other lawyers, their practices will be more profitable. Although the struggle to separate yourself from the rest and stand out in the sea of potential clients is real, you continue to just fall in line with the same crap everyone else does.

Is there nothing you're interested in other than what you do for a living and selling it on the same platforms as everyone else?

About 10 years ago someone gave me a really good glass of wine. I then began to travel around town to various tastings, learning about wines, and getting to know the people who collect, buy, sell, and spend much of their free time enjoying the types of events and gatherings that involve wine. I studied wine, became proficient, and now spend a nice amount of time educating people about wine and helping them select and enjoy it as well. I talk to them about traveling to wineries and answer "It's my anniversary, got a recommendation?" texts on a lone Friday night. Recently I was asked to speak to a once-a-month dinner meeting of a business group. I assumed they wanted me to talk about something law-related, but "No, we want you to talk about wine." Do all these people know what I do for a living? Yes.

So man, it must be killing my business that I'm asked about wine about as much as I'm asked about legal issues.

Yeah, maybe I'll increase my SEO instead.

Like any other hobby, wine is a great equalizer. It is enjoyed by doctors, CEOs, celebrities, small business owners, and yes, even a lawyer or two. It would take much too long to talk about the people I've met, the relationships I've developed, the things I've been able to do for others, and donations I've made around town, all based on a hobby. My intention in getting into wine was to get into wine, to learn about something other than law. The unintended consequence has been to increase my network of referrals tenfold.

Hobbies make it easier to meet people you would not otherwise meet, or want to meet. When I'm trying to make a connection for someone, saying "She's a lawyer too" doesn't sound as interesting as "You're both avid runners."

When it comes to typical networking or advertising, the same question is asked by those who couldn't contemplate doing anything that doesn't directly bring them business—they robotically ask, "Does it bring in business?" People never ask me whether my involvement in the wine world brings me business. But I'll answer that question: yes—tons. Do we all stand around and talk business? Hardly.

While the traveling crowd knows what everyone does, the topic of discussion is almost never about business. The only thing that is happening is real talk about what's in the glass, or the great new restaurant in town, someone's recent trip, or what their kid is doing. When we introduce someone to someone new, we'll mention what they do for a living, but no one really wants to engage in a conversation about "getting business." Maybe a card is exchanged, maybe a call comes in a few days, weeks, or months.

If you're sitting around wondering why doing the same thing everyone else is doing is not working for you, get a hobby. Develop relationships that are guaranteed to turn into business based on the non-lawyer connection you have with the people involved.

People may actually start to think you're as special and interesting as you think you are.

POLITICAL NETWORKING

Although lawyers make up 43 percent of Congress and 60 percent of the U.S. Senate, according to *Governing* magazine,[10] "Since 1976, the number of lawyers in legislatures has declined by nearly a quarter, from more than 22 percent of all lawmakers to less than 17 percent." Of course, there is a natural path from lawyer to legislator. But the low pay, travel, time commitment, and mudslinging that we see on TV and the Internet turn many lawyers away from public service.

This is a mistake.

I know there is a notion that there should be fewer lawyers in politics, but remember that many "lawyers" in office are not practicing lawyers, have never been practicing lawyers, and have no clue how the law works. They have law degrees, but they don't have clients. In the halls where laws are advocated and passed, I say the more practicing (and former practicing) lawyers, the better. Lawyers think the same as non-lawyers—politics is something that goes on in Washington or their state capitol. But politics affects everything in our court system, and the statutory schemes that govern your practice area.

And the point?

Practicing law is not solely about the pleadings and arguments; it's about advocating to those who make law, or are running for office to make law. Where does most criminal and personal injury law come from? Prosecutors, cops, and insurance companies. Nothing wrong with them trying to make law, but are you involved in this process?

The old "call your legislator" may be meaningless to you, but it wouldn't be if the person on the other end of the call was someone whose campaign you worked on, someone you raised money for, made phone calls for, or encouraged to run. Candidates and elected officials listen to those who give them money, but also to those they trust—people from their small circle of advisors, paid and unpaid.

Many lawyers stay out of politics because they don't have the money to donate. But politicians aren't just looking for money. They need votes, places to speak, places to put signs, advice from those in the know. The first time you hear a politician ask a question that's right out of your mouth to your adversary at a hearing, you'll understand. Participate enough, help out with enough campaigns, and you'll see a lot of the same people. I'm not talking about the Biglaw show where the associates are invited to the conference room at 5:30 to meet some candidate and fill up the room. Get involved at a deeper level and you'll develop relationships that can open important doors for you and your clients.

Today's city commissioner is tomorrow's U.S. senator. Just ask lawyer and former West Miami City Council member and current U.S. Senator Marco Rubio. Do you think the people who helped start his career have their calls put through in Washington? And that mayoral candidate you got a speaking invitation for at your bar association dinner? She now needs someone to help her daughter with a legal matter, and she remembers what type of law you practice. You assume she knows a bunch of lawyers that do what you do, but she doesn't.

It's not solely about your ability to donate; it's about your ability to be relevant to the candidate or elected official. Next time you are invited to an event, if you can't donate (or don't want to yet), be up-front about it, and let the host know you'd like to meet the candidate. It's better than sneaking out without leaving a check.

Running for office is a life-changing commitment, but short of that, there are a lot of ways to be involved in politics—to be important to those who are in and running for office, and make some important, lifelong connections in the process. It's not only good for your profession, but it's good for you as a professional.

CHAPTER 6

MARKETING— IN REAL LIFE

WHAT WILL ALWAYS MATTER IN THE LEGAL PROFESSION

The Internet flows with messages to lawyers about what they need to have to be successful. No longer is it about cross-examination skills, negotiation skills, people skills—it's all about toys, apps, and placement on the World Wide Web. It's sad, and we lawyers have done nothing to attack the commoditization of our profession.

Mark Britton of Avvo.com frequently says "If you are not on the Internet, you don't exist." He tells the story of his search for a toy for a child. It didn't matter how many toy stores sold this toy, all that mattered was which merchant came up (on the first page of Google) and was a click away from shipping the toy. Mark makes a good point, but his point is not inclusive. I've spoken at the same conferences as Mark a couple of times, and always tell the audience that Mark's statement is true, with a caveat: If you are not on the Internet, you don't exist *to those looking for products and services* on the Internet.

The Internet is a wonderful source of information and merchandise, including information about services—like lawyers. At its lowest common denominator, the Internet is where people go to find the best deal on whatever they are going to buy. If your goal is to be the best deal as a lawyer, then I recommend you put every single marketing dollar, dime, and penny into Internet marketing.

This is not a criticism. Clients need low-fee lawyers. People need access to legal representation and if someone can do it, or claim they can do it, for $500 instead of $5,000, then the client should have that choice. We just hope they make an informed one. But not every lawyer is in that market. Not every lawyer is looking for every client with a few dollars to spare. And not every client is looking for the lawyer with the most toys, or best ability to get to the top (of Google).

So we come to my point.

Regardless of who is telling you otherwise, there are things about the legal profession that will never change, no matter how many toys Apple makes, how many social networking sites are invented, or how many tips and tricks exist out there to play the marketing game. There are so many techs and toy-related "10 tips," "5 tips," "20 things every lawyer needs to know" lists.

But here is what will always matter about the profession:

1. Most clients come to a lawyer when they have a problem. They are looking for someone to understand the problem. People understand problems; toys don't understand problems. It will always require a person to understand a problem.
2. Cases and disputes are resolved between people. They will always be resolved with people talking to people. Always.
3. Reputations of lawyers are not ever going to be determined by which lawyer has which toy or placement on the Internet.
4. Real clients with real problems will never hire a lawyer because of the toys they own, or the tech they use, ever.
5. The best tech a lawyer can have is ears.
6. Marketing may get you a call or an appointment, but it will never get you a happy client.
7. Happy clients will always be the best source of referrals, not Google.
8. Even unhappy clients will be a good source of referrals, if their unhappiness is not viewed as your fault.
9. Being on the first page of Google means just that: you are on the first page of Google. There are plenty of unethical, crappy lawyers on the first page of Google, and the clients will never know that until it's too late.
10. Your ability to persuade a judge, jury, prosecutor, opposing civil counsel, client's boss, client's wife, or licensing board will never be determined by the success of your marketing.
11. There will never be a toy or app that will make a client feel better about their situation. Only you and your words and actions will ever make a client feel like he or she is in the right hands.

12. Machines have no emotion, no ability to care, and they break. The best thing your client gets from you is your voice, after you use your ears.
13. No one will ever become great merely because they own something.
14. There is no app, toy, or marketing technique that will get you a thank-you from a client for saving their life or making it better.
15. The number of people you "know" online has nothing to do with you getting a client who needs a good lawyer.

So go, be on the front page of Google, exist on the Internet, buy all the cool new toys. There is a whole world out there that doesn't care about any of it, but they are looking for good lawyers.

Maybe a good lawyer like you.

ARE YOU A GREAT LAWYER, OR A GREAT MARKETER?

Over at Simple Justice,[11] a must-read blog for anyone who wants to know what a real lawyer blog should look like, Scott Greenfield asked whether we are trying to create a new generation of great lawyers or great marketers. Scott was frustrated. He, like me, knows that on Twitter and other social networking sites, there are those that parade as lawyers who have no clients. There are those who parade as the answer to all those wanting a "profitable" career, who have specious backgrounds not worthy of any lawyer's time.

When I started practicing in 1995, a respected criminal defense lawyer told me what he learned at the outset of his career: "Do a good job for your client and the calls will come." We no longer teach that philosophy. We teach that there are too many lawyers and getting clients is more about "slick" then it is about substance. We have lost the notion that in order to market yourself, you must first be good at what you do.

By encouraging "going solo" out of law school, we are saying that being a good lawyer is irrelevant to just about everything. No, I don't agree with going solo out of law school, even if this means you have to volunteer for a while with a lawyer in order to learn how to practice law. Law school doesn't teach you how to be a practicing lawyer, and it never will. The public, mostly hiring lawyers for the first and only time, don't know better. They like what they see and hear, and they hire. Those who seek referrals from other lawyers pale in comparison to those who read a colorful ad with a pretty picture, or listen to the lawyer saying he will "fight" for them, while watching *Matlock*.

Social media is an opportunity for two things: it allows good lawyers to converse with others and develop new relationships with debates, blog posts, and other discussions. It also allows those who are barely lawyers to create an online presence that is, well, a complete lie.

Lawyers are important to society. So are marketers. According to Wikipedia, marketing is defined by the American Marketing Association as the activity, set of institutions, and processes for creating, communicating, delivering, and exchanging offerings *that have value* for customers, clients, partners, and society at large.

"That have value."

Value.

Lawyers that have "value."

Value to clients, or value to a marketer?

WHY WOULD ANYONE HIRE YOU?

You want to know what the future of law entails for you? Probably not much. You do the same crap everyone else does. You're some run-of-the-mill commercial litigator, or you write the same wills as every other estate planning lawyer, or you're an "aggressive" and "caring" and "passionate" criminal defense lawyer that will "fight for your (client's) rights."

It's all garbage. You don't matter. You compete on price and spend your day wondering what works better, pay-per-click or your Facebook fan page. You'll pay the bills and get a nice case every so often, but you're just another lawyer wondering why the world hasn't lined up to hire you.

The future of law is specialization. I'm not just talking about niche practices, I'm talking about specialization within your practice. I'm talking about being a resource in your practice area, or knowing more about a specific issue than others. And yes, I have examples, calm down, I'll lay this out for you in simple, easy terms that you can understand. Maybe you can even put some of this to work in the middle of contemplating your miserable life as a lawyer.

WRITE SOMETHING

No, contrary to what you learned in law school or before you escaped from Biglaw, it doesn't have to be a law review article. Write something—an article on a specific issue relevant to your practice. You're an estate planning lawyer? Here is your article: "Estate Planning for the Young Family—Issues to Consider after Your First Child is Born." Post it, wherever you can. Send it to your friends, send it (really?) to your competition. I'm thinking one of your competitors does big-time estate planning and isn't interested in a young family who can only spend a couple grand on some documents.

TAKE THAT ARTICLE AND TALK ABOUT IT

Lawyers love to hear themselves speak. For some reason, people love to hear lawyers speak—and not just lawyers. Let's continue on the "estate planning for young families" article. Where do young families go? Temple, church, schools. Offer to give a talk on the article, copies to be provided to the attendees. And don't forget about the local bar associations—there is nothing like walking into a room of lawyers from various practice areas.

REFERENCE THE ARTICLE IN YOUR E-MAIL SIGNATURE BLOCK WITH A LINK

I need to explain this?

EXPAND THE ARTICLE

The topic of "estate planning for young families" will evolve. There will be tax code changes, issues regarding the definition of "family" and "spouse," and case law that affects the practice. You must stay on top of this. If your one-page article becomes a 15-page e-book, great. You will become the go-to lawyer on this issue. You will be consulted on issues regarding estate planning for young families. You will be hired because you have put yourself out there on this issue. Do you actually know more about this issue than other lawyers? Maybe. But whether you like it or not, when clients are making a decision on hiring a lawyer, often perception wins out. Does a lawyer who wrote a book on his practice area know more than one who hasn't? Doesn't matter. The book author has the reputation that "she wrote the book."

What I am suggesting works in any practice area. No one cares what type of law you practice. They only care if you appear to know more about their problem than the others who do what you do. Find something within your practice area that clients want or need to know, and become the lawyer who provides the information.

You don't even need to pay a marketer to help you.

You're welcome.

A GOOGLE SEARCH TELLS ALL: "HOW TO MARKET YOURSELF AS A GOOD LAWYER"

In today's world of lawyering, it is not the lawyer, but the perception of the lawyer, that brings in the cash. No longer does a lawyer need to work to become a good lawyer by handling cases to the satisfaction of clients.

It's all about the marketing. Pretend you are a good lawyer, and convince the unknowing public of the bullshit you are trying to peddle. It's not about reputation, it's about making money. Present yourself as a good lawyer on your website, on Facebook, on Twitter, and maybe even with the aid of those who have left their "wildly successful" law practices to now teach you not how to practice, but how to market.

You want to be a good marketer, hire a marketing maven. Going down that road, I'd be wildly suspicious of any "former lawyer" who claims to have the secrets.

You want to be a good lawyer, then lawyer. Practice law.

A marketing maven can't teach you to try cases, or how to get a judge or other respected lawyer to say you are a good lawyer. A marketing maven can only teach you how to create an image that is not necessarily your reality.

Even when you're not, you can market yourself as a good lawyer all day. It's called lying.

Be a good lawyer, don't just play one on the web.

HOW TO GET THE CLIENT AND LOSE YOUR LAW LICENSE

There is no better collection of BS than the attorney section of the yellow pages. Lawyers presenting themselves to the unknowing public as "aggressive," or whatever other adjective hits the emotions of the recently arrested, injured, or those preparing for divorce. Sometimes though, it goes beyond BS and becomes a flat-out lie.

Take the case a few years ago of the lawyer who told a client he had won a $1.1 million medical malpractice settlement.[12]

Except he didn't. He didn't even file a suit.

The New Jersey Supreme Court ordered his immediate disbarment.

Seems harsh, except that the lawyer was already serving a one-year suspension for lying to another client.

I know, you would never do that. But that's you.

WRITING FOR LAWYERS

One of the things I hear from lawyers is "I want to write, but I don't have the time/know where to post/want to start a blog." I'm not in the blog-selling business and I don't believe that every lawyer should have a blog—because I'm not in the blog-selling business. Not every lawyer can write, but if you want to write, I'll offer my thoughts.

The first thing you have to determine when thinking about writing is your audience. Unfortunately, many of you law-review types actually think anyone out there wants to read something closely resembling a law review article. You can't write anything without citing case law or other articles no one has read or wants to read. You believe you're still writing for adoration of your ability to analyze the history of some statute. You believe you can't write anything unless it takes you weeks to research and is perfectly cited. You believe writing is done to impress rather than educate or inform.

If most of your business comes from law professors, go for it. But if your audience is other lawyers or, heaven forbid, clients, dumb it down. Write as if you're talking like a normal person. Writing is marketing. Clients don't pay attention to the writings of lawyers because "Man, that guy has the best footnotes." They pay attention because the article conveys that this lawyer seems to know this issue.

When you write, you'll see—ahem—comments about the writing style. These are coming from those that can't write like normal people. They spent months writing some over-cited, boring article that no one read and are raging against anyone who writes something interesting that contains a non-law review writing style.

As a PI lawyer, do you think you're going to get more hits (what we used to call "readers") writing about the history of comparative fault, or an article about the five things not to do after an injury? As a civil litigator, do you think it's better to write about the evolution of notice pleading, or the pros and cons of mediation versus litigation? If you need a guide, write something that would be a good speaking topic. Would you find an interested audience as a corporate lawyer if your topic was "(some obscure UCC code) and its effect on (some international convention)" or "tax consequences of various corporate structures"?

If you're going to post online, and you should, know that most people search for legal issues, not lawyers or law firms. Write about things that interest people, not just things that interest you. Now let's talk about publishing.

If you want to start a blog, first make sure that if you work for someone, you get permission. Then consider how often you will post. A new blog will get nowhere unless you post at least once a week. If you don't have 10 to 20 topics in mind, forget it. Also consider whether you'll want to write about recent news in your practice area. If so, you'll need to post more often.

Do not outsource your posts to some shorts-wearing, mommy's-basement-dwelling hipster. If you're too busy to write and post, do not write and post.

When you write something, send it to your friends, online and offline. Tell your clients, current and former. You shouldn't tell them every time you write something, as not everything you write is interesting (despite what mommy tells you), and people will get bored and annoyed.

Determine whether there are any publications that may be interested in an article from you. Many legal publications are constantly looking for content, and even if you can't get something in right away, they will give you space in a later issue. Remember that if you are writing something that will not be published right away, you need to stay away from current events and stick to something that will be timely regardless of its publication date.

Finally, one issue I hear a lot about is length. Who said that anything a lawyer writes has to be a certain length? You don't impress readers with the amount of words; you'll put them to sleep. A 300-word informational article will get you more readers than a 2,000-word, citation-filled analysis of something about which no one cares.

So cut the crap about time and length and your fear that your old law professors will be disappointed in your down-to-earth article geared toward the public. Most people reading your articles are just looking for information, or your point of view on an issue.

THE TRUTH ABOUT MEDIA APPEARANCES

Lawyers who practice in small law firms are frequently in the media. The reason is simple: the cases we handle are interesting. When was the last time your local TV station wanted to interview a Biglaw partner about a corporate transaction? Stories of divorce, crime, ethics violations, catastrophic injuries caused by plane crashes, and whether a building collapse was caused by a construction defect are why Don Henley had a hit with "Dirty Laundry." (I love the fact I was able to weave in a comment about Don Henley. Big fan.) At some point, you may get a call from a local reporter because you either have a high-profile client, or the reporter knows you and there is a case in your practice area where your comments are requested.

Let's begin with the obvious: Lawyers like to talk. Lawyers like to talk when lots of people are listening. Lawyers like to get calls about cases. Lawyers like to get calls instead of another lawyer getting calls. Media appearances are often considered free advertising. One of the best things about media appearances, paper or TV, is that most people don't remember what you said, just that they saw you or your name. It goes like this: "I saw you in the paper." "Oh yeah, what did you see?" "I don't remember, I just remember seeing your name." Thankfully, no one seems to remember if you said something so ridiculous that it made you look borderline incompetent.

Let me first talk about media appearances (paper and TV) regarding your clients. I disagree with the notion that "no comment" is always the best advice when the media comes calling about your client. There is no reason (other than a gag order) to refrain from saying something good about a client who is getting pounded in the press. You're the lawyer for heaven's sake—say something. Say you look forward to addressing the allegations in court, say the truth will come out, say your client is a well-respected professional and you look forward to defending him. If the other side is out there lying about your client, tell the truth, even if you must in a general way in order to prevent something coming back to bite you in the ass. Pretend you care. Pretend it matters that everyone is trashing your client.

Know that you may be on the phone for 20 minutes and then see the story without a mention of you, or worse, your long rambling quote was cut to a sentence. It's always the editor who does this. Speak in sound bites. Getting quoted out of context, meaning your original quote was shortened, is never fun to have to explain to your client or others. Should you go on TV and give an hour-long interview about your case while it's pending? Probably not, but again, say *something* if you can.

Now let's talk about cases that don't involve your client.

As you go through your career, chances are that your media appearances will have less to do with your own high-profile cases and more to do with cases being handled by other lawyers in your community or around the country. Before you get excited about jumping in front of a camera or talking to a reporter on the phone, here are some things to consider.

1. Never talk about something about which you know nothing. I know CNN wants to interview you about a local criminal case, but you're an estate planning lawyer that was a prosecutor for 10 minutes, 15 years ago. Do us a favor and refer the interview to someone else. I know giving an opportunity like this to someone else is going to kill you, but do it.

2. Never agree to be interviewed by a reporter who has an angle. You can tell if this is the case if you ask prior to the interview what the issues are and as you are talking with the reporter you frequently hear "But don't you think . . . ?" That reporter isn't interested in your opinion, they're interested in you validating their opinion. Click.

3. Decline the opportunity to play backseat driver. Of course you would handle the case differently, you're not sitting in the courtroom. You're too smart to actually be there listening to the evidence. You didn't get the case, but that doesn't mean it's your job to second-guess everything the lawyer in the case is doing. We know, you are an awesome lawyer and know everything, and the client was stupid not to call you, the perfect lawyer. Talk about why the lawyer may be doing

this and the options, but don't sit there and create ratings by allowing the anchor to make it about the lawyer's competence or strategy. Educate people.

4. No matter how much publicity you will get, never agree to talk in-depth about a case in another state unless you know the law in that state. How they do things in your state is of no interest to anyone but you, and the more you say that, the more you look like you're doing the interview just for attention.

5. Don't make people dumber. I'll say it again: educate people. Know the law and procedure, explain how things work, and be bold enough to dispel the public's (wrong) perception about the process and the evidence.

6. Whether you get a phone call or are approached in person, unless you must, don't give an interview unprepared—especially if it's about your own case. Sometimes you're walking out of court or somewhere else and are approached by the media for a comment. If you feel the need, say something quick, and then ask the media to meet you at your office later. The same goes for the paper. When they call, ask to call them back. Do some research, see if there is a recent development you don't know about, and then engage in the interview. When the paper calls, always ask for the reporter's deadline so you don't waste your time preparing for an interview only to realize the deadline is in 30 minutes.

7. Always return the call, even if you're not going to say much. Reading that someone didn't return a call or was unavailable is annoying.

8. Remember that reporters can often be a valuable part of the process. In a high-profile case, you may find that a friendly reporter is an essential source of information. You will also find that the reporter/lawyer relationship can be one of the most important ongoing relationships you have in your career.

Finally, and please don't cry, media appearances don't bring you clients. Current clients think it's cool when they see their lawyers on TV, but other than that, all you will get from frequent media appearances is your friends and family saying that they saw you on TV or in the paper. That's it.
Sorry.

LAWYER CONSULTANT ON LAWYER DIRECTORIES

While today's lawyer runs, as fast as possible, to put their profile on every single website promising to get them to the first page of Google and bring them more clients than they ever dreamed of, a lawyer marketing consultant actually questions the practice. Dave Lorenzo of Rainmakerlawyer. com asks, "Do Internet Directory Services Work for Lawyer Marketing?"[13]

As the economy deteriorated these services ramped up their marketing efforts so that almost every lawyer in America received a call from one of them at some point (or so it seemed).

Dave correctly notes that directory services are essentially the Internet replacement of the phone book. But then he makes this point:

You list your law firm in there with other attorneys who do the same thing as you do. You provide your information packaged in the same way as all the other lawyers marketing their services. You even have the opportunity to list prices for your services. Then people call you. Some call seeking free advice and some call shopping around for the least expensive lawyer.

He makes the desperate-for-business lawyer feel good:

You will get phone calls from most of these services. And in many cases you will get clients. In a few cases, you may even get enough clients to do better than break even on your investment. Many people would say this is a good lawyer-marketing tactic since you are receiving a positive return on investment.

Then he drops the bomb, engaging in what few lawyer marketers are willing to discuss—the truth:

> The problem with directory services is that they make you a commodity. You become the same as a can of peas on the shelf in a supermarket. Potential clients cannot see the difference in your service from all the other attorneys in the directory. You all look the same. When everything looks the same the only criteria the client has to make a decision is price. This is not good.

This is "not good"?
Damn.
Dave believes that placing yourself on these "please hire me" sites will give you visibility, but not much—if any—credibility. He gives a big fat "no" on the subject of differentiation:

> This is where we put the nail in the coffin. These directory services offer no way to differentiate you from everyone else. In fact, they make you a commodity which is the opposite of what good lawyer marketing is supposed to do.

Dave's analysis is focused on those directories that claim your clients are waiting to hire you. Noticeably absent from his analysis are the typical directories that serve as place cards for lawyers. I personally think every lawyer should have a profile on the most popular sites—the ones people go to for information on a lawyer. But I've never participated in these "I need clients" sites, and Dave's post nails the reason why.

AN ACTUAL TRUE (NO, REALLY) FOR-REAL MARKETING SECRET BY A CREDIBLE PERSON (SERIOUSLY)

Before there was Twitter or Facebook, or the slew of social media sites where you can auto-post to death your desire for business, there existed blogs. Because there wasn't any place to post links to the blog, except on other blogs, people actually read blogs and because of that, people often wrote things that mattered (without links to their website(s)). One of the people who has maintained a presence of real blogging is Thom Singer.[14] Thom is a speaker, author of more than nine books, and actually says things that make sense. He doesn't like to be pigeonholed as a networking guy, but if you want to learn about networking and business development, Thom's not a bad choice for daily reading.

Today, there is a new marketing secret for every hour of the day. Most of those tweeting or copying other people's posts about marketing "secrets" have never achieved any level of business success, nor is their secret a secret. Of course, there are always the groupies who think if they hear from one of their idols that they should try to give business rather than get business, they have just heard the cure for cancer.

I don't see many secrets because most are just called secrets to attract readers, but Thom wrote a blog post on how to refer him business. In that post he revealed some actual secrets:[15]

(1) No one knows what you do for a living. (2) Because of that, you have to make sure you let people know not only what you do, but what you are looking for in terms of clients. Stop wasting time on potential clients and instead spend your time educating those who refer you business.

Lawyers love to waste time. Potential clients call and want to "come in." Sure, spend a free hour (free consultations, except for contingent cases, are for losers) with me so I can realize that we aren't a good fit. Yeah, I know, the young, desperate lawyer is thrilled to have an actual live person come and meet them at their Regus office or Starbucks, but what is the point if five minutes into the coffee, the lawyer realizes that the client needs an employment lawyer instead of a divorce lawyer? Wouldn't it be better if your referral source knew exactly the type of cases you want, and more importantly, *don't* want?

We're scared to do this. We're scared to be negative. Send us clients, we'll ferret them out. We'll meet with four and maybe one will retain our services. We'll spend all day screening bad referrals. Thom says we need to be clear to people that refer us business.

"I've spoken to networking groups about this. I tell them the cases I don't want. I tell them to ask potential clients what they are prepared to spend on a lawyer. I am occasionally told that I probably scare people into never calling me to refer a case. Good. They're the people who hear "I need a lawyer," and immediately send the broke jerk with a "great case" to my office.

I have a history of telling my referral sources that they sent me a dud. It's called educating your referral sources. Try it.

If you don't like my advice, take Thom's.

ARE PUBLIC RELATIONS FIRMS STILL RELEVANT?

Yes.

Now you can go back to work, or your Xbox, or continue reading. Whatever makes your precious self happy.

After I was solo for five years, I started Tannebaum Weiss—new office space, business cards, stationery, phone number, all the bells and whistles. I know in today's world you may wonder, "Why didn't you just get a new laptop," but back then, it was OK for lawyers to operate like professionals and interact with other human beings in office buildings.

I also hired a public relations firm. I wanted to get the word out about our practice and thought this was the best way. We didn't have Facebook or Twitter, and the media was still interested in reporting about things other than, well, what was on Facebook and Twitter. It was important to be at events where potential relationships could be started, because we couldn't just hire some kid to tweet all day about how awesome we were. We wanted to establish the firm in the community and couldn't do it with a Facebook fan page.

We retained the PR firm for one year. It was expensive. We couldn't really afford it, but I thought it was important and that it would somehow pay for itself. Of course, this was also back in the day when investing in your law firm meant more than just finding an outlet at the local Starbucks and hoping it all worked out without having to invest a dime. It was a learning experience, from the initial interviews (we interviewed two firms) to the working relationship.

The first thing to know is that PR is not marketing. Both have elements of each other, but marketing is closer to advertising. Public relations is closer to relationship building. Public relations requires the clients to participate. Marketing can require as little as a check and a kid with a keyboard.

The first firm we interviewed was well-known. Every time a hotel, restaurant, or club opened up, they seemed to be behind the promotion. Their agents were mini-celebrities and it appeared that working with them was going to get us noticed in the community, so we brought them in for an interview. At the outset, the owner said: "We would love to work with you, but we don't have experience with lawyers." I asked why that mattered. We were looking to be promoted, this firm seemed to do a great job with promotion, we had some money, let's go.

"We would first need to learn about your practice, who you are looking to meet, what events you would want to be involved with, and what your message would be." So lesson one, if you're looking for a PR firm, they're like law firms—all are not created equal. Some firms have particular divisions, while others concentrate on a certain segment of the business community.

The second interview went something like this: "We only represent professional firms, government bodies, and corporate entities. We've read up on your practice and think we can put you together with some of our other clients and introduce you to some of our media contacts that would be interested in speaking with you about stories they are writing." I asked about press releases, as at that time this was my perception of PR firms—they spent their days sending out press releases and waiting for a bite. "We can send out press releases, but we'd rather set up meetings with our media contacts so that when they are doing a story, they know someone to call."

With the onslaught of social media, you may believe that your best move is to invest in a digital marketing firm. I hate to break it to you, but many of those are former traditional marketers that now want you to believe they have the secrets to the Internet because no one wants them to produce a brochure anymore. I get it—everyone wants to be found on the Internet, and there is no question that lawyers need to have some Internet presence. Unfortunately, developing relationships that will provide good clients over the long term is not something worth waiting for as much anymore. We want our clients to buy us like they buy a pair of shoes—point, click, overnight shipping, done.

While I understand that everyone needs to make a living, there is still room for traditional public relations services. A good PR agent puts you together with the right people and events and keeps you away from the wrong ones. This may mean a one-on-one meeting, a sponsorship at a key event, or making you available to the media (and I'm not talking about those pathetic e-mails about how so-and-so lawyer is available to comment on the latest court opinion, or verdict, or tragic news story).

While every lawyer in town is running to the so-called digital marketing firms, consider a public relations firm. You may find it better to actually meet the people that can help you build your business, rather than hope they are pointing and clicking their way to your bank account.

THE BEST MARKETING TOOL FOR LAWYERS

I was talking to a lawyer marketing guy. He sells blogs. He told me he gets calls from new bloggers: "I've been blogging for three months and I don't have a single new client from the blog." His response: "Get out and meet some people."

I scan the Internet and see lawyers typing "how to get rich as a lawyer" on the hour on Google. I see former lawyers parading as coaches; their practices having failed, they're ready to tell you how to be successful. Some of them practiced for a fleeting moment, and were never hired by a client. I see former lawyers trying to claim star status by convincing you that Apple's newest device is the key to your future.

Here, today, for free, I give you the best marketing tool for lawyers.

Here it is.

Ready?

The lawyer. You, the lawyer, and other lawyers.

So while you're typing your brains out and buying every new gadget that the online world cheers about, answer the questions below. When you are done, you can let me know that I am wrong, that it is really all about blogs and toys, or start thinking about getting the hell away from technology for a while and trying a little human interaction for a bit.

1. How many lawyers do you know?
2. When is the last time you had a conversation with a lawyer about your practice?
3. When is the last time another lawyer referred you a client?
4. At what point did you start to think that typing blog posts and playing with the iPad was the answer to building your practice?
5. When is the last time you sponsored an event?
6. When is the last time you went to an event?
7. When is the last time you spoke to a group of lawyers? Real lawyers, discussing real things—like law, not battery life and phone reception?

8. Under what theory did you think you would get great clients with good cases by writing blog posts? (Hint: Clients hire lawyers, not blog posts.)

9. Who are you and what relevance do you have in your legal community? Are you known for something important that a client would need, or do you just know how to scan a document in a parking lot of a Starbucks?

10. Who was it that convinced you that all it takes is a computer and some SEO work, and what relevance does that person have in the legal community?

11. When did you take yourself out of the mix?

LESSONS LEARNED FROM HANGING OUT WITH 75-YEAR-OLD LAWYERS

I had just returned from my annual bar convention. Have you been? Hundreds of lawyers, judges, and a smattering of law students attending meetings, receptions, CLE seminars, and having chance meetings at the real bar with opposing counsel. It's a day or two to realize you're part of something bigger than your law office.

I know, some of you hate your state bar. You don't hang out with "bar types" and see no value in spending a day or two running around a hotel and saying hello to lawyers you know and don't know. But being involved in my state bar has been one of the most important components of building my practice.

Three years into practice, I became friends with someone prominent in my state bar. He told me of the importance of being involved, encouraged me to get involved, and said if I wanted to be on a committee, he would make it happen. I picked a rules committee, but was told I needed more experience to be on that committee and was instead appointed to another rules committee.

When I first attended this meeting, I walked into a room of about 50 people—lawyers from all over the state in various practice areas, as well as judges. The practice area of the rules committee was not an area in which I spent much time, but I soon realized that others on the committee practiced in different areas as well. One member was a prosecutor. He and I disagreed on every single issue. In fact, he disagreed with most people on the committee. Often he was the one dissenting vote. As I write this article, he's sitting right next to me on another committee, a decade, many cases, and a developed friendship later.

I have many stories like that. I sit on my third committee now, full of the many familiar faces of people I've called on for advice and help, and those who have done the same to me. Yes, I know, you're wondering, because it's all you care about, "Do you get cases from it?" Yes, idiots, relationships turn into cases—have you not learned that yet?

It's not just sitting on the committees, discussing the issues of the day; it's the estate planning lawyers going to the business law reception, or the family lawyers going to the appellate reception. After a few years, it becomes a day or two of packed events, people to see again, and people to meet for the first time.

Now to the 75-year-old lawyer.

Among the suits walking the conference center, name tags prominently displayed, I saw him in the lobby, in a polo shirt and shorts. He had no name tag, he had no iPad or stack of materials for his next meeting. This year, as last year, he was getting an award for his lifetime of service to the bar. He's one of the giants of the profession.

I walked over to him to say congratulations and asked why he was dressed so casually. He said, "It is a resort, right?" I asked him what he had planned for the day. He had a meeting, a lunch, all the usual stuff. But he had one event he was looking forward to more than the award dinner. See, back in the '70s he was a member of the young lawyers section. For the first time, they were holding a reunion. Although he was receiving one of the highest awards the bar gives, he was more excited about seeing old friends.

At 75 years old, and with 51 years practicing law, what really mattered to him was the relationships he'd developed—the relationships he developed by showing up to the bar conventions.

WHAT MATTERS IN A LAWYER'S OFFLINE PRESENCE?

While we're busy creating a generation of "lawyers" obsessed with their online presence, I wonder if the lawyer's offline presence is even a consideration anymore.

I'm not talking about the Starbucks lawyer with no clients whose only offline presence involves remaining quiet enough not to disturb the college students enjoying cafe lattes; I'm talking about the lawyer that goes to court, or meets with clients, or actually carries around a file or two and wears an occasional suit. And I'm not just talking about dress.

I'm talking about presence.

I'm talking about the way a lawyer conducts him- or herself in and out of court, around clients, around other lawyers. My personal belief is that a lawyer's presence is about how they conduct themselves from the time he or she walks out of their house to the time they get home.

I once was in court before the judge took the bench and observed four prosecutors laughingly discuss the weekend. The discussion was loud enough for the defendants in the courtroom to hear. I wondered what they thought. I wondered if they were either relieved to know that the people who in a few minutes would ask the judge to sentence them, take them into custody, or otherwise advocate that their lives change in a significant way were happily discussing their social lives, or whether that made them feel like this courtroom was not a serious place to the government.

I then saw a tweet from a business professional criticizing lawyers tweeting from court. I explained that there is a lot of downtime in court waiting for the judge to call cases, to which he responded that regardless, he would immediately fire his lawyer if he saw him tweeting from court.

Some clients don't like when opposing counsel appears friendly in court. Some lawyers can't wear a matching jacket and pants to save their life. Some lawyers put on a dramatic show at every court appearance, thinking the client will be like a proud parent and say "that's my lawyer!"

This leads me to a question, really directed at clients:

What do clients expect from their lawyer regarding his or her behavior, conduct, dress, and overall presence? Have you ever asked a client who has been to court with a lawyer what bothered them about their lawyer's conduct, or the conduct of another lawyer? When clients hire a lawyer, is it for the lawyer's ability alone, or does it matter how clean their office is, how professional they look, or how they carry themselves in court?

Once you get past the lawyer's BS website and Vegas-style marketing brochure, what really matters?

CREATING A "BRAND" WHILE OTHERS CREATE YOUR REPUTATION

Spirit Airlines is a cheap airline. They advertise a $9 fare club. They advertise a lot. Their goal appears to be to let everyone know—to create the reputation—that they are the low-cost alternative to other airlines, just like you want everyone to know you are the aggressive alternative to all other aggressive lawyers out there who will "fight" for their clients (free consultations and payment plans available of course as well). In fact, when you Google "Spirit Airlines," you get this:

Spirit Airlines—cheap tickets, cheap flights, discount airfare, cheap . . .

I've never flown Spirit, and I don't know if anyone has actually flown anywhere for $9, but I do know that I've never heard anything good about this airline. They call themselves "cheap," while others say they're "bad." They do make a ton of money, which should bring a smile to the growing number of cheap and bad lawyers out there.

Maybe there are people who have had great experiences on Spirit, but I haven't heard from them. Those voices seem to be quieter. I heard, and I think you did too, that they wouldn't give a $197 refund to a dying veteran who was too sick to use his ticket because it would have violated their refund policy. Policies are great, until they piss off the wrong person or segment of society. After several weeks of bad publicity, including this lone man protesting outside Tampa International Airport, and a bunch of angry veterans and others typing away on Facebook, they refunded the fare, plus committed to making a $5,000 donation to his charity of choice: Wounded Warriors.

You may think Spirit really screwed this one up, but you'd be wrong. They won't miss the extra $5,000, and don't bet that all those threatening to never fly Spirit again won't be settling in for a half-can of Diet Coke on a Spirit flight near you soon. People are happy to protest and join the crowd on social media, until that terrible, unfair, mean company can save them a dollar next time they need something. Spirit will be fine. As long as they are cheaper than the others, the angry crowds will still be pointing and clicking for airline tickets. I'm not sure, though, that you and your "hire us, we're cheap" small firm could take a hit like Spirit and not feel the effects.

So I bring you the bad news that while you and your small firm are buying a reputation, trying to create a reputation, sorry, "personal brand" (back in the old days of the early 2000s we used to call them reputations, but I know, I'm out of touch), things happen that prevent you from continuing the charade. As a young, hungry lawyer you try so hard to control the message, but you can't control what others say. You spend all that money on reputation management and pay-per-click advertising, while some lone, old, dying guy is managing your reputation just fine for free. Damn.

Reputations aren't created or bought, they are earned. Personal branding is nothing more than a new way for people to create form over substance. You have nothing to offer, so let's make you look good, even if it's all garbage. The intelligent clients, those looking for more than cheap, will go beyond your online and offline fake reputation and learn the truth. They will ask people in your community about your real reputation; they will go beyond what you've tried to project.

Spirit's problem was a failure to understand the broader consequences of their policy. But they are bigger and cheaper than you (and you can't fly anyone anywhere on a big jet), and their market is those people only looking for the cheapest way to get from point A to point B. Apparently though, no one in the inner circle at Spirit thought to mention, or if they did, failed to initially convince anyone, that adhering to the refund policy could have negative effects on their reputation—or Spirit didn't care. I don't know.

Spirit has created a reputation for themselves as cheap, and that's exactly the message they projected to the public. If your only goal is to create a reputation that you are cheaper than the rest, then maybe you don't care what your real reputation is either.

FREE ADVERTISING

A retail business owner asked me why I don't believe in pay-per-click advertising or spending money on SEO strategies for my practice, as it has worked well for his stores. So I asked him, "What would you do if you needed a lawyer?"

"I would call someone, get a name, and then look that person up," he said.

"You wouldn't just do a Google search?"

"No, never. After I got a name, I would check out the lawyer's background, maybe see if he's written anything that gives him credibility."

No kids, he's not talking about cute tweets or postings with links on a Facebook fan page. He's talking about real writing, and he's talking about getting your name from real people. But I know that I'm wrong, don't know what I'm talking about, and my practice is facing a sure death when I suggest that there are other ways of getting your name out there besides vomiting all over every social media platform.

For those wondering if the life of a lawyer will ever be anything more than keeping track of your Google prowess by taking calls like "I found you on the Internet. How much do you charge?" I have good news—it can be. There are actually real people out there who are looking for quality. It's not that they found you first; it's that they found you after a little research. If you're going to be the type of lawyer that is found after someone gives your name, you might as well have something on the Internet that evidences you have done more than just listen to some unemployed lawyer's advice on building a practice.

My ideas are mostly all free, and if you're not afraid to use your real name, you may get some benefit from using them.

1. Those community newspapers you see at the local deli need a recurring column written by a lawyer. They'll publish your name and picture and a little bio. They'll need you to write basic stuff about law. Maybe you can do that. Post the articles to your JD Supra account. Of course you have a JD Supra account, it's where lawyers post documents and other items. By the way, your state bar also has

a publication. Distribution? Every lawyer and judge in your state. Submit an article.

2. Besides local bar associations, your town has a few business organizations. You've never heard of them. See number 1 for where they advertise their meetings. They want you to come speak to them for 20 minutes about anything. You'll have to wear something that makes you look like a lawyer, so maybe tuck in your T-shirt. They may want you to sponsor the breakfast or lunch. Consider doing that, even if you're one of those new lawyers who believes you can and should build a practice without investing a dime.

3. You have friends who actually leave their homes and do more than pimp themselves on the Internet. They're in bar organizations, business networks, nonprofits, cults—tell them you are inviting yourself to their next event. If you have more than a few friends, you now have a fairly decent social schedule and you can get introduced to people who won't say they found you on the Internet.

4. Write an op-ed piece in the local newspaper. Yes, people still read the paper. An op-ed piece gives you the opportunity to write a decent-sized analysis of a current event related to your practice. A new law is passed? Express your opinion. A caveat: because you are using your real name, you probably have to be truthful and know what you are talking about.

5. Introduce yourself to local media. Instead of quietly cursing local reporters for their lack of knowledge about the law, personally tell them they are wrong (or right, if that happens). All reporters have e-mail. Good reporters don't want to be wrong, but many don't have connections in the legal community. Be a resource. They'll call you five times and mention your name only once, but eventually, if you develop good relationships, you'll be able to call a reporter about your case instead of sending out those silly worthless press releases that no one cares about.

Actually, now that I've read through these again, forget it. These things take too long. Do the pay-per-click advertising thing, and ask people to "like" and "follow" you. Keep taking those calls asking how much you charge. It's much easier, and you don't have to think much or get dressed.

THE ETHICS OF LAWYER MARKETING, AND OTHER LOST IDEALS

When I was in law school, the Internet was in its infancy. Cheesy lawyer marketing was limited to billboards, bus benches, and sending "I heard you got arrested" brochures to clients' homes. I remember my torts professor (of all subjects) say "I better never see any of your names on the back of a bus." The funny thing is that I never have—seen any of my classmates names on the back of a bus, that is—and yes, I always look.

Yesterday's lawyer marketing still exists; the billboards are still the darling of personal injury lawyers and the bus benches are mostly reserved for ticket and foreclosure defense lawyers. But today, it's all about the Internet. It's all about getting to the top of Google, and nothing more. Every day lawyers get e-mails about how some kid in shorts and a T-shirt sitting at Starbucks can get us to the number 1 spot on Google. I always wonder how everyone can be number 1 in this "race to the top," which is really a race to the depths of shameless marketing.

Here is the secret to Google: linking. Every chance you get, link to your website. Google will pick it up. This was better said by a commenter to one of my blog posts:

> How does Google do it? Is it magic? . . . sleight of hand? . . . divine intervention? No, it's done by robots. Yes, robots. They mindlessly crawl around the web and look for magic words that people like you and me use to find plumbers, dentists and lawyers.

When I wrote about this, I received these comments:

The Ethics of Lawyer Marketing, and Other Lost Ideals 129

I'm working with Justia to create a better blog platform (will be up in a few weeks), and they want me to write that way. They've got some good ideas but that one is lame.

It is just advertising. If you are practicing law to make your living and not as the ideological lawyer for a cause, what is the problem?

Exactly—this is the lawyer marketing being taught today, and those whose Biglaw dreams have been shattered and have to suffer through trying it on their own find nothing wrong with the race to depths of shameless marketing. It's all about getting clients, even if getting those clients means typing mindlessly for the sole purpose of being number 1 on Google.

I guess after all those years of college and law school, you have to try to be good at something.

CHAPTER 7

OF COURSE, SOCIAL MEDIA

THE DEFINITIVE (ALL YOU NEED TO KNOW) GUIDE (THIS IS IT) TO SOCIAL MEDIA FOR LAWYERS

Sorry to disappoint the snake-oil salesmen, but I am going to buck the trend, and debunk the fallacy of nonpracticing lawyers who write books about social media for lawyers. Here, today, my friends, I will tell you everything you need to know about the complicated and scary topic of how to talk to people on the Internet like a normal person.

FACEBOOK

If you think Facebook is code for "high school," you're correct. But if you live in the same town you went to high school, why not connect with your loser friends who have some midlevel job? They need lawyers. Yes, as part of reconnecting with your past you'll experience the joy of seeing that girl you wanted to date has moved to some small crap town and married Jim, who is prematurely bald and "an awesome husband," but so what?

Do not post every single picture you take of your kids, dogs, in-laws with your kids, kids with your dogs, the 189 pictures of your vacation, or fake complain about the first-class service on some airline. You're practicing law, not creating a family scrapbook.

Do not have a Facebook fan page for your law firm. No one should ever be a fan of a law firm. You are not a rock star, and even if you were, rock stars do not ask people to be their fans. It just happens with good music. Asking people to be your fan may also violate your state bar ethics rules, if that kind of nuisance interests you—you know, ethics rules.

TWITTER

Everything important in the world is referenced on Twitter. Watch the news for 27 seconds and a story will either revolve around some celebrity tweeting something stupid or a rumor that was confirmed via someone's Twitter account.

Here is where I give you, the young, desperate-to-make-money lawyer, a huge cost savings. You don't need to pay someone to teach you Twitter. You don't need to buy any Twitter books.

Here is everything you need to know about Twitter:

Open an account. Talk to people.

I know, you're thinking, "Talk to people? I need to sell to people!"

No.

Don't spend your Twitter time linking to your website, and don't listen to your SEO guy who tells you he will set up various accounts to post links to your website under fake names. You're a lawyer, an officer of the court; you should have no issue using your real name.

Do not protect your tweets and do not ask people to follow you. Do not thank people for retweeting what you wrote and do not thank people for following you. Talk to people like you would in real life (if you do that kind of thing). If you write a blog, post a link to a recent post. Follow people you have things in common with both in and out of your professional life. What you do as a lawyer is not that interesting. Trust me.

LINKEDIN

LinkedIn is a complete waste of time. The proof of this is the various hysterical posts and books written in an attempt to convince you that LinkedIn is not a complete waste of time. It is. Yes, you should have a profile there. You should have a profile on every social media site. Yes, you should connect with people on LinkedIn, but that's it. Move on.

GOOGLE+

See LinkedIn section above.

KLOUT

Seriously?

CAN WE ALL JUST SHUT UP ABOUT SOCIAL MEDIA CHANGING THE WORLD, AND ACTUALLY CHANGE THE WORLD?

Self-fulfilling prophecy:[16] A self-fulfilling prophecy is a prediction that directly or indirectly causes itself to become true, by the very terms of the prophecy itself, due to positive feedback between belief and behavior.

The self-fulfilling prophecy is, in the beginning, a false definition of the situation evoking a new behavior which makes the original false conception come "true."

In other words, a prophecy declared as truth when it is actually false may sufficiently influence people, either through fear or logical confusion, so that their reactions ultimately fulfill the once-false prophecy.

There is no question, no debate, that social media has changed the way we communicate. The telephone did that too. So did the fax machine, and e-mail. But we still talk to people (though not as much), and we still fill restaurants with groups of people wanting good food and good conversation.

What we fail to understand is that there is a group of people out there who are selling social media as a career, and it is they who spend their days telling everyone else that they are either involved in social media or dead. If I sold Toyotas, I would spend my days trying to convince others that Toyota was the best car. Sure, there are other ways to get around, but according to me, it would be about the Toyota, and nothing else.

This is how people in social media work. Their "jobs" are nothing more than selling all of us on something that is otherwise free and readily available. They try to convince others that they know the secrets, and that even though they have never had business success, you can if you just write them a check.

You think I'm kidding? People, lawyers, do it every day. The drum continues to beat, because it has to in order for these social media salespeople to survive.

And I'm tired of it.

Here's a recent defense of social media is from Entrepreneur.com, "How Social Media Is Changing Business":[17]

> Up until now, social media has been optional for businesses. But Charlene Li, one of the world's leading thinkers on social media and co-founder of the Altimeter Group, a research-based advisory firm in San Mateo, Calif., predicts that companies that do not get on the social media bandwagon soon—within three to five years—will not survive. It's not an overstatement to say social media is transforming every aspect of business.

Hear that? That's the cheer of social media salespeople everywhere. "We are no longer optional." In fact, read the article; it quotes a bunch of people about how social media will take over the business world—and everyone quoted is in the social media business. It's not even subtle.

I think social media is great. I like being on Facebook and Twitter. I think LinkedIn and Plaxo are a complete waste of time—for me. All these other sites? I have no use for them. I'm not a restaurant hoping the Internet-surfing tourist comes upon my site, and I'm not selling anything to the masses. I provide legal representation to clients who have serious problems. My clients ask around. While they may find my name on the Internet, it's usually (75 percent I predict) after getting my name from someone. While I think it's important that people can find me on the Internet, I'm not looking to grow my business via social media.

So, social media marketing as a huge part of my practice is not my thing. If you're a lawyer, it shouldn't be yours either.

Most lawyers who have a big social media presence based on some paid strategy are worthless. I wouldn't hire them to tell me the time of day. They have invested in a big presence on the Internet because it's the only way they can get clients. Stop telling me that social media is taking over everything. It's not. People are still looking for real lawyers, who handle real cases, and get real referrals based on real results.

My clients don't want customer service via Facebook, and they don't want to interact on Twitter.

There are real people doing real things and causing real change—to the world, to the country, or to an individual sitting in their office.

The others are just talking.

About nothing.

THE ART AND SCIENCE (AND SCAMS) OF LAWYER BIOS

Bob Ambrogi has given a lot of thought to lawyer bios:[18]

What was clear to me from the outset about lawyer bios was how poorly written they were.

Bob goes on to give his basic philosophy about a lawyer bio:

It should have a theme.
It should use facts to back up that theme.
It should be written in a compelling style that draws in and holds the reader.
All of this should be done in no more than six paragraphs.
In the case of a lawyer's biography, the theme should emphasize what makes that lawyer distinct—what makes that lawyer stand out from the competition.

Bob makes the point that

consumers of any product or service want to feel confident that they are making the right choice. There are two ways consumers most commonly reassure themselves. The first is by word-of-mouth referrals. The other is through objective information. Thus, if we are buying a product, we want to hear from friends and reviewers who've used that product. We also want to see data on repairs, safety, reliability, performance, etc.

Bob then kills the theory of the social media mavens out there that Facebook and Twitter accounts with lots of followers are the silver bullet to a lawyer's success:

> In the legal context, word-of-mouth referrals remain the most powerful drivers of new business. Whether it is corporate counsel to corporate counsel or neighbor to neighbor, legal consumers are strongly influenced by the positive (or negative) experiences of others.

He believes that where a lawyer went to law school is important (although in reality it is not), and he believes in highlighting things like law review, clerkships, and specific cases. Bob then makes a point that can be taken two different ways:

> Different consumers look for different things, of course, and part of marketing is knowing how to position yourself to your target audience.

Positioning yourself to your target audience. Meaning what? Well, what Bob is talking about is the following:

> I have spoken directly to corporate counsel who tell me they most definitely want to see evidence that the lawyer has handled the type of case or matter they have—and has handled it successfully.

Good point. The lesson is that lawyers should be specific about what they do and their experience. It's not good enough to say "commercial litigation" when the lawyer mainly represents banks in disputes over international fund transfers, or to say the lawyer does family law, but in reality he or she concentrates on adoption, not the run-of-the-mill divorce work. A potential client from France with a tax matter wants to know that the lawyer has represented "French nationals in disputes with the IRS," not just that the lawyer practices tax law. But I go back to the prior comment:

Different consumers look for different things, of course, and part of marketing is knowing how to position yourself to your target audience.

This is part of the problem on the Internet.

Lawyers *know* that part of marketing is knowing how to position yourself to your target audience. So they lie, or fudge, or exaggerate. The best way to spot this is when a lawyer doesn't list his or her year of graduation. That means he or she has been a lawyer less than five years. This is what the marketers tell them to do, because people are looking for experienced lawyers.

Here are my thoughts on lawyer bios:

1. Always look to see if the lawyer fails to state their year of graduation or admission to the bar, or doesn't have a link to easily access that information.
2. Disregard any value you may put into someone being a member of anything. If they practice law, they are required to be a member of a bar. Stating that in a bio is nice, but means nothing. Basic memberships in other bar organizations are also meaningless.
3. Plenty of morons went to great schools.
4. Plenty of stellar lawyers went to unknown schools.
5. The lawyer's bio was probably written by the lawyer—a lawyer looking for clients. People say a lot of interesting things when they are looking for clients. Only some of those interesting things are actually true.

THE TWEET HEARD 'ROUND THE SOCIAL MEDIA MARKETING WORLD

Before the unemployed marketers found a way to sell it for a living and convince lawyers that clients were going to line up with every online tweet or status update, no one thought of creating a fake persona for the purpose of lying to get business. No one thought of puffing up qualifications, or, in legal terms, making shit up, in an effort to appear experienced, aggressive, and here to fight for you 10 minutes out of law school.

When Facebook and Twitter and other social media sites came online, the first thing people started doing was talking to each other. When the marketers, unable to truly assist in marketing those who were qualified to be marketed, started swarming, they made it a profession to help lawyers create an online image—true or not.

Lawyers are sheep. Proof? They are the most scammed segment of society as a result of Nigerian e-mail solicitations and other "may I deposit millions of dollars in your account?" jokes.[19] Want to make money? Convince a lawyer you can make them money. They will give you money. It doesn't matter whether you know how to make money. As a marketer told me recently in response to my wonderment about how lawyers give certain morons money to give them marketing advice: "No one asks about qualifications—no one."

In the middle of watching the resident Internet hucksters try and peddle their wares, I saw this article from a social media marketer: "Separate Social Media from Marketing" by Anthony J. Bradley and Mark P. McDonald, *Harvard Business Review*.[20]

Harvard Business Review. Hehe.

We need to break out social media and talk about more than marketing and technology. Instead, we need to talk about what social media enables: the ability to collaborate in new ways—which is particularly important for business leaders interested in creating more collaborative, innovative, and engaging organizations.

Huh?

An executive may boast, "We have Twitter and SharePoint, and we're on Facebook." But if you were to ask the executive how social media is positively impacting business results, you may raise a significant issue. When social media is applied to marketing, it creates activity—and in marketing, activity is a good thing. But activity alone does not create business results.

Now wait just a minute.
You can't just type things on social media sites and things will happen?

Just because you've opened the door doesn't mean you've crossed the threshold into a new way of working, managing, and leading. To achieve those ends—we've described these as attributes of a "social organization"—it takes more than setting loose the technology and praying that something good will happen.

So wait, there has to be something behind your online fakery that is actually true?
We need to move beyond social media as a technology tool. This article basically says that if the organization behind all the social media lights and sirens is not social, then it doesn't matter.
Taken a step further, if your law firm, solo practice, reputation, or credentials don't comport with the crap you are spewing on the Internet, then all you are doing is using a marketing tool to project something that doesn't exist.
And for some, that's OK.

If it's not, then maybe it's time to think about whether you should be spending more time working on who you truly are rather than who you are on social media.

THE FINEST EXPOSÉ (EVER) OF THE (FRAUD THAT IS THE) SOCIAL MEDIA GURU

The industry that calls themselves "social media gurus" is an industry of nothing. It is an industry of liars and failures from other careers now selling air. I've been writing about this for a long time, wondering if anyone else saw what I saw. Some did, but many are just so enamored with the possibility of making money that they don't care that the industry is a complete fraud.

Milo Yiannopoulos[21] does, and here are some spectacular observations from his article.[22] He begins:

> On the outskirts of a regional city in Britain—Bristol, perhaps—two hundred people gather to discuss "radical engagement strategies." They are oddballs: a mixture of chippy girls with unruly fringes and sweaty, overweight blokes with bits of burger stuck in their beards.
>
> These are the social media gurus, a rag-tag crew of blood-sucking hucksters who are infesting companies of all sizes, on both sides of the Atlantic, blogging their way into consultancy roles and siphoning off valuable recession-era marketing spend to feed their comic book addictions. They claim to be able to improve your relationships with your customers by "executing 360 degree reignition programs." But who are these people? Where did they come from? And how on earth have they managed to hoodwink so many big companies so quickly and so comprehensively?
>
> So the gurus are hired, and promptly set about cutting and pasting "social media strategy guidelines" into PowerPoint presentations and swanning around the office instructing secretaries about "social

media for social good" and how Twitter's going to change the world, all the while leeching off the productive bit of the organisation.

He says that beneath the social media guru cover are:

> layers of life coaches, yoga teachers, acupuncturists and feng shui consultants. That's the level of business insight and mission-critical expertise we're talking about here.

He nails it on why these frauds are able to exist:

> One of the conditions that has allowed the faux-academic colloquy of the social media industry to grow so fast is a lack of checks and balances online, especially within social networks. Highly questionable practices go either unremarked upon or purposefully ignored by the Twitter bubble. When someone gets caught with their trousers down, you're more likely to see messages of support than opprobrium. Plus, the industry is well mobilised, and dishes out a number of ludicrous awards to itself.

Milo sees the groupie nature of these scam artists, referring to it as the "poisonous cult of the social media guru." He then makes the point:

> Social media consulting amounts to little more than mastering the art of the bleeding obvious and no company, no matter what its size, should even consider hiring external social media consultants. Internally, the most you need is a couple of interns with laptops.
>
> All is not lost though. Milo predicts the end of the social media guru. I hope he's right. Fortunately, there are signs that the window of opportunity for all this silliness is closing. Firms are cottoning on to people who misrepresent and overstate their achievements and add no value to businesses while showing off to other "like minds" about how many Twitter followers they have.

In describing social media conferences, Milo says the red thread running through these events is, "I can't believe we're still getting away with this."

As the character Bob Sugar said in Jerry Maguire: "Finally! Someone said it."

THE ONLINE ETHICS SLIDE: WHEN DOES IT HIT THE GROUND?

After I signed on to Twitter for the first time, I quickly signed off.

It wasn't because I didn't like it, or I was getting spammed. It was because I didn't understand it. What was the purpose of this site? Sending 140 character messages to people? Was anyone reading it? Who was on this site sending messages to me and others?

Then I had dinner with someone who said, "Hey, why did you stop using Twitter?"

"I didn't get it."

"Just go on there and talk to people."

So I did.

Now, a few years later, I've talked to a bunch of people, even met some of them in person, and yes, I've even established some pretty nice relationships.

Twitter has also brought to light the immense amount of scum in the legal profession that live by the phrase "on the Internet, no one knows you're a dog." In just a few short years, I've discovered the following, all on Twitter:

1. A disbarred lawyer parading as a blog salesman, while saying he went into blog sales because he loved it so much, not because he was disbarred.

2. This same blog salesman signing on as a professor to an online "university" for lawyers to learn about solo practice three months after his disbarment, and then terminated after the head of the university was advised of his disbarment. The head of the university claimed no knowledge of the disbarment, although it was discovered with a quick Google search.

3. A laid-off lawyer (laid off after less than a year) claiming to be an experienced corporate lawyer and to have the ability to teach Biglaw how to bring in business through social media.

4. This same laid-off lawyer claiming to have been part of a $450 million deal, who then later confessed his role was document review.

5. A lawyer claiming to be a practicing attorney due to an of-counsel relationship in which there was no evidence of any legal work being done, and anger and hysterics anytime someone inquired about the practice.

6. A lawyer pleading guilty to felony real estate fraud and still parading as a partner in a law firm. When confronted, this lawyer angrily said that she was innocent and was not going to leave her law partner to be the sole rainmaker. She's since changed her bio several times, eventually settling on "real estate law," as if it's an interest and not her profession.

7. A lawyer claiming she doesn't practice because she has chosen not to, when the record of her state bar shows her suspended.

8. A lawyer posting a picture of a tall, glass office building on his website, when the attorney's presence in that building is simply that he has paid a time-share-type company to accept his mail there.

9. A lawyer raging against the use of ethics against young lawyers, to then only have to post her recent correspondence from the bar, initiated by a complaint concerning the possible unauthorized practice of law.

This is just what I have found, and there is probably more that I can't remember off the top of my head. It's like exterminators tell you: when you see a roach, it means there are many others somewhere nearby.

So where does it stop? When do we stop drawing lines between young lawyers and old lawyers and start thinking of the vast hundreds of thousands of lawyers as a profession?

Have we stopped being concerned with the profession? I think so. I think it's every lawyer for him- or herself. It's all about paying the bills, paying the student loans, paying for the house you can't afford, paying for the marketer to put you on the first page of everything that matters in life.

When did the iPad become more important than the networking lunch? When did your social media presence become more important than who you truly are? When will we stop getting excited about every new social media platform (and charging lawyers to teach us how to use them), and start getting excited when a lawyer does something good for a client? When did the lying, marketing fake biographies, and skirting ethics rules to push your way to the front of the line (which used to be called hard work) all become acceptable?

When do we stop congratulating those who see the practice of law as a readily available outlet at a coffee shop and a few documents to sell, or stop letting those who failed as lawyers advise other lawyers on rainmaking through social media, and start wanting to learn from those who have taken on the government, or helped a person become a citizen, or prevented a developer from tearing down history, or just did something that didn't involve an avatar and a keyboard?

There is a phrase I learned in college from a roommate. He said, "While we concentrate on the mice, the elephant walks out of the room." Maybe you've heard that, or a variation of that phrase, which means that we spend too much time concentrating on the irrelevant. What it means to me is just that—we spend so much time on the irrelevant that we don't even notice the relevant is right there, and leaving.

Let's rid ourselves of those who are receiving a pass on the Internet. You, yes, you, start calling them out as well. Let's become a profession again. Let's at least try. Stop pretending that the scum populating the Internet don't matter to you. They do. There is nothing to be scared of, these people are small, weak, and don't deserve to be a part of a profession that requires an oath.

I can see the bottom, it's not too far away.

BECAUSE FIRST YOU HAVE TO BE DEAD

Long before I signed a lease for my office space, the cleaning crew in the building was there, and I trust they'll be there long after I leave. There are a few things they do that keep them coming back every day as the sun sets. One, they clean the place. Two, you could leave a diamond ring, two Rolex watches, and a stack of cash on your desk and it would be there the next day. And three, they have a policy where unless a box, container, or other thing on the floor that looks like it's garbage actually says "GARBAGE" (I write "BASURA" because I actually know these folks), they don't throw it out. That's right, that empty cardboard box appearing to have no relevance or future will remain in the middle of the hallway the next morning if there are no instructions on what to do with it.

Sometimes that third thing is a bit annoying, but it sends the appropriate message: we have a job to do, and begging for forgiveness is not helpful at contract renewal time. You want the box thrown out, just say the word, literally.

In contrast, the philosophy that there is a hierarchy of authority in the business world was rejected at the "Marketing Partner Forum." That's right, Sally in marketing is on her way to becoming a "marketing partner." This group is just a few motivational conference quotes away from relevance in the 70 percent of law firms that don't have a marketing partner.

The following platitude went viral in the conference Twitter stream and I'm sure emptied a few tissue boxes:

@cindygallop: You heard @silviacoulter, #MPF12 peeps: BREAK THE RULES and ask forgiveness, not permission.

That's right, the marketers have had it with lawyers, especially when it comes to social media, saying "no, not for us, not our image, no, just no". If the gray-hairs, whose only significance was to grow a successful law firm, won't listen to the 28-year-old social media star, well, they're going to just do their own thing, start pounding away on Twitter and LinkedIn and blogging, and apologize later.

They don't ever discuss rules, like this rule:

Rule 5.3 Responsibilities Regarding Nonlawyer Assistants:
With respect to a nonlawyer employed or retained by or associated with a lawyer:

(a) a partner, and a lawyer who individually or together with other lawyers possesses comparable managerial authority in a law firm shall make reasonable efforts to ensure that the firm has in effect measures giving reasonable assurance that the person's conduct is compatible with the professional obligations of the lawyer;

(b) a lawyer having direct supervisory authority over the nonlawyer shall make reasonable efforts to ensure that the person's conduct is compatible with the professional obligations of the lawyer; and

(c) a lawyer shall be responsible for conduct of such a person that would be a violation of the Rules of Professional Conduct if engaged in by a lawyer if:

(1) the lawyer orders or, with the knowledge of the specific conduct, ratifies the conduct involved; or

(2) the lawyer is a partner or has comparable managerial authority in the law firm in which the person is employed, or has direct supervisory authority over the person, and knows of the conduct at a time when its consequences can be avoided or mitigated but fails to take reasonable remedial action.

When it comes to rules, the marketers have an easy out: one, the rules don't apply to them, and two, the rules are seen as scare tactics by lawyers like me who constantly throw them in their face and, well, maybe hurt business. Anything that hurts business is wrong, and communist, and part of the past, and mean. Marketing folks didn't have to swear to their state Supreme Court to follow rules; some reject the constant droning of "be careful with social media" and reject any notion that anyone should be scared of the consequences of stupidity on the Internet.

I responded that I thought their "seek forgiveness not permission" nonsense was a good way to get fired, to which one of the merry group of morons replied with something about how you wouldn't want to work for someone who didn't "follow" that premise.

Who are the lawyers to tell the marketers how to run a law practice?

Of course, the marketers would like my cleaning crew to take a page from them and just start throwing out boxes, then saying "oops." And there was really no example of how this philosophy (other than my mean, mean rants) was actually detrimental to someone's career.

Then I saw this:

> The managing editor of a student-run news organization that covers Penn State resigned Saturday after the publication's Twitter account sent messages saying former coach Joe Paterno had died, according to a letter on the publication's website.[23]

That's right, the kid woke up, probably threw back some badly needed coffee, some cold two-day-old pizza, went for a run, did a little homework, had some tweets pop up from the paper's Twitter account about Joe Paterno dying, and, well, he's out of a job.

Just like that.

Yeah, see, the problem was, Joe Paterno hadn't died yet. The family spokesman never said he died, because he wasn't dead. News about a death is sad, and even sadder when you hear about it while you're still trying to live.

He's not a marketer, but he's begging for forgiveness right now. "I never, in a million years, would have thought that Onward State might be cited by the national media," his letter said. "Today, I sincerely wish it never had been."

Yeah, I know, you're just some local student-run paper at Penn State, and when you tweet something about the death of Penn State football's Joe Paterno, why think that anyone else may read it?

The kid had some help from some other, better-known media outlets that couldn't be bothered with that old, dying journalistic concept of "verification":

> The incorrect information found its way onto media websites, including CBSSports.com, People.com and the Huffington Post.
>
> CBSSports.com had run a photo of Paterno with a caption saying the longtime Penn State coach "loses his battle with lung cancer at 85." The blurb did not include the source of the information.
>
> In an apology on its site, CBSSports.com said the mistake "was the result of a failure to verify the original report. CBSSports.com holds itself to high journalistic standards, and in this circumstance tonight, we fell well short of those expectations."[24]

Oops. Sorry.

The now-former editor did say something that was true, of which the perfect "verification" is his own stupidity. "In this day and age, getting it first often conflicts with getting it right, but our intention was never to fall into that chasm," the letter said. "All I can do now is promise that in the future, we will exercise caution, restraint, and humility."

Caution, restraint, humility.

Not really exciting buzzwords like "thought leader," "game changer," "rock star," "evangelist," or "epic."

They're terms of the past—that have caught up with the future.

BLOGGING AND OTHER SOCIAL MEDIA: LIKE A SEARCH ENGINE WHORE

You're still in the race to page one of Google. Nothing is more important. It's tiring. Your marketeer tells you that blogging is king. You don't have time to blog, you need clients now. You aren't interested in waiting for some client to think you had something interesting to say in your blog, and in turn, call your office, or for some lawyer to read what you wrote and refer you a case.

Not a problem, says the marketeer. It doesn't matter what you write, as long as your website is linked throughout the posts, like this:

> Recently, this Craptown family lawyer read about a father being held in contempt for failing to pay child support. This case was not in Craptown and did not involve a Craptown family lawyer. As a Craptown family lawyer, it is important that anyone in Craptown who has a problem with Craptown family law call a Craptown family lawyer. It is unclear whether the father sought the services of a Craptown family lawyer, but contempt is a bad thing and is a reason to seek out a Craptown family lawyer. So for those of you fathers that are broke, it may be time to call a Craptown family lawyer.

These blogs all suck, say nothing, and exist based only on the marketeer's promise of clients finding you via Google and dropping off a pile of cash at your office. The authors are very, very, very proud of their prose, as the marketeers cheer on their attempts to game Google. "Hey man, that last post was great, you had 27 links to your website."

I have a question: Does it work?

Do clients call your office and say, "I read that great post you wrote and couldn't get enough of your website every time I clicked a link"?

I often get accused of being a hypocrite when it comes to the Internet and Internet marketing. I understand the criticism; people are just that stupid that their ability to read doesn't extend to an ability to comprehend.

I think the Internet is a great and horrible tool for lawyers. I participate on Facebook, Twitter, to a lesser extent that worthless site, LinkedIn, and I blog. I blog. I write things. I don't write things for the search engines, and I don't write things hoping to get clients. If a client reads something I wrote and it causes them to call me, great. But it is not the reason I write. I know, it's impossible for you to believe. That's because you do nothing that doesn't involve an attempt to get clients.

I do not, nor have I ever, paid someone to teach me to use the Internet or social media. I do not, nor have I ever, paid someone to blog for me, teach me to blog, or ask others to link to my blog. The fact that no client has ever asked if I'm on Twitter doesn't mean I'm not on Twitter. I am. I do things on Twitter like talk to people. I don't repeatedly post automated links to my website. So when I say in my Above the Law bio that no client has ever asked if I'm on Twitter, it simply means that no client has ever hired me because "Hey, I saw you posting links over and over and over and over again on Twitter."

Are clients hiring you for that reason?

Again, and again, and again, I think Internet marketing can be a great thing. If you're honest, clients can get an honest picture of who you are. If you're lying or an automated or link-baiting piece of crap, there is a place for you in Internet marketing as well. If your goal is simply to be read *first*, then it doesn't matter to you what you write, and you will continue to just be a target for calls from shoppers and broke clients looking for a shoulder to cry on.

So I ask again, does it work? Does your fake, automated, link-filled Internet presence work? Do you like telling other lawyers the name of the company that blogs for you? Do you get satisfaction writing a blog post that has 48 links to your website? Does that make you proud to be a lawyer? Do you like giving up your ethics to a marketing company that has the keys to your Facebook page or Twitter account? Do you like when a national story explodes on Twitter and your marketer has automated your tweets so that in between all the talk of another school shooting, you keep coming up with posts about personal injury with links to your firm?

Here is some free marketing advice: stop the multiple links in your blogs, and stop automating your social media accounts. Fire anyone who you hired to do this for you.

Stop being an Internet marketing whore, and start being a lawyer.

FINAL (FREE) TIPS

Social Media is just that—social. "So-shul." It means you act like you would offline. People will tell you to brand yourself, or not to be "mean" or offend people because you won't get clients. Heh.

The idiots who say this want you to believe the conversation goes like this: "Hey, you know a personal injury lawyer in Chicago? My cousin fell out of a 747 at 35,000 feet."

"Yes, I know a great one. He's well-respected, and has a few verdicts in excess of $5 million."

"Wait, is he the guy that's mean to people on social media?"

How do you get clients with social media? The same way you do offline: people see what you do, what you say, take an interest, and when they need a referral, maybe they'll think of you. They won't think of you simply because you are constantly in their face with your business card. Would you stand in a room with a megaphone and tell people what you do over and over again? I know, some of you would. But if you wouldn't, don't do it on social media.

There is no need to create a social media strategy. Anyone who tells you there is a need for this is in the business of selling social media strategy. Don't have one. If you do, it's obvious, and it's a turnoff. Open your accounts, talk to people, have your profile speak for what you do. And for God's sake, do not ever spend a dime on social media advice, in a book, on the phone, on the Internet, anywhere. Let the idiots at Biglaw continue to do that.

CHAPTER 8

REFERRALS, AND THE FEEDING AND PROPER CARE OF REFERRAL SOURCES

WHO'S THE IDIOT THAT INVENTED THREE NAME REFERRALS?

I want to know when lawyers will stop using opportunities to give referrals as a panicked strategy of covering their asses. You know what I'm talking about—the "three names" idiocy?

Whether you're on a listserv and the 27th "I'm looking for an excellent, aggressive, and inexpensive lawyer" request of the day has donned your computer screen, or someone actually thinks you are worthy of a phone call or e-mail requesting a lawyer to save their life or fortune, let's just agree to stop being wimps and meaninglessly passing along names, and start giving real referrals.

I know, you were taught this. You never give one name. Why? Because what if it doesn't work out? Then you're going to have some sort of imagined problem that someone told you could be very, very bad. And yes, I know, people like choices. You feel like you're doing them a service by giving them lawyers from which to choose. But you're not. You're just uselessly giving out names.

One of the deep, dark secrets (shh) of being successful in a small-firm world is your ability to be more than just a paper-pushing, time-keeping drone. The ability to be a connector is just as important, or more, than your ability to practice your trade. If you are in a niche practice, there are more people who won't need your services than will, but that doesn't mean they shouldn't have a reason to call you—for example, that you are the one person who always gives them the best referrals.

Have you received those e-mails? "I know you don't do this work, but you always seem to put me in touch with the best people, so I'm now looking for _____."

No?

Let me help you.

DON'T KNOW ANYONE, DON'T REFER ANYONE

I know, sounds basic. But I also know what you do—you go to Google and find a sweet website and tell your friend that "this guy looks competent." You don't know anyone—admit it. Keep your credibility. Sure, if you are being asked for a probate lawyer in Houston and you happen to know a great corporate lawyer there, give that name as the person who would be able to make the referral. Try to make some connection if you can, but only if you have a personal connection.

ASK QUESTIONS

It always amazes me that while lawyers are trained to ask questions, when it comes to referring other lawyers, they never do. When someone calls and says they need "the best pit bull meanest bestest divorce lawyer in town," I recommend you ask a question like, "How long have you been married?" If the answer is 18 months, and the couple rents an apartment and has a dog, why not do them a favor and tell them they don't need the bestest lawyer in town? We know those lawyers: they deal with multimillion-dollar divorce cases where the couple is too stupid to realize that after $500,000 in attorney's fees, they each basically got what they talked about splitting in the beginning, minus the $500,000.

The key is not to just "make a referral," but to put the client with the right lawyer.

THE LAWYER YOU TRIED A CASE WITH 20 YEARS AGO ISN'T ALWAYS THE BEST REFERRAL

I see this in criminal defense referrals all the time. Someone asks for a referral for a college student charged with marijuana possession. A 60-year-old lawyer responds with the name of the guy he tried a federal drug trafficking case with in the '80s. Everyone else on the list knows that the lawyer is retired, or is now handling one federal, multi-defendant, white-collar case a year.

Lawyers within disciplines specialize. Before making the referral, do something really old school: call the lawyer you are thinking of referring the case to, and see if she's the one for the case. Maybe you'll find out she's dead. (That's actually happened.)

STOP WITH THE "THREE NAMES"

Even if the clients insist on three names, I tell them, "I don't give three names, this is the person I think is right for you. You want three names, call two other lawyers for referrals."

ONE MORE THING

Don't ask for referral fees. Make money on your own cases, not another lawyer's. You don't deserve a percentage of another lawyer's fee just for making a phone call, you cheap bastard. Most states actually require participation beyond the phone call. But we won't get into that here.

ARE YOU A REFERRAL SOURCE OR A NAME COLLECTOR?

You've read my thoughts on the three-names game and the fact that to me, that's not a referral, that's giving three names and saying[25] "pick whomever." In 2009, I said:

> Why tell the client the best Italian restaurant in town, when you can give them a list of three? That way if they don't like the one they choose, it's not the lawyer's fault.
>
> In football, we call that "punting." You can't get the ball where you need it to go, so you just give it to the other team and see what they can do with it.
>
> If you're referring three lawyers, you're referring no one. You're punting.

Later, I said: "We are the profession known best for referring business and we suck at it."

Now it's getting worse.

Here is the new trend. An e-mail goes out on a listserv:

> Anyone know a good, reasonably priced, not too expensive divorce lawyer (everyone on a listserv wants a good, reasonably priced, not too expensive lawyer) in (small town no one has ever heard of)?

Fifteen minutes later:

> Thanks for all the responses, wow this listserv is great, I've passed along all the names to the client.

Way to go. The guy just asked you to recommend someone for him and you told him to choose between 13 names of friends of your friends, and probably some of your friends who in this economy told you they will fly there and handle the case themselves, for $500 down.

Question: What is your fear of becoming a good source for referrals to good lawyers? Why can't you take those 13, 19, or 57 names and take a few minutes and look up a couple of them? Maybe call one or two.

I think you're better off saying you don't know anyone, because you don't.

Clients are looking for referrals, not looking to pin the tail on the donkey on the Internet. They're asking you for a name, a recommendation. Give one, or don't.

DO YOUR REFERRAL SOURCES GET IT?

If you're trying to build a word-of-mouth-based referral practice (is anyone doing that anymore?), you may be frustrated with two things about some of your referral sources: they don't appear to know what it is you do, and they don't make a real effort to get you the case/client.

Let's talk about the bad referrals first.

We've all been there. The call comes in, the client was referred by a familiar name, and he wants to hire you to do something you don't do or don't want to do. Maybe you're a divorce lawyer but don't want to handle child custody modifications, or you're a commercial litigator who has said many times that you don't do collections work.

If you're getting the wrong referrals, it's your fault.

You're getting bad referrals because you haven't spent enough time educating your referral sources. The first time you get the wrong type of matter referred to you, the next call is to set up a meeting with the referral source. As you're buying them lunch or coffee to say thank you, along with the gift you're bringing them for thinking about you, make it clear why the referral didn't work. Don't be a wimp, don't think that you're going to hurt someone's feelings. Be honest. Do you really think the referral source wants to keep referring people to you that you can't help? It makes them look clueless.

Another thing to tell your referral sources is to call you first before just telling the client to call you. This way you avoid the wasted call from the client, and the referral source will look better to the client as the source will give them the right lawyer to call.

Now let's talk about the lack of effort by the referral source in getting you the case.

I've previously talked about the "three names" garbage. The pin the tail on the donkey, "I don't care who you call" crap. For the referral sources that are intelligent enough to give one name, and that name is you, encourage them to tell the client why they should hire you. Often the client is referred, the referral source lets you know, and the client never calls or doesn't hire you. When this has happened to me, I'll call the referral source and ask about the conversation. "What did you tell him about me?" "Nothing, I just gave him your name, told him I knew you, and you did this work."

That's why the client never called. He called another referral source that gave him more details about the other lawyer. The client was sold before even calling that lawyer.

Encourage your referral sources to be more vocal about why they are referring you. If they don't know much about you, educate them. If you're going to build a referral-based practice, you will learn sooner or later that the direction of your practice is mostly based on the people that are referring you cases.

THE ULTIMATE SMALL-LAW GIFT GUIDE (EVEN IF YOU'RE CHEAP)

For those of you who have clients, and in turn, those who have referred them to you, you may be wondering how to say thank you to them. Not to worry, as always, I am here to help. No, no, no need to thank me, it's my pleasure. The following is based on years of receiving both crappy and awesome gifts provided in an effort to make the gift-giver look like at one time before he or she became a lawyer, someone taught him or her good manners.

First, I know you like your name or your firm's name or logo. No one else does. I've thrown out more leather binders with law firm logos, coffee mugs, pens, Godforsaken calendars, and things I'm supposed to carry around in my golf bag that have a law firm name or logo than you've received.

Gift giving is not a time to blatantly market your firm, it's a time to say, "Thank you, you did something important for me." The truly valuable marketing aspect comes from making an impression without having to get your logo into the hands of your referral source or client. I know you got excited when you opened up the box of firm logo trinkets ("Oh, awesome, this is my name on something!"), but please, throw them away.

Second, if you know what the recipient likes, focus on that. I know you want to buy 30 of the same thing and just send them out. That's OK, but what's the point of your gift? Is it just to send something, or to have the recipient know you put some thought in to it? Trust me, they won't be talking about the five similar gift baskets they received with food they'll never eat and cheap wine; they'll be talking about how you sent them a book on the wine chateaus of France knowing that they are going there next year, or something that recognizes you heard all 54 stories about their college football team this year.

Third, if your recipient is local, use a courier. Things arrive in boxes all the time. Rarely does a person hand you a gift and say, "Joe Lawyer wanted me to give this to you."

Fourth, if you are sending something out of state, try to use a well-known local company in yours or the recipient's community, or at least send something that is unique to your community. If you live in Maine (do any lawyers actually live in Maine? It seems like too nice a place for lawyers), send one of those live lobster packages. (Those are awesome by the way. The lobster arrives in a pot, claws taped, ready for boil. You can order a bunch of sides. Is this part getting annoying yet?) Anyway, it's a cool gift. Amazon is easy, but it's more meaningful when your recipient receives something that shows thought beyond just sending something.

Fifth, be different in whatever you send. Instead of a bottle of wine (let me know if you need my address) send a magnum (double the size of a regular bottle, for you jug wine drinkers). The recipient and (warning: subtle marketing tip) anyone seeing it will ask, "Who sent you that bottle?"

Sixth, your goal is to impressively say thank you. The blatant marketing of your law firm name may not be there, but by sending a gift, you are marketing. You will be remembered as a thoughtful, generous lawyer, or you won't be remembered, or worse, you'll be the office joke.

Let me end by saying that the cost is irrelevant. For those that I've simply given some quick advice, or put a few bucks in their pocket, a handwritten thank-you card is quite meaningful—mainly because no one sends them anymore. I am also a big fan of books on topics of interest to the recipient. For example, someone gave me a book of insults. It was one of those little books and probably cost $6. There was nothing new in there I haven't used, but I appreciated the thought. Obviously if the recipient put thousands of dollars in your pocket, a gift that recognizes that is required, in my opinion. If someone put ten grand in your pocket, it's time to think about something in the range of hundred(s).

Remember that in giving a gift, even if it's just your thoughts in words, you are not only saying thank you, but ensuring that the recipient remembers you positively, throughout the next year. In that light, don't hesitate to write on the card, "I'll be in touch to set up lunch early next year." You all still do have lunch with people, yes?

Happy shopping.

FOLLOWING UP ON REFERRALS (NON-BEGGAR EDITION)

I rarely follow up on potential clients anymore. You want to hire me, you'll let me know. I'm not playing your game of calling you back after the initial interview so you can tell me you're "thinking about it," but "the fee is really big." Yeah, the fee is really big; so is your problem. You want to take your big problem to a bargain basement lawyer, knock yourself out. I don't run a booth at the Straw Market in the Bahamas. If I'm going to negotiate, it's going to be with opposing counsel, not you.

It's killing you, though. You spoke with the client, they seemed interested, they asked all the right questions, and you gave all the right answers. They told you "money is no issue" (first clue they have no money). It's been a day or two, and nothing. No call, no e-mail, and no questions about the retainer agreement you gave them.

What to do?

First, assume nothing. The client may not see the urgency in hiring a lawyer. The client may have spoken with you and then encountered an emergency or other issue that put their legal issue on the back burner, or they may be trying to get the money together and don't want to waste your time until they can pay.

The anxiety you have about where the client may be in the hiring process can be resolved by being direct either at or before the initial consultation. When someone calls my office, they are asked certain questions before I speak to them, including, "Are you meeting with other lawyers?" and "Are you the one hiring the lawyer?" If they are meeting with other lawyers, I tell them to meet with the other lawyers first. I know, you car salesmen out there are thinking, "That's a terrible idea, Brian."

Listen, if the client is going to hire the first lawyer that tells them what they want to hear, including the price, that lawyer can have the case. I'm looking for clients who are looking for a good lawyer, not the first person who tells them they love them.

Second, if you must follow up, do not ask if the client has any questions or whether they have made a decision. Send an e-mail thanking the client for contacting you, and wish them good luck. Basically, say goodbye. If they're interested, they'll let you know. Any indication you give that you want, need, or must have this case, makes you look like a beggar. If you want the case that bad and the client hasn't called you back in a day, call the client and tell them you've rethought the fee and it's now discounted 30 percent. Just don't tell the client you are a complete loser and they own you—they just figured that out.

Also, do not give the client a retainer agreement unless they agree to hire you. I don't care if you have a form retainer agreement that never changes (which is stupid for many other reasons). I do not let the client walk out of my office with a single piece of paper until they've agreed to retain me. You want me to have something typed for you, pay me. You want me to send you a retainer agreement, send me a check. I'll explain my fee structure to you, but nothing goes on paper until I'm paid.

You want the best follow-up? Forget the client, and follow up with the person who referred you the case. Be direct with your referral sources about the guy that wasted your time and hired some moron, or the one who said they were coming by with a check yesterday and didn't show. Referral sources need to be thanked for good referrals, advised when things didn't go so well, and asked to follow up. It's always better for the client to get a call from the referral source asking, "How did things go?" The client will be more honest with the referral source than they will with you, especially if you came off as an incompetent slob.

DO YOU WANT MORE CLIENTS, OR MORE REFERRALS?

There are plenty of people running around the Internet claiming to know how to get you more clients (for a fee) and referrals (for a fee). There are plenty of lawyers, pen and check or credit card in hand, ready to pay. The same lawyers searching the Internet for their financial future are also looking for someone who will teach them the secrets of social media.

Sad news: there are no secrets. There are no secrets to getting more clients, referrals, or writing 140-character messages. There are only people who claim there are secrets in order to convince you that (for a fee) you can know something your competition doesn't. Marketers will tell you that just doing a good job is not enough. I agree. Others need to know you did a good job. In order to get more clients and referrals, you need to make yourself known.

There are a few ways to do this. First though, as I said in the beginning of this book, you have to decide what type of lawyer you want to be.

There are two types of lawyers (there are actually about eight types of lawyers but for this discussion, there are two): there are lawyers who want clients, and lawyers who want referrals. If you want more *clients*, here are my suggestions:

1. Direct mail
2. Google AdWords
3. Billboards

You'll get a ton of calls, and a ton of cases. Most will be clients looking for a low fee, but that's OK. You can do a bunch of cases cheap and hopefully have a practice that can handle the number of clients. Calls will come in droves, clients will be happy with a nice payment plan over several months, and the real tools you need are a credit card machine and a good calendar program for your computer.

If you want more *referrals*, you'll first have to understand that what you are seeking is another person, lawyer or otherwise, who will put their credibility on the line and tell someone else that you should be hired. Here is how you do that, in no particular order:

1. Do not take advice from anyone who has no experience getting referrals, and only experience getting clients.
2. Get off the computer, except to write something about your practice. This can be as simple as a short article about the different types of procedures in your practice area, or a complex page-turner about a recent decision affecting your type of clients. Where do you write this? Start a blog—but only if you're committed to posting at least once a week.
3. Talk to your current clients about other things besides the case; ask them about their lives. When you develop a relationship with a client where they feel they can discuss anything with you, they will. Some clients will refer you cases during their representation, others you will need to ask when the case is over (assuming you weren't fired). If you are not willing to ask a client to refer you clients, you have a problem.
4. Meet non-lawyers, go to non-lawyer events, have non-lawyer conversations. If you think you need to sell your practice to get referrals, you'll be the one at the cocktail party standing alone in the corner on the phone. Clients aren't hiring your practice, they are hiring you.
5. Never assume a meeting with someone was a waste of time because 10 minutes later there was no referral. My rule is that within six months of meeting someone who may be in a position to refer me a client, I get a call. Sometimes it's a year. It just happens that way.
6. Pay attention to what is going on in the community. Pay attention to people you know, even if you just know them by name or reputation. If someone you know won a case, or received some other type of accolade, say congratulations. No need for a formal typewritten letter—an e-mail will do. Do not include in the e-mail an invitation to lunch, unless you know the person well and it would be natural for you to hang out with them. There are people who scour media and

send letters to lawyers who win awards—most of them are financial advisors looking for clients.

7. Spend your advertising and marketing money on things that allow you to be in the presence of others. Small ads in the local paper are fine, but your $1,500 is better spent on a foursome at a golf tournament than on a four-color ad in a lawyers' magazine. Those seeking clients would never consider taking time from the office to work on their practice instead of in their practice.

8. Always make time to talk to people seeking advice—especially those that are in a position to refer you a client. I take a lot of calls, and receive a lot of e-mails seeking opinions and advice. I return them when I have time, but usually pretty quickly, because "thanks for calling me back so quickly" makes you the lawyer who deserves an important client.

9. The best and worst part of having a referral-based practice is that you never know who will refer you a client. That is why number 8 is vital.

10. Always, always, always show appreciation—even (especially) if it doesn't work out. I received an e-mail from a lawyer who told me my referral didn't work out, but thank you. I do this as well. I want to follow up, and let my referral source know why the case didn't work out. Many lawyers don't like to do this because it appears negative. I think it's essential. You can also take the opportunity when a referral doesn't work out to take the referring individual to lunch and talk more about your practice. No one expects anything when a referral doesn't work out, especially a free lunch. There are a few lawyers who have referred me multiple clients—none hired me. Those lawyers all received holiday gifts. The phrase "it's the thought that counts" is actually true.

11. Be patient. Again, if you just want clients, you shouldn't have read this far in the post—type away on AdWords and start stamping mailers. None of your clients will care about anything else but that you charge a reasonable fee (read: cheaper than the guy down the street). Good referrals take time. It requires you to have a reputation—not necessarily as a great lawyer, but as a good lawyer. The definition of a good lawyer is not just based on legal skills—it comprises many things.

Becoming a good lawyer happens one client at a time. If you want to have a volume practice of small cases, that's fine—you will get there through advertising, especially Internet advertising. But if you want a smaller practice with better cases and higher fees, you'll have to stop seeing the computer as the key to your future. Unfortunately, that suggestion pisses off a lot of people that are making a living telling you otherwise.

WHEN THE REFERRAL SOURCE IS A ONE-WAY STREET

For those ignoring the unemployed "future of law" idiots typing away from their kitchen table in some crap city with a regional airport and instead still living in the universe where you believe practices can be built and survive on the referrals of others, I have some advice on maintaining your referral base. Some good stuff here, so keep reading if you actually practice law and have to bring in business instead of living off the income of rainmaking lawyers who people actually hire.

A referral base is sometimes, but not always, a two-way street. This is where honesty comes into the equation. There may be a lawyer who refers you business to whom you would never refer business. There may be lawyers who refer you business, but you have never had the opportunity to send them any. On the other hand, there are those lawyers to whom you send business, who haven't sent you anything.

Referrals from other lawyers happen for two reasons: either the lawyer is your BFF, or they know your reputation in the practice area. It's sad news for some of you that your reputation, as I've said before, is not based on how many people have accepted your invitation to write online testimonials about you.

Let's talk first about the second type of referral: the call from the lawyer with whom you have no relationship.

I don't pay referral fees or take them from other lawyers, except in significant personal injury cases, of which I've had three. PI lawyers have a thing with referral fees: they like to pay them because they think it will ensure they get the next case. They won't take no for an answer. On typical hourly or flat-fee work, I'm not taking a piece just because I sent the client your way.

You should check your state bar ethics rules. In Florida, we have partial participation fees, meaning you must do something other than make the referral in order to get a portion of the fee, and the client must be advised. The way it's done in Florida is that lawyers make the referral, do nothing, and take a partial participation fee. I mean, they *did* make a phone call, so why shouldn't they be entitled to 25 percent of the fee?

Some lawyers make a practice of taking referral fees. They'll call, have a referral, and start the conversation with, "Will you pay me a referral fee?" I never get to hear about the case, because that's where the conversation ends with me. Years ago a young lawyer kept trying to refer me cases. He also kept asking for referral fees. I finally asked, "Are you looking for a relationship with me, or a check?" Never heard from him again.

Some lawyers I discuss this with, the ones who take referral fees, think I look down on them for doing so. I do. I think it's cheesy. I think it's cheap. If you understood relationship-based referrals, you would too. Tell a lawyer you don't want a piece of the fee and see where that gets you.

So this local lawyer that you don't know has just helped pay for your next iPad or maybe the annual salary of your associate. What to do? May I suggest after the retainer is signed you pick up the phone? I know, e-mail and text is so much easier. During that phone call, how about an invitation to a meal? (And not a "let's have lunch" at some point in the next year.) A gift is sent, or a handwritten note, and then again at Christmas (Hanukkah, Kwanzaa, whatever).

If you've never sent this lawyer any business, you need to learn everything that you can about his practice and unless he's some incompetent dope, make an effort to reciprocate. You may not be in a position to send him business, but at least try to introduce him to someone, or try to set him up for a speaking engagement, or invite him to an event where there will be people for him to meet. There is no reason to limit your relationship to trading business. Saying "I hope to send you something" gets old. If you can't send business the other way, try something else.

Remember this: one of the most important things you can do in the area of developing relationships is to connect others. There are plenty of lawyers in my network that for various reasons I can't or don't send them business. So what? I can connect them with others that are in a better position to refer them work, and I can make sure they know I appreciate what they've done for me.

Now let's talk about the lawyers you send work to and get nothing back. There are two reasons for this: either it's the same scenario, where the other lawyer doesn't have the ability to send you work, or there is another issue (his firm has a lawyer that does what you do, he thinks you are an incompetent dope, or he doesn't really understand what you do). Whatever the reason, you've got to know.

While I don't believe in a quid pro quo, I am not going to spend my time repeatedly sending you work when you don't send me any, don't make an effort to connect me with others, and show no appreciation. I owe you nothing. There are plenty of lawyers out there. So I'm going to do the same thing. I'm going to invite you to lunch, my treat, and I'm going to ask you why this is a one-way street. Maybe the reason is innocent—the lawyer just doesn't get calls for the type of work I do. Maybe it's something else. Maybe he hasn't thought about the people he knows that may be a good referral source for me.

Some people just don't understand the concept of relationship-based referrals—that it's not about the relationship between two people, it's who each of you know. If you can't send or receive business to or from someone, figure out who can, especially when they are lining your pockets.

THE MOST IMPORTANT REFERRAL YOU'LL EVER RECEIVE

One of the good moments in the practice is when you see the result of a networking event, online introduction, hit on that marketing blog that you've never written a post on, or God forbid, a happy former client.

The result being a referral.

A real referral. A real case, a paying client who wants to meet with you as soon as possible. This person calls and says they got your name from someone you know. They read your canned post on the latest fatal accident, they think your automated Twitter feed with links to your website is awesome, or they heard you did a great job for their good friend and now they need you (but I hear that never happens anymore and that lawyers that rely on doing a good job and getting referrals as a result of that are part of the past and are going to go out of business very, very, very soon).

So this is all very nice. It shows that something you are doing is working. It may for a while take your mind off suing your law school for lying about getting you a job.

But then there is the call that goes something like this . . .

"Hi, I was referred to you by [someone you've never heard of]. He speaks highly of you and said you are the best lawyer for my issue."

Now, when someone calls my office, there is a protocol. One of the questions asked is "Who referred you?" It's the most important question. I know, you're thinking, isn't the most important question "Can you pay?" No. That answer comes from "Who referred you?" Sometimes the caller can't remember who referred them, or the person who referred them has asked to remain anonymous. Nothing I can do about that.

When the potential client mentions a name I don't recognize, I used to say, "Who?" Now I just brush it off and say something like, "That's great, glad to hear from you." I'm happy that there is someone I don't know who apparently knows me and is willing to tell someone to hire me as their lawyer, but I don't want to embarrass them by letting them know I haven't got a clue who they are. They're not part of my—what do those idiots call it?—"target audience."

As far as an audience, lawyers have several. We may have our courthouse audience, our bar association audience, our networking group audience, our blogging audience, or our pay-per-click audience. Let's talk about blogging as an example. I know in that audience I have lawyers, law students, unemployed, bitter, basement-dwelling "I blame everyone else for my lot in life" lawyers and law students, professors, Biglaw haters and apologists (both in and out of Biglaw), and non-lawyers who are trying desperately to peddle their marketing and tech wares to lawyers and who e-mail to tell me that they are "different," and please stop saying bad things about marketers because some lawyers actually believe this crap.

But there are others in the audience—others I don't know. Every so often I hear from someone I would never think would read the writings of a lawyer. They are in businesses having nothing to do with lawyers, or they do things I didn't know people did for a living.

And that's just from blogging.

No matter whether your marketing is mostly on- or offline, or a combination, there is no way to ever know your complete audience. You realize this when that call comes in and someone is about to give you money based on the referral of someone you don't know.

I not only want—and need—to know who this person is, and how they know of me, but what it was that caused this person to refer me a client. This outlier type of referral is something I need to explore. It may be that an article I wrote came up on an e-mail listserv for a group of lawyers I've never heard of, or that some business owner was talking to a customer about me. I have no idea. I do know that I am more interested in the source of this referral than those that come in from people I know or are part of my *expected* audience.

The question becomes "What's your reach?"

The problem is that I don't spend the time exploring these types of referrals. I blow it off, and it's wrong. If I don't know the person, I don't take the time to figure out who it is. Often I'll ask, the client says they don't remember the last name, and I let it go at that. I need to do a better job learning about these unknown people who are comfortable enough to send along my name. This is how you learn about your real audience. It's a continuing effort.

You can listen to your marketer talk about your target audience all you want. If you're a good lawyer and other lawyers and current and former clients are spreading the word, and you're getting some play with your online marketing, that's great—that's expected.

I'm more interested in those that aren't targeted. Do you know who those people are? Neither do I. But I'm going to spend more time trying to find out.

CHAPTER 9
MONEY

IS IT OK TO MAKE MONEY AS A LAWYER?

There is no Google search that I see more than "how to make money as a lawyer." One of the reasons people hate lawyers is because we are perceived as making a lot of money, and that creates jealousy and anger. I have no problem with lawyers or anyone else that makes a lot of money. I just don't think people should go to law school for the sole purpose of making money.

A comment I made on Twitter caused a raging debate about lawyers and money. I said, "People who go to law school to become lawyers for the purpose of making money are no different than prostitutes."

My meaning? Prostitutes are engaged in an important function: sex. In some relationships sex is part of love; in others, it's just superficial, like prostitution.

My comment was interpreted as being critical of lawyers who make good money. After an hour so of debate, some got it. My point was that those who enter law only to make money are part of the problem.

If your only purpose for going to law school, for practicing law, is to make money, then you have no sense of the higher calling that is the profession.

Being a lawyer is important.

Making money is a nice thing.

I believe one of the reasons we are so hated in society is because of the notion that we are all rich. Truth be told, most lawyers are not rich, but "rich" is usually defined as someone who makes $1 more than the person making the accusation.

That being said, we did not take an oath to poverty. When I hear a PI lawyer obtained a $100 million verdict, or a fellow criminal lawyer got a six-figure fee for a big case, or a divorce lawyer is working on a multimillion-dollar divorce, I say "Way to go."

Doctors make good money, health care costs are out of control, but you don't hear people being critical of doctor's salaries. It's not sexy. Unless it's a charity medical procedure, you never hear that a patient received a heart transplant and the doctor received $50,000. When we hear how much people make, the worst in us comes out.

Lawyers work hard to build practices. We go to school at least three years longer than most others, and the stresses of the career are not well understood. Many of us lay awake at night, having absorbed as our own the problems of our clients. And yes, there are scumbags among us, those that give us a bad name. There is bad in every profession. No segment of the workforce is exempt. Unfortunately, when lawyers are criticized, it's often preceded by the term "money-grubbing."

I just wish we could weed out those lawyers in law school.

HOW TO MAKE MONEY AS A LAWYER: FORGET LAW SCHOOL

A few years ago my electrician showed up at my house in a BMW. A few days later he showed up in a Porsche. I asked whose Porsche it was, and he said, "mine, the BMW is in the shop."

Recently, there has been some discussion about this country developing an economy of lawyers, doctors, and accountants. No one wants to be a plumber, electrician, or other tradesperson. It's demeaning. Mom and Dad won't be proud, and all the money to be made is in lawyering.

Yeah, right.

I will tell you this:iIf I graduated plumbing school 20 years ago, I'd be making as much or more than I am now. I'd have 10 trucks, ads running around the clock, and my name plastered everywhere around town—from bus benches, billboards, airplanes over stadiums, and charity events. No fancy office, no bar regulations, no judges wanting me in court NOW, no sleepless nights wondering if Mr. Jones' hot water is working.

With all the discussion about "the future of lawyers," I haven't seen one post about "the future of plumbers."

Will there be a time where people no longer stop up a toilet? Will sinks no longer need to be installed? Will giant condominiums be built in 2023 without bathrooms and kitchens?

Will we be taking a shit on our iPads?

From the *ABA Journal*::

Hedge fund manager Daniel Ades of Kawa Capital Management tells the *Wall Street Journal* that students should seek an education that pays the highest salaries relative to the cost of education. According to that analysis, technical colleges are the best. "We're in a skills-based economy and what we need is more computer programmers, more [nurses]," he tells the newspaper. "It's less glamorous but it's what we need."

The article is geared toward the discussion of loans, and why it's more cost-effective to pay for a trade school education in terms of making money in a career than it is to pay for law school.

So there's the answer: forget law school. If money is the goal, go to trade school. It costs less, you don't need to wear a suit, you can use all your shiny toys for business, and you don't have to worry about social media for lawyers.

Let me know if you do it. I'll hire you to fix my toilet, and bitch about how much it costs as you drive away in your Porsche.

HOW TO MAKE MONEY AS A LAWYER: RAINMAKING IS FOR LOSERS

Whenever I look at my handy little website that tells me what Google searches lead people to my blog, I am of course not surprised to see that "how to make money as a lawyer" still leads the pack.

This is not a search done with the same attitude that someone searches for, let's say, "how to remove gum from a shoe." This search is done with anger, frustration, and the desire for immediate relief. The search is really "I went to law school, have $100,000 in loans, I missed the cut on the entitlement to my Biglaw job and mahogany desk, and I want my damn money so tell me how to make money as a lawyer, NOW."

But there is another term that is running around the Internet as much as unemployed social media experts who used to be lawyers before they were laid off, disbarred, arrested, or otherwise just got tired of working in an office that didn't have young people in green shirts working behind a counter and asking "room for cream?"

Rainmaker.

Rainmaker: an influential employee who creates a great deal of business or revenue for his or her firm.[26]

One who is known for achieving excellent results in a profession or field, such as business or politics.[27]

A rainmaker is also a person who can initiate progress, take a leadership role, and has the drive to succeed.[28]

Well, here is my advice if you are trolling the Internet looking to make money as a lawyer: forget rainmaking.

At its core, a rainmaker is someone who has deep relationships with a vast number of people who send business their way just like an open cloud sends rain from the sky. This method, the true method of becoming a rainmaker, takes way too long. It can take 10 years before a lawyer, a real lawyer with clients, becomes known as a rainmaker. You don't really want to be a rainmaker, you want to make money as a lawyer, and waiting is not an option.

So spam.

Advertise like there is no tomorrow.

Plaster your card and name everywhere you can.

A rainmaker is an influential person who creates a great deal of business or revenue for his or her firm. You don't want that. It takes becoming a good lawyer, gaining the respect of your colleagues and others in the community. It will only wind up causing you to have big cases, great clients, and a wonderful practice. You're focused on making money as a lawyer.

That's not a rainmaker.

So stop frustrating yourself by asking how you become a rainmaker. If you want to make money as a lawyer, your time is better spent with the guy from the yellow pages, the dude that can teach you to play on Twitter, or the life coach that can help you create a fan page on Facebook.

It's simple. Easy.

That's what you wanted upon graduation, right? A simple, easy way to make money?

There you have it.

Screw the rainmakers. They're too busy establishing themselves as influential professionals.

SETTING, EARNING, AND KEEPING FEES IN SMALL LAW FIRMS

As I've said preivously, one of the most popular Google searches by law students and lawyers is "how to make money as a lawyer." I rarely see searches for "how to cross-examine the expert witness," or "building a reputation, one case at a time." It's all about the cash.

So here it is; here's your red meat.

CHARGING WHAT EVERYONE ELSE CHARGES IS FOR LOSERS

Good clients know you get what you pay for. Cheap, annoying, time-sucking, bar-complaint-filing clients try to own someone for nothing. If you want the same clients everyone else has, charge the same legal fees. You can be Wal-Mart, or you can be Saks. More people shop at Wal-Mart, but people looking for quality shop at Saks, and they know the difference. They go in, they see something they want, and they pay for it (without a payment plan). (And don't tell me credit cards are payment plans. The seller gets the full amount, the buyer makes payments to the bank.) Saks doesn't have low prices, and customers aren't going there for low prices. They're looking for quality. Price is secondary.

You can have ten $1,000 cases, or one $10,000 case. Part of the difference is whether you practice in shorts at Starbucks, or online selling documents, or actually have a door, and behind that door is a desk, and a pen or two. The difference is also whether your name is one that causes people to say you are a "good" lawyer. Yes, it takes time to build a reputation, but good reputations bring good clients, and good clients bring good fees. If you want quick money, attract bad clients with little money who will make you hate what you do. You'll make money, but it's a crappy way to practice.

If you don't have the time to build a reputation, I can't help you. If you're scared to charge more than the four guys down the street, you'll always be another dime-a-dozen lawyer. If you can't sell value to the client, you are worthless. Figure out what makes you different, and make it apparent to the client.

THE BILLABLE HOUR IS NOT DEAD

It will never die, and it must be a part of your fee schedule. I'm not telling you to charge by the hour—I try not to. But whether your fee is going to be a closed-end flat fee, combination of contingent and flat, or straight hourly, at some point, someone is going to want to know how you arrived at that amount. And whether it's the client, a judge, or the bar, it's nice to say, "My hourly rate is _____, now pay me."

DETERMINE YOUR HOURLY RATE

Start with the cost of running your office for one hour (determined by cost of rent, utilities, staff, insurance, tall or venti coffee, etc.). Let's say rent is $1,000, other overhead is $1,500 a month (we're talking solo, no secretary, no frills). Eight hours a day, 20 days a month. So $2,500 divided by 160. Your hourly cost is about 15 bucks. How does $150 an hour work out for you? It's probably lower than you hear most lawyers charge these days, and even if you don't bill 160 hours a month, you're still ahead of the game if you bill half that. (By the way, hourly rates are all BS. They're really determined by the formula "What is everyone else charging?" Trust me, ask any lawyer.)

IF YOUR STATE BAR ALLOWS NONREFUNDABLE, BE NONREFUNDABLE

I've never understood, outside of a bar requirement, why lawyers don't embrace nonrefundable fees more often. Who taught you that you are merely a place to hold money for a client until they ask (or threaten) for it back? If permitted, at least some portion of the fee should always be nonrefundable. You should also consider the term "earned upon receipt," and make clear in the retainer what is earned, and when. Contracts are great. We're lawyers, we should understand that.

So if allowed, put in your retainer that the fee is $X, and a portion is nonrefundable and earned upon receipt based on "the initial consultation, opening of the file, preparing initial documentation, initial research, etc."

FINAL WORD ON FEES

Don't negotiate, don't undercut your competition, don't take payment plans, and don't reduce your fee because things are slow. If your fee structure just isn't working, change it, but change it across the board, not just per client. If the main concern of the client is the fee, then it doesn't matter how good you are. If the main concern of the lawyer is getting the cash, then it doesn't matter to you how good you are, either. You can always make money as a lawyer—it just depends how you want to make it.

WHEN YOU'RE NOT GETTING PAID AT YOUR SMALL LAW FIRM

I've always marveled at lawyers who continue to represent clients when they're not getting paid, or are too weak and fragile to engage in a serious conversation with the client over the unpaid bill(s). It happens more in the civil arena, as any halfway intelligent criminal lawyer knows you get the money up-front. Bad results with open bills is never a good way to pay the rent. There are criminal lawyers who are too stupid to get the money up-front. They claim where they practice, they have to offer payment plans. The problem is, there is no such thing as a payment plan. What I call it is a non-payment plan.

I can count on one hand, well, maybe one and a half hands, the amount of times I've been stiffed by a client. In most cases, it was because I was waiting for the money up-front and decided to do some work in the interim because I (wrongly) believed the client was good for it. The client wasn't good for it, and I quickly withdrew from the court case or ceased doing work.

I know there are those out there who believe it's pure arrogance to ask that they get paid or they don't work, that chasing money or waiting for money that will never come is part of the practice. There *are* criminal defense lawyers who get paid, (sorry if you don't know any) and not getting paid is not part of your practice, unless you let your practice run you instead of running your practice.

Let me tell you what I hear—you probably hear it too, or say it to yourself—and how to make it stop, and stop now.

Never do a stitch of work without being paid. No exceptions. If you do work without being paid and don't get paid, that's your fault, not the client's.

Never enter into a payment plan that will take longer than three months, as long as the case will take at least six. These numbers are not hard and fast, but you morons out there quoting $5,000 fees and taking $500 down and $500 a month on a case that will take 90 days to resolve, what the hell are you doing? You just quoted a $1,500 fee. You want $1,500, quote $1,500. You're not a bank. If the client needs a payment plan, that's for a bank, family member, or a friend, not you.

Never, ever take a case for less than half of what you are quoting if it's a flat fee. This is of course if you're too weak-kneed to get it all up-front. If it's hourly, never take a case for less than 10 hours up-front.

Clients have the money, they just don't want to spend it. They will hold onto as much as they can, and if they can screw you for the balance, they will. They're not stupid, they know you are too much of a wimp to sue them (oh God, my malpractice carrier will get mad at me, or my deadbeat client will lie to the bar about me). Grow up, you're a lawyer, and you deserve to be paid for your services. If you want to be a bank, and you want to get screwed, keep doing your silly affordable payment plans and complaining about how you're not getting paid.

Now let's talk about the deadbeats.

Working on hourly cases is where you can get screwed. You took a $5,000 retainer (but you didn't make it nonrefundable because "civil lawyers don't do that," or more importantly, your state doesn't allow it), and after a couple of months of sending bills for a few thousand dollars a month, you hear crickets. Your calls to the client go unreturned, and you're aware that the client is getting your e-mails and calls and just hiding from you.

Why do you keep working on the case?

My guess is that your retainer agreement doesn't say "The client agrees that should any invoice remain unpaid for (whatever time period is good for you, 30, 60, 90) days, the attorney will cease working on the matter, and if the matter is in court, the client agrees to the attorney's withdrawal."

No, here is what you love to say: "I don't want to do anything because of my relationship with this client."

Relationship? Are you kidding me? Are you sleeping with the client? (I and your state bar hope not.) Is the client your mother or best friend?

No, you just don't want to lose the client because they've sent you work or have had other matters and may have more.

I don't care. You have got to be completely stupid to think that you actually have a relationship with that client when they are not paying you. Don't you realize that all they are doing is taking advantage of your precious relationship?

Get. Out.

Lawyers who treat getting paid as an afterthought will be an afterthought themselves. This is not a charity, this is a profession, and professions are about both business and service.

One of the reasons you don't get paid is because at the initial consultation you don't take the time to discuss the retainer agreement and how you work. You're too busy selling yourself and smiling when the check is written. Forget about that crap, and explain in detail all the scenarios in which lack of payment can create a problem. Explain that when money issues get in the way of your representation it creates a conflict, and you'd rather not have that conflict. Let the client know that if money issues arise, you'd really appreciate a call four days before the payment is due instead of 12 days after you've made two calls.

Paying is the client's responsibility. Getting paid is yours. Stop pretending it's OK for the client not to pay. Stop proving to deadbeat clients what they already know—that they picked a great lawyer because he does the work and doesn't hassle them about the fee.

Or just continue to think it's part of the practice because you're scared.

HOW MUCH MONEY CAN YOU MAKE AT A SMALL LAW FIRM?

One thing that the Biglaw mentality creates is the thought that the only lawyers making money are in Biglaw. Small-firm lawyers are all just scraping along trying to pay rent while Biglaw lawyers are rolling in it. I thought I'd address this myth. The title above is one of those phrases that bloggers see typed in all day by lawyers and law students, particularly those who claim to love Biglaw, but would jump to their own place or a smaller firm in a second if they could make the same money. They are looking for the magic bullet.

This is the issue—money. I know.

I know when I get the calls, when lawyers want to discuss the "possibility of leaving," that it's the only thing on their mind. Sure, they want their name on the door, more freedom, more client contact. But they just have one real question. One real fear. One real concern. One thing they need to convince their better half of before making "the jump."

Can I make the same money?

Here is the answer . . .

Sure.

You can make the same money. You can make less money. You can make more money. There is no magic answer. No magic. Really. It's all going to depend on your ability to make rain. Office-dwelling drones with bad suits need not apply.

Let's play with some numbers. You're a couple years in at Biglaw. Your salary is still a bit below $200K. You have the adjustable rate mortgage for the house you can't afford, and two BMWs because you need to show the wife that you've "made it." With your debt and need to maintain the lifestyle of a high-flying, glorified paralegal, you can't leave unless you can make $200,000, so you think.

Question: Are you taking any clients with you? If so, what are the clients paying your firm, and what are they going to pay you? We're not talking about you taking GE or Google in to your new small firm, so the question is, will Bob's Bait and Tackle, with six locations, pay you enough to maintain the life?

For the rest of you—most of you—who won't be taking any clients with you, understand a few things. First, if you're going to work for a small firm, you're not going to make the same money right away unless you are a rainmaker and have an agreement with them that you get a piece of any business you bring to the firm. If you are a rainmaker and don't negotiate this into your financial package, you are a moron. Small firms, even the ones that make a lot of money, aren't stupid enough to pay young lawyers more than they're worth. So unless you bring them dollars, you may have to get the wife a Camry and start eating at Applebee's once a month.

Second, if you are striking out on your own, don't work from home or a coffee shop. I don't care what the "futurists" say. They're just being cheap because they're too scared to try and become real lawyers. Get an office. Even if it's a part-time office. Get one. The best situation for you is going to be a small firm or a group of solos sharing space that have an office for you. Try to trade work for rent, but if that's not possible, find something where all the extras are there—Internet, copier, receptionist, and so on. You should figure about $2,000 a month for this type of arrangement, and yes, I know real estate is more expensive in certain cities, but you're looking for a decent office by the courthouse, or in the central business district, or somewhere convenient for your clients, not the 50th floor of the most expensive building in the city. You want nice clients, get a nice office. You want crappy clients, work around the baristas.

Third, the most important relationship you should immediately establish is with a bank. Get a line of credit (if you're not a deadbeat). Occasionally ask to increase the line, even if you don't need it. One day you might, or one day another bank may want your business, and the fact that you've had a line of credit will be important. You may not need $50,000 or $100,000 right now, but one day you may need $500,000 to finance a case.

Finally, understand that the question is not "Can I make the same money?" It's "What do I need to survive?" Anyone who starts a business (and that includes leaving Biglaw for a small firm) knows that for the most part, for the first couple of years you're building something. So you're going to need to prepare for the possibility of living within a new means. If that's equivalent to suicide for you, well, then, good luck.

But most of the people I know that left Biglaw made as much or more their first year out.

Yep.

THE FREE CONSULTATION AND THE FEE SECRET

A few years ago I was at a seminar where one of the speakers asked, "Who invented the free consultation?" The answer is PI lawyers. They take no fees up-front and are paid nothing unless they recover damages. It's an all-risk, some-reward practice. It's the closest thing to Vegas in the legal profession. Take on a case for free, and if you win, you get paid. If you lose, you get nothing, and lose what you put into the case.

Most lawyers charge an hourly or flat fee. That fee is either paid up-front or in monthly installments based on invoices. That fee is set at the initial consultation. Long ago, lawyers would routinely charge a consultation fee. Often clients would go see a lawyer simply for a consultation. There was no reason to consult for free, as a few consultations a day would add up to real hours. It still does today, in an age where the free consultation has become the norm in every practice area.

Take the lawyer who charges $250 an hour and does two free consultations a day. That's $120,000 in free consultations a year. But lawyers who charge for a consultation are deemed arrogant or out of the mainstream. The sense of most lawyers is that a free consultation is good business practice and gets the client in the door. Many lawyers waive the consultation fee if they are retained on the case, so it's really only there to discourage "shoppers" and people who have no intention of hiring a lawyer at all.

I've gone back and forth with consultation fees. My practice now is that if the client comes from a good referral source, I waive the fee. If the client found me on the Internet, or otherwise "found" me somewhere, I advise of the consultation fee policy. I do not understand why lawyers act as car salesmen, thinking that getting the customer in the door, and in the car, will get them to buy. Car salesmen are great at what they do. They never discuss price until they've confirmed the customer loves the car, and the answer to price is "What would you like your monthly payment to be?" It's a game, and it's not for lawyers.

Many lawyers scoff at the notion of a consultation fee because "no one in my area charges one." That's a great way to distinguish yourself as a law-yer—do what everyone else does.

I find that a consultation fee sets the tone with the potential client that your time is valuable and your advice is worthwhile. A consultation with-out a fee is not a consultation, it's an audition. I also think it's time we stopped talking fees at the end of the consultation. Lawyers who consult with potential clients regularly know that every meeting with a potential client has unspoken concerns: "Can I afford this lawyer?" and "Can the client afford me?" It is a waste of time for both the lawyer and potential client to spend 30 minutes or an hour or more discussing a case when the client has $500 to his name and the lawyer wouldn't consider representa-tion for less than $5,000.

Still, lawyers shudder to think about telling a potential client over the phone, "I don't take cases for less than _____." Lawyers are fans of the car salesman model: "If the client meets me, he'll hire me."

It's time for lawyers to reevaluate the free consultation and "hiding the ball" on the fee until the end. We are simply wasting time—our time, and the potential client's time.

FEWER CLIENTS

Fewer clients. This is the ideal that began the story of the transformation of Jerry Maguire.[29] Haven't seen the movie? Watch it. Absorb it. It's a great premise on which to build your practice.

In prior years I attempted to mentally keep track of who called me and who hired me, but I wound up forgetting a lot of the details. This year I've made some changes. On a monthly basis, I'm reviewing prospective clients who called, as well as who referred them, who took their calls, their case types, and whether I was retained. The percentage of calls-to-retained used to be "most." Most potential clients that came to my office retained me. I made it easy. I'd bring them in, spend some free time, smile a lot, negotiate the fee, and get the case.

Now that percentage has gone down, way down.

In one month it was 39 percent. Eighteen calls, seven new cases.

Eleven potential clients didn't hire me.

I am thrilled.

There's more. Of the 18 calls, my office passed 11 along to me pursuant to another new policy. Potential clients calling are asked (after determining their legal matter is something I know about) if they are calling to retain me, and then they are told my fee structure. To both issues these 11 didn't immediately hang up. I was eventually retained by seven of those 11. Now we're at 64 percent of the people who claimed they were calling to retain me, and aware of the fees, eventually hiring me. The remaining seven callers ended their conversation with the receptionist or another lawyer in the office, and were either referred to other lawyers or told "thanks for calling."

What about the other four I spoke to who did not become clients? One caller had a type of case I don't handle, but he was referred by a lawyer. One decided to handle it on his own, and another said he'd think about it. I told the last one that he didn't need me. It was worth stopping work on other cases and having a conversation with all of these people.

I know you are thinking, "Why didn't you bring the others in and do a free consultation? Why not at least talk to them?" You know, say happy things. Try to sell the client. Why? I'm not a car salesman. I'm no longer interested in people coming in and taking an hour of my time to kick the tires and sit on the leather interior. Yes, I'm aware free consultations are a staple of contingent fee lawyers. I'm not one of them. With few exceptions, I don't do free consultations anymore. You want to engage in the show, the audition, knock yourself out. I did that my first 10 years in practice—and you should too if you're building a practice or your only reputation is a perceived one on the Internet.

In my early days of private practice I took cases all over the place, negotiated fees, did free consultations, met clients outside the office. Understand that what I'm advising is not going to work if you are a dime-a-dozen lawyer or have no reputation in the community (and that doesn't mean the online community).

In this age of an ongoing crappy economy, lawyers are undercutting each other on fees, and plunging their brains out on the Internet, hoping for this kind of call 37 times a day: "I found you on the Internet and have $500 in my pocket." So, the notion of fewer clients is blasphemy. I may ask whether you want ten $1,000 clients or one $10,000 client, but more and more the answer is "No one is going to pay me $10,000, because I practice from Starbucks in my shorts, and I sell documents on the Internet. I need every person that breathes and has a few dollars to hire me so I can pay my SEO guy."

There is nothing wrong with a competent volume lawyer. People need access to lawyers, and if there is a lawyer who will charge $69 to competently handle a traffic ticket, or $150 to write an airtight will, that's great. You have to do a lot of those to make a decent living. But if you want to handle serious and complex matters for clients who want that one lawyer to give them the attention and skill they need, you have to set a goal of fewer clients. You have to have a good screening process, even if it's just you doing the screening. Do not invite everyone in your office to take up your time when they don't even have the money to pay for the free coffee you poured them or the candy you gave their kids.

I know, you don't quote fees over the phone. But you're wasting your time.

Regardless of the whining that everyone wants a virtual lawyer and no one will have a law office in three years, there are still clients out there whose main concern is not how cheap they can get representation. They're not looking to buy their business contract on the Internet or hire some liar with a cool website. These clients aren't looking to waste your time. They want your attention, and they're willing to pay for it.

When you stop trying to collect clients and start choosing them instead, your numbers will go down. But the important numbers will go up. Way up.

WHEN THINGS ARE SLOW

Lawyers don't like to be honest about not making money.

I went out on my own in March of 1998. I did no advertising. The first month, I made three times what I was making monthly at the small firm I worked at for nine months. I was well on my way.

April was about the same, and so was May. This was awesome. No looking back. Who said starting your own firm would be hard?

Then came June.

Nothing. No new cases, no money. The phone didn't ring.

It was over. Three good months, and now I was done. I, of course, freaked out.

A few days into July the phone rang, and I was back. Whew. So I had one slow month. Now it would all be fine.

Then it happened again, and again, and again.

While I've learned to actually appreciate the slow times and use them to my benefit, I never forgot my first June. "June" became code for the slow months. I had one or two a year. One year, I had six slow months—it was right after 9/11. I considered shutting down, until my dad yelled at me. At the time, I was sharing space with a partnership of two successful lawyers in practice for 20 years. I asked one of them, "When do you stop worrying about money?"

"You don't."

While the public face of Biglaw may convince you that slow times only occur in small law firms, don't be fooled. The bigger they are, the harder they fall. Slow months happen everywhere. We've seen whole departments in Biglaw firms doing "other" work. Ask any real estate lawyer about his business over the last seven years.

In small firms, it just matters more because you may not be handed a paycheck every two weeks just for showing up. Rent comes due, the new iPad is out and yours is seven months old, and you are generally more aware of firm finances because there is no accounting office on another floor that is not your concern. Your money is a click away on QuickBooks, or written on a checkbook register in a drawer.

Small-firm lawyers take slow times personally. When you're young, you fear telling your colleagues that things have been slow. You think it's just you, and you start to rethink your decision to go out on your own. It can consume you. But unless you have a volume practice where you send out mailers or help fund Google AdWords and undercut your colleagues $500 so you can get the case, you're going to have slow months. You can't create cases or legal matters, and depending on your reputation and referral sources, sometimes the phone just doesn't ring for a few days, or weeks, or months.

I'm not here to tell you that you get to a point where there are no slow times. If you think slow times are not a general part of the profession, you are probably one of those people who says "But they looked so happy" when you hear of a divorcing couple.

When you're just starting out, slow times can mentally consume you. You've got to learn to work through them. The first thing you need to do is to try to base everything on months, not weeks. There are too many weeks, and you'll just get depressed. There are only 12 months. (I know this even though I went to a third-tier law school.)

You also need to determine whether it's you. In the beginning, I never asked if other lawyers were slow. That was a no-no. I was in private practice, and everything was wonderful. No room to admit weakness or failure. Then one day I asked a friend, "How's business?" "Slow." "Yeah, me too." Then I spoke with others. I felt better. It wasn't me, it was just a slow time. One caveat: never brag if you're doing well. Misery loves company. If you're not slow and your friend is, then things are "fine." And don't be afraid to give some advice, if you have any.

If you're the only one that's slow, then you need to evaluate why. Are your fees too high? Is your name not out there enough? Did you jump into a practice area because it was "hot," and now it's crowded with cheap lawyers? Did your SEO guy get a real job and abandon your account? Regardless of how long you've been practicing, you should always be reevaluating the business side of your firm—and not just when things slow down.

At some point, you'll reach a level where you appreciate a few slow weeks. It will give you time to refocus on the work at hand and plan for the future.

You'll also learn to use the slow times to get out of the office (or coffee shop, or dining room) and go talk to real people about real things. While I am a proponent of lawyers taking a break from their work to actually live life a little, you can also take the time to maybe drum up a conversation with someone who will become a new referral source.

Eventually, and that may be 10 years into it, the slow times will be just part of the year, and you'll use the time to your advantage. The economy may dictate your income, but at least you can control how you use your time when you're busy and when you're slow.

THE DANGERS OF HITTING YOUR STRIDE AT A SMALL LAW FIRM

I know it's not popular to write about lawyers doing well, because misery loves company, but the sad truth is, there are lawyers who don't spend their days blaming their law school for the fact that they should have never thought of becoming lawyers, or trying to figure out how every new "future of law" tool on the Internet can bring them clients. There are lawyers, regardless of what you've been convinced of, who are actually making a living off the time and sweat they have put into their practice. These are the lawyers getting multiple calls a week, whose main concern is not counting the days until their worthless LinkedIn connections bear fruit, but how they are going to get all the work done, and if the stride will continue.

So for the whiners out there, the heartbroken dreamers, the ones who believe expressing their anonymous anger on the Internet will one day result in something positive, take the week off. I want to talk to the success stories out there in Small-Law-Ville (anyone own that term yet?).

Hitting a stride is a great and dangerous thing. You start to feel comfortable. You're getting a good number of calls per week and signing up one or more clients. The operating account is looking good, the workload is increasing, and then for 10 days no one calls. The first time this happens you wonder, "Is it over? Is that it?" Then the calls start up again, but for the next week or so, no new clients. You thought this four-to-five calls a week, one-to-two clients thing was on autopilot, but now you're starting to be concerned for upcoming expenses.

I don't care how long you have been practicing, your reputation, or how much money you make—you will have slow times. Sometimes they will be measured in days, sometimes weeks, and yes, months and years. Slow, by the way, usually means nothing is coming in, or just enough to pay expenses, maybe. When a lawyer tells you things are slow, bet that nothing has come in for at least several weeks.

Oh, the advice.

As I said before, measure everything in months. If you brought in $100,000 in January, $5,000 in February, and $40,000 in March, you're averaging just under $50,000 a month. Never look at things in terms of weeks, you'll just drive yourself crazy.

Unless you've been practicing for long enough where big money cases are expected throughout the year, never get stupid with money. If you just brought in your first six-figure case, or even a high five-figure case, that's not the time to buy a boat, or other lawyer toy—that's the time to park a chunk away for next month when you believe your phone is going to be disconnected. You want to treat yourself to something, great, but keep it reasonable, and that means an amount you won't miss.

Do not get lazy. This applies to two things lawyers love to do.

Do not immediately convince yourself you need to hire someone. You get more work, work harder. When it gets to the point where it is almost impossible to do all the work, then consider expanding. If you have too many deadlines, too many appearances, that's the time to bring someone on, not just because you don't want to do all the work.

The second way lawyers get lazy is to disappear. I mean this in the networking and relationship-building sense. All of a sudden, all the time you've spent meeting people and developing relationships has found you some success, so you stop going out, you stop going to lunch, you quit the nonprofit board—you cut out all the things that helped bring you to where you are. Don't do that. When things get slow is not the time to reenter the world of building relationships. I saw this in 2008 and 2009, when the bottom dropped out. Lawyers came out of the woodwork in both online and offline networking.

Finally, talk about it. Lawyers don't like to talk about when things are slow, but when they are for you, you'll feel much better knowing it's not just you. This is equally important when things are good. You struggle with practice decisions just as much when things are good as when they are slow. When you hit your stride, seek more advice. Never brag, but if, for example, you are a real estate attorney, you know that things are getting better. Lawyers know this, even if they are not doing real estate. There is nothing wrong with saying in response to a question about your practice,

"Things are coming back." Perhaps it results in a conversation that helps you make a decision about your next move.

If you've hit your stride, congratulations, now get to work.

THE LAWYER ECONOMY: IT'S LIKE AN ART FESTIVAL

Spending a few hours at the Coconut Grove Arts Festival in Miami was a good analogy to the state of the legal economy. There were hundreds of artists, each with a booth. There were categories: jewelry, paintings, photography, sculpture, and so on. Each artist was different. Some were solo artists, some were couples. Some were expensive, some were affordable. Some artists were friendly, others were hiding in the back of their booths seemingly uninterested in who was browsing.

Few people were buying.

What was selling? Necessities. The most profitable booth was the guy selling lemonade. There was also a moderate line for the Italian Ice. Kids love that.

I overheard conversations of artists saying they sold nothing all weekend, and many people were hiding their embarrassment over a lack of funds by asking the artist, "Do you have a card?" I noticed something interesting. Many of these artists, in fact most, needed to sell quite a bit of art to break even on their expenses for the booth, travel, and motel. The stress was most likely overwhelming.

Then I looked across from the rows and rows of similar looking white tent booths to the grassy area across the street. There I saw moving sculptures of animals made out of metal, moving their heads and other body parts by the power of the wind. They were colorful, different, and separate from the crowd.

The small alligator was $10,500.

"Who's buying this stuff in this economy?" I thought. Then it hit me. This artist probably needed to sell one, maybe two pieces to make some money. Out of over 150,000 people, someone had to buy. He just needed one, maybe two.

Others needed dozens just to break even.

Maybe he dropped the price a bit, maybe he put some people on payment plans, but he didn't need to do a volume business to make some money. Sure, he probably wondered if anyone would make such a large purchase in this economy, but the odds were pretty good. No matter the economy, there are always people who will spend money. To find those people, you need to have something that attracts them.

He was different, and by being different he was able to charge a premium. Even in a bad economy.

TALE OF THE BIG LEGAL FEE

I wrote a post on a shooting at the Las Vegas Federal Courthouse. The following comment resulted: "But yet, Brian would defend this person if the price was right! Spare us Brian . . . " I don't know who wrote this. It's no one who knows me well, just a person that judges from afar. These people don't bother me, they entertain me—those who assume, without asking.

I remember having a high-profile case in 2002. It was on the news almost daily. It was in *The New York Times*. It was everywhere. One day, walking into the courthouse, a fellow lawyer said, "Wow Brian, you sure are milking the fees in this case." My response: "I was appointed." Anyway, the purpose of the post was to recall the time (and possibly give some pause to young lawyers out there) when I lost a really big fee.

It was nine years ago. I was representing someone under investigation. He paid me a small retainer to communicate with the prosecutor during the investigation and do all the other things criminal defense lawyers do during investigations. Then the arrest came. The bond was over $2 million. After a quick conversation with the prosecutor it was lowered to $1 million. The only holdup was that the prosecutor wanted proof the bond money was clean. This would take a little time—gathering bank statements and other documents.

I quoted a mid-six figure fee. It was the biggest fee I had ever quoted.

The client hemmed and hawed, and then offered to pay me a substantial amount of money for the bond work, the fee for the case to be solidified after he was released. I received half of the fee for the bond work, and was told I would receive the other half "next week."

The bond work was all I could do. I dropped everything. My entire office was working every minute of every day to get all the documents together. I was getting ready to head out of town for the annual criminal defense conference, and everything was moving along. I left for the conference and my cell phone rang constantly from 7:30 a.m. throughout the day. It was the prosecutor, the family, my office, the family, the family, and the family. When was he getting out?

Then I got the call—the prosecutor was told that my client had a substantial amount of funds in an offshore account. My client denied this, but the prosecutor, apologetic, revoked the bond offer. This was on a Friday. We would now go to court and have the judge set bond. The judge wouldn't hear the case Monday; it would be days before we could get a hearing. There was nothing that could be done on the weekend, but the family continued to call, Saturday and Sunday, throughout the day, beginning with my wake-up call. I took every call, missing almost all of the conference.

When I came back home, I ran to the jail to see my client. Looking over the sign-in book, I saw another criminal defense lawyer had been to see him. I asked him what this was about, and he told me his family sent this (very good) lawyer to see him. I told him I would get him a bond hearing as soon as possible. He was not happy I went out of town over the weekend. I called the other lawyer and was told I was probably out. The client's uncle called and told me the same within the hour. He asked me for money back, and got an earful. I went back to my office and told everyone I was out.

They were thrilled.

They told me they put off other clients, other work, and like me, were also bombarded with nasty calls throughout the day. They told me I was not pleasant over the past week or so, and they wanted to get back to our normal way of doing things. I was still devastated over losing the client, and yes, the big fee. I went home and told my wife.

She was equally as happy.

It's been nine years since I lost that big fee, and the case went on for years. The big fee would actually have been a big loss.

The point is obvious: big fees look nice from afar, and they are when you have a good client and good case. But never forget that when someone pays you a large amount of money, sometimes they believe they own you. If you're OK with that, then this take is meaningless to you.

Taking a case shouldn't ever be just about the fee, and sometimes, the best case is the case you don't get or the one you choose not to take.

CHAPTER 10

WHAT LAW
SCHOOL DOESN'T
TEACH YOU ABOUT
THE PRACTICE

WHAT NO ONE CAN TEACH OR SELL A LAWYER

It's hard for any lawyer who spends any time on the Internet to think that to be successful they need anything but a few toys with power switches and apps, and some tips from a nonpracticing lawyer on how to run their office. Sure, there are all kinds of "lawyering," just as there are all kinds of clients. If every client needed to have a conversation with a person in order to have a will written, LegalZoom wouldn't exist. Some people who get traffic tickets want to tell a real, live human being what happened; others just want to fax in the ticket and a credit card number to a faceless lawyer who probably won't be the one in court handling the case.

But for the most part, clients go to lawyers because they have problems. That, or they are trying to avoid problems. The lawyers they hire will be required to do something that cannot be done by a machine, or anything on that machine.

The lawyer will need to understand the problem.

This is often not too difficult for the average lawyer. But what separates the average lawyer from the great ones is not how much technology they own, how advanced their filing system is, or how well their marketing plan is put together.

What great lawyers do, is establish a connection with their clients.

Connections are established in ways that snake-oil salesmen can't understand or explain. A connection is established when a client feels that you as the lawyer understand not only the problem at hand, but the relevance it has to the client.

Don't ever think it's less important to understand not only what the problem is, but who the client is. When a client knows that you understand the total package, that's when you become not only a lawyer, but their lawyer.

Now back to your toys, apps, and race to the front page of Google.

MANNERS

Lawyers, you are the worst at valuing your colleagues' time. If you have a legal issue or question, you feel entitled to advice, case law, representation. You feel entitled to the extent that your appreciation is often nonexistent. You often want referrals to lawyers who will help you or your client for free because, well, now that you've been paid, there is no more money.

Relax, I actually do have some examples.

You e-mail a fellow lawyer your seven-paragraph issue. You don't have the time to do the work yourself (you're too busy billing clients for your legal work). The answer to your question will possibly resolve a major issue in your case or with your client. I've seen your issue before. It's not as complicated as you think. I had the same issue (you contacted me because you thought I might know the answer). I send you a road map of how to deal with the issue along with a couple cases and a memo I did on the issue.

Your response?

"Thanks."

Now I have an issue in general with the e-mail response of "Thanks." It's a waste of my time to click on an e-mail to read one word that basically says, "Yeah." I'd prefer a response like, "Thanks, I appreciate it. Let me know if I can do anything for you." I won't get into sending a bottle of wine or offering lunch or coffee. No need to scare anyone. Remember, it is all about you and what you need for you and your client. All your colleagues exist merely to help you.

You may also have some of the new tech advances like a pen, paper, envelopes, and stamps. Don't let the "future of law" people convince you that a handwritten thank-you note is illegal in the twenty-first century.

Then there is the lack of appreciation for a referral. If you send me a client, you're going to know about it. Sometimes when you are sent a client the conversation goes like this:

"That guy call I sent your way?"

"Oh, yeah, been working on his case a few months now."

"Oh, great."

A**hole.

And you law students? Now listen, I know you send résumés by the stack and receive no response—and I think that's wrong. You, though, do not need to behave the same way rude lawyers do. Maybe in the middle of your whining and crying about the fact that law firms and lawyers don't find you as fabulous and entitled as you think you are, you can learn a thing or two about not acting like an entitled, spoiled brat.

I hate to break it to you, but (to those of you who are takers) you are not entitled to career advice from a lawyer. You are not entitled to free legal advice. When you receive either career or legal advice, you have to pay for it. Maybe not in the form of money, but in the form of appreciation—well-written, thank-you e-mails or notes, or maybe you can muster up a few dollars for some coffee. Lawyers remember those who appreciated their time, and those that expected it.

The legal profession is one based on relationships. Especially for you law students desperate to gain the attention of a lawyer—you never know if the lawyer on the phone or in front of you is going to have an impact on your future. Yes, there are a lot of lawyers and law students, but it still amazes me how many times I look at a list of lawyers on a committee or in an organization and remember an encounter we had. You lawyers and law students who believe these types of pathetic displays of a lack of manners aren't remembered, are sorely mistaken. Anyone who takes the time to help you in any way is taking time away from something else they could be doing. Make sure they know you understand this. It's called manners.

DO YOU AND YOUR CLIENT UNDERSTAND THE SCOPE OF REPRESENTATION?

PART I

There are two things lawyers are doing wrong when it comes to scope of representation, as in, "What is your obligation to this client?" The failure to comprehend this critical concept begins when you are retained, and rears its head again when the representation is over. So let's talk about the dumbass things you are doing to complicate your life, and how to fix them.

First, understand that there are few things more important than a "scope of representation" clause in your retainer agreement.

Case in point: *SCB Diversified Municipal Portfolio et al. v. Crews & Associates et al.*, 2012 WL 13708 (E.D. La. Jan. 4, 2012). The Crews firm was hired on a residential community project and was sued for malpractice.

> The Court reviewed the engagement letter and found that the letter was clearly drafted, providing a successful defense to the allegation of a duty of due diligence for an environmental report. The Court also rejected the client's assertion that the law firm had invalidly limited its representation without consent, finding instead that the law firm had properly created a narrow and clear scope of representation in the engagement letter.

By the way, I got that case from a "Lawyers for the Profession" alert from Hinshaw & Culbertson, one of the premier firms representing lawyers in malpractice cases. They also have some cool lawyers there, and if you want to subscribe to their alerts, know that they don't bombard you with e-mails. End of Hinshaw commercial.

Retainer agreement, engagement letter, whatever you want to call them. Have one.

Don't make it a bunch of much-too-long, written "understandings" of too many things that the client isn't absorbing at the initial consultation. These documents are not tools to attempt to impress the client with your ability to expand on the basics: "You are going to pay me this, and I am going to do this, and I'm not paying for this, and if anything else comes up, we'll talk about a separate retainer/fee/cost, and I'm not guaranteeing anything or giving you money back, and we have no other agreements, so sign here." One unbelievable question I've been asked (by a 25-year Biglaw lawyer) (yes, they ask me questions) (stop crying) was whether to have the client sign the engagement letter.

My retainer agreement is two pages, double-spaced. It has never been an issue. Every so often, I change a phrase, or add or delete something, but it never gets longer. You know when you go to the doctor for the first time, and after three pages of "have you ever been asked this many questions?" you think to yourself, "I'm sick. I have my insurance card and copay. I just want to see the doctor and get some meds." That's how your clients feel after they meet you, want to pay you, and you throw a way-too-long and embarrassing contract in front of them. So cut the crap.

In whatever document you give to your client to sign, you must make clear what you are doing for them, otherwise they will assume that other things are included, and that can become costly. You may be retained to do various tasks for a client, and there is an understanding (agreement) that anything they ask you to do as their outside general counsel is billed at a certain hourly rate, but that's different.

What I'm talking about is the client who hires you to handle a contract dispute for their company and in the interim is sued on the same contract by another party, in another state, and the client assumes that the fee they paid you covers that as well. Simply putting the style of the case and a case number or description of the matter will help you when you discuss with the client the additional fees that will be needed, or when you tell the client you are not going to handle the matter for whatever reason.

For those of you who don't do retainer agreements in every case, *every case* (and there are a lot of you), you are morons and deserve the heartache that comes with that stupid, sloppy practice.

The second issue regarding scope of representation is what you actually do at the end of the case. We'll discuss that next.

PART II

So the matter/case (whatever you call it) is over. You've resolved the contract dispute, formed the corporate entity, ended the marriage, had the criminal case dismissed, resolved whatever the client's issue was for which you were retained. You've taken my advice and narrowly defined the scope of representation in your written, signed retainer agreement. Now what?

Your guess is that you send a nice letter advising the client that you're done here, thanking them for retaining you, and possibly reminding them that there is a balance due. Not a bad idea.

Not the best idea, but not a bad idea.

I suggest that the end of your representation is where you give the free consultation, instead of at the beginning. It's time for a face-to-face meeting with the client to continue the relationship. It's time to ask, "Is there anything else I can do for you?"

I'm terrible at this. I rarely do it. I generally say goodbye to the client in court, or with a phone call and tell them to take care. I may say, "Call me if you need anything," but I don't often take the extra step to continue the client relationship. Many times the relationship is already established through the representation, so I don't feel the need for the face-to-face exit interview, but I'm missing out on an opportunity, and I know that.

Much of what I'm hinting at I do at the initial consultation. While other lawyers are immediately assessing the case, I'm learning about the client. I always begin the relationship (representation) asking about the client, their family, their background, and staying away from the facts and circumstances of their legal issue—we'll get to that. It's important that the client realizes they are talking to a person that actually gives a crap about them as a person, and not just a case.

If you're not doing that at the beginning, do it at the end. I should do it at the end too, I just don't. You can hand them a termination letter at that meeting, after you discuss with them that you would like them to call you any time they have a legal issue. You may not handle that specific issue, but you'd be happy to put them in the right hands. You can also ask the client about their plans for the future, and whether you can help them meet someone in town that you may know. Clients don't expect this— they don't expect you to be a resource to them other than a hired gun to resolve a legal issue. They see us as a fee-for-service industry. Be different, convince them otherwise.

Some lawyers fear termination letters are bad for business, especially when there are several different legal matters going on for the client at one time. You can resolve the issue of when representation ends on a specific matter with face-to-face meetings when a specific issue resolves. Our number one ethical obligation that gets us in trouble is communication. So communicate.

Communication with the client is more than a .3 letter. Representation begins and ends, but never forget the opportunity you have to continue a relationship with a client after you're done representing them. They're your best referral sources, and always will be.

THE MID-REPRESENTATION CONVERSATION

It's not part of a legal strategy or a way to churn the file; it's an attorney-initiated discussion about the client smack in the middle of the case. What usually happens is that the attorney is retained, legal work begins, the client is updated as to the status of the case/matter, asked to weigh in occasionally on strategy, and reminded about the pending bill. We see this as part of the job, but how does the client perceive the representation?

At some point in the representation, the best chance you have to hear what the client is really thinking is when they are not happy. You'll get that anxious phone call, that question that is really a criticism, and it is during those times that you focus on trying to make the client happy. What if you were proactive? What if you scheduled a nonbillable meeting with the client, outside your office, for the sole purpose of allowing the client to voice their overall concerns after you've been representing them for a while?

This isn't a meeting to ask what the client thought of your motion for summary judgment, or your performance at the last deposition. This is a meeting to ask, "What do you think of all of this, of me, of what you thought would happen as opposed to what has happened?" The definition of a good lawyer is not tied solely to motion practice and oral argument—a big part of it is about the attorney/client *relationship*.

Unless a client is experienced in litigation or other legal disputes, they feel like they have their place. That place is to listen to their lawyer, receive updates from the lawyer, and pay their lawyer. Some clients are more involved than others, but usually not at the invitation of the lawyer. Many lawyers, including me, take the position of "Let me do my job, it's what you paid me for." What we forget is that the most important feedback we can receive is from our clients. There are plenty of lawyers out there to say "good job," and congratulate us when we are successful, but when you ask for feedback from a client, you'll get it. While clients may not know the law like we do, they do understand relationships and how we are dealing with their issues.

To make this happen, you've got to put away the ego, stop the time clock, and be willing to hear the truth. I've done this at the end of a case, but not in the middle. Call it a break, call it a time out, call it an opportunity to possibly change the way you are handling the case. Maybe the client's goals have changed, maybe something in his or her personal life has arisen and he or she hasn't had the guts to tell you—or doesn't want to call because "he charges me every time I call him."

The client in front of you has the best ability to send you more clients. They'll send you more clients because you do a good job for them, but also because you asked them if they think you are doing a good job, before the job is done.

DEALING WITH THREATENING, DEMANDING, OPPOSING COUNSEL

I imagine there are a few dozen articles on the Internet about dealing with difficult opposing counsel. There is probably some good advice in some of them, but I thought I'd offer my own as well. I deal with difficult lawyers and have found a way to cast them into the abyss of irrelevancy, causing them to either question their own disgraceful way of practicing law or wonder how to proceed. First, I'll tell you where I learned how to deal with these self-important blowhards.

When I was a young lawyer, I had the opportunity to work on a case where a well-known securities lawyer was involved; he was on our side. I went to see him at his New York office, and after an all-day session with the client, he invited me to dinner. He told me the story of an opposing counsel in another case that sent him a "lawyer letter" laying out his position on the case, and making several threats and demands.

My friend responded with a letter of his own. It was two words: "I disagree."

That dinner taught me two things. One, there is no requirement that your response be as wordy as the initial screed of threats and demands. Two, there is no need to respond in detail to bluster, regardless of who is blustering.

I've used this tactic many times. I read every e-mail with this question in mind: "Does this require a response?" I also maintain a philosophy that I practice law my way, not opposing counsel's way. Just because you yell, doesn't mean I need to yell. Just because you're a piece of crap, doesn't mean I need to join you in the gutter. Clients can be stressful, but what I hear often is lawyers stressing about their dealings with opposing counsel. My question is, why do you engage these idiots at their level?

Going back to the "I disagree" story, last year I received a lengthy e-mail from a lawyer telling me what I was going to do and when. He used all the buzzwords and phrases: "immediately," "by everything, I mean everything," and "if I don't hear from you in 35 seconds . . . "

My response? "Was this e-mail meant for me?"

I never heard from him again. Someone else called me a few weeks later and we worked it all out. The initial dope had no idea how to deal with a lawyer who didn't travel down to the gutter to deal with him.

Lawyers often ask how to deal with these types of chest-beaters. The problem is that they are looking for a way to respond on the same level. There is a different approach. When someone is yelling, be quiet. When someone threatens, ignore. When someone sets their own deadlines, say you can't meet it, but will be happy to discuss it over the phone. Disarm those who spend their days making threats and demands.

The problem is that lawyers who spend their days making threats and demands are used to invoking a response. I don't respond in a way that indicates I give a crap. Judges set deadlines; lawyers can ask me if I agree to their request for a date to respond. Obviously if a lawyer says he's going to file a lawsuit in 30 days if he doesn't hear from me, he'll hear from me. I'll probably call. No e-mails, no faxed letters, no three-page response to his three-page demand letter. We'll have a conversation and then I'll determine whether writing "lawyer letters" is time better spent on behalf of my client. While I know that a .2 conversation isn't as lucrative as a .5 response to "this office represents so and so and you will now shake in your boots as I lay out your life for the next 10 days," you may find that responding like a human being gets you further than playing that game with the baseball bat where you see whose hand makes it in on top.

Part of the problem is that we've all been trained to do things a certain way. Someone writes a letter, you write back. Someone threatens, you threaten back. Someone raises his voice, you speak louder. Why are you doing this? What are you accomplishing?

A few years ago, a lawyer set a hearing without contacting me. That's a no-no. When I called him—*called him*—to ask why he did this, he responded, "That's what everyone does to me." He then apologized. We settled the case and have remained friends ever since.

Don't ever let your boss, your supervisor, or your partner at your firm tell you that the way you practice law is the way the other guy does. When people are trying to invoke a response from you, the worst thing you can do is respond. I'm not telling you to ignore opposing counsel; I'm just telling you to respond in your own way, not anyone else's.

IT'S NOT ALWAYS ABOUT THE CLIENTS

Lawyers often let themselves be abused by clients. After all, the clients pay the fees, and because they pay the fees, they are entitled to behave how they want. Part of being a lawyer is learning that you have to accept clients who treat you and your staff like garbage.

I've never understood that.

Sure, lawyers have clients that are emotional, anxious, demanding, time-consuming, or confused, but our job is to try and use the "counselor" part of "attorney and counselor at law" and help them through the journey as best as possible. Why that has to mean we just take their crap to no end is a ridiculous notion.

Small-firm lawyers are more often the recipients of abusive clients. The fees are usually being paid by an individual or small company instead of by some insurance company in another state. Instead of dealing with a legal issue that affects a whole company, it's often someone's marriage, injury, arrest, or contract dispute—something personal. The client has more of a one-on-one relationship with a lawyer and sees that lawyer as the reason for both success and failure.

The reason lawyers think state bars go after small-firm lawyers more than Biglaw lawyers is simple: there are more of us, and Biglaw clients usually (but not always) don't see the bar disciplinary process as a worthy forum for their issues. So we get threatened more, asked for fees back more, and often feel under siege by bad clients.

When I was a young lawyer, I had a client who couldn't stay out of trouble. His mom couldn't understand how I allowed him to continue to get arrested because, of course, he had done nothing wrong, and there was no way he was going to jail, not for case 1, 2, 3, or 4. When I presented the state's position on the case(s) to the family, I was threatened with a bar complaint if I didn't refund all monies ever received for every case.

I got scared. Real scared. Now I laugh about it, but I didn't back then.

Now I wouldn't take that client. I would see mom's attitude (more than the dollar signs) at the initial consultation, and politely refer them to someone else. I can do that now, but I understand maybe you can't because you need that fee, and you're willing to deal with this. I used to be more interested in the fee than the fit between lawyer and client. I had to be. It sucks, but it's part of building a practice. I've realized I'd rather lose the fee than take on a headache. Yes, I still need to make money, but not to the extent that I'm willing to accept a client I know is a problem from the start. Which leads me to my strategy for dealing with clients who you realize aren't a good fit, and who are abusive with you, your time, and your staff (even if your staff is just you).

First, I try to fix things. Always. I try real hard. I tell the client my job is only to help them, but I need them to help as well. The receptionist didn't deny the motion, and she's not the reason I'm in court and can't return your call for a couple hours. I explain that their strategy may have seemed like a good idea, but that's why they hired me, so I could tell them it's a really bad idea, and that there is a better idea. I try to tone down the client.

Some clients, though, have no ability to act like normal people. They're just angry, abusive, and because "I'm paying your fee," feel they have the right to do whatever they want. The clients get fired. I embrace the philosophy of the former CEO of Southwest Airlines, Herb Kelleher. From the must-read *Nuts! Southwest Airlines' Crazy Recipe for Business and Personal Success*:[30]

> One woman who frequently flew on Southwest, was constantly disappointed with every aspect of the company's operation. In fact, she became known as the "Pen Pal" because after every flight she wrote in with a complaint.
>
> In sixty seconds, Kelleher wrote back and said, "Dear Mrs. Crabapple, We will miss you. Love, Herb."[31]

Kelleher's philosophy?

The customer is sometimes wrong. We don't carry those sorts of customers. We write to them and say, "Fly somebody else. Don't abuse our people."[32]

Obviously, there are cases in which you cannot fire the client, because of court obligations or other reasons. And I know that you may be scared of having to give money back, or a bar complaint, or bad review on Yelp, but you cannot operate from weakness. There are those who will abuse you if they can, if you let them.

Don't.

FIRING CLIENTS

To the chagrin of happy marketeers everywhere, I want to talk about getting rid of clients. Can I never just jump on board and play along?

Usually, it's the client who fires the lawyer because they are not satisfied for whatever reason. Lawyers though, are gun shy to fire clients. Lawyers fear bar complaints, malpractice suits, and negative online reviews, or they grew up being taught that clients are always right. A lawyer will put up with almost anything to keep the client.

I can only speak from 19 years of experience as a lawyer with clients, so maybe some failed lawyer with eight months' experience or some former lawyer "selling the dream" can advise you better, but there is certain conduct clients exhibit that should lead you to fire them.

UNCOOPERATIVE CLIENTS

"Uncooperative" doesn't mean they disagree with you. Uncooperative, in the "fire the client" sense, means clients who miss appointments, are constantly late, don't respond to communication, and believe you are on their schedule. I think every retainer agreement should have a "client cooperation" clause. Something as simple as:

> Client agrees to timely return phone calls and respond to e-mails (based on the agreed form of communication). Client agrees, but for emergencies, to advise of the need to reschedule appointments no less than 24 hours before the appointment. Client agrees to timely provide requested documents to avoid the need to seek repeated delays in a pending case. Failure to cooperate with the attorney, at the sole discretion of the attorney, will result in termination of this agreement, and if there is a pending court proceeding, a motion to withdraw.

You can put whatever you want (subject to ethics considerations), and use the clause to remind the client that this type of behavior is not only important to your ability to properly represent the client, but is also part of your agreement. Obviously things happen and you need to be flexible, but by having a written agreement on more than just fees, you let the client know how you expect the relationship to work.

Uncooperative clients should be fired.

CLIENTS WHO HAVE A "SHADOW" LAWYER

These are clients who shouldn't be your clients in the first place but you took them on anyway. The client came in and wanted his "friend," or worse, his brother-in-law who is a lawyer in another state, on the phone. The lawyer doesn't do what you do, but the client wants this other lawyer copied on everything. Every strategy you come up with has to be run by this other lawyer. Every pleading you draft is reviewed by him. The other lawyer says he "doesn't want to step on your toes," but questions every single thing you suggest, do, think of, and write. Every time you ask the client for authority to do something, he doesn't respond right away because he's waiting to talk to the other lawyer.

Fire this client. Your professional independence is being affected, the client will find a way to blame you for anything that goes wrong, and more importantly, it's just freaking annoying.

LIARS

I often wonder if clients realize that the same behavior they swear they didn't exhibit is the same type of behavior they are exhibiting toward you as their lawyer. Yes, I know, clients lie. I'm not talking about clients who lie about what happened or about the circumstances of their plight. I'm talking about clients that lie to you, about almost everything. This includes the payment of attorney's fees.

I remember being taught not to be judgmental of clients. Some lawyers believe that means you should just calmly nod your head at everything the client says. I'm not going to pretend I don't know the client is lying. Not being judgmental doesn't mean you shouldn't let the client know you think he is full of crap. Even if you're stupid enough to ignore the fact that you don't believe what the client is saying about his case, you shouldn't tolerate the client adding to that by lying to you about matters relating to the representation, such as why fees or costs haven't been paid, why the client is missing appointments, or why the client continues to tell you he will meet deadlines and doesn't.

When do you fire a client for lying to you? When your gut tells you to do so.

CLIENTS WHO DON'T NEED YOU

These types of clients do two things. One, they tell you at the initial consultation that "this is how we're going to handle this," and two, they never want to get to the issue at hand, using you to delay everything. They are going to make things worse for themselves, and they want you to help them.

When you are representing a client, the paramount concern is protection of the client. Inherent in the protection of the client is maintaining the ethics of the profession. There is also that thing called a reputation. No client should manipulate you into putting ethics or reputation on the back burner. If you find yourself being used as a tool, whether for delay or to file some motion that has no merit, or any other reason, put a stop to it (unless, of course, you are a lawyer who prides himself on being used as a tool).

Obviously there are cases in which delay benefits the parties, but this is another gut check. If every time there is a deadline, the client calls you the night before and says, "Can we just get more time?" you need to have a heart-to-heart with the client. If you get no resolution, fire the client. This type of client didn't hire you for your legal work and advice; this client just expects you to "put this off" until he or she is ready to deal with it.

BEFORE YOU FIRE THE CLIENT

Always try to work things out with the client. Sometimes the conduct is due to anxiety or something else, and sometimes it's just that the client has other ideas about how to handle the attorney/client relationship. But never hold on to a client who sucks the lifeblood out of you by doing the types of things I've described here and won't stop. Difficult, demanding clients are one thing, but clients who have no concept of the way you ethically and professionally practice law, need to go.

"MONEY'S NOT A PROBLEM" AND OTHER REASONS TO HANG UP THE PHONE

One of the main differences between small law firms and Biglaw is who hires the lawyer. While both receive calls from the actual individual (person) client, general counsel, or corporate representative, the consumer-type disciplines (personal injury, criminal, divorce, employment, and immigration) are usually smaller shops, and normally get the call from the actual person needing representation. Most of the time this person has never hired a lawyer, so the conversation will be much different than the call from a general counsel who understands typical billing formats, or an insurance company agent who tells you what you're going to bill and not bill.

I'm writing this post for those who have been in small law firms for less than five years. The rest of you know the drill, you've heard the buzzwords and phrases, and (hopefully) you've taken control of your time in a way that shortcuts the worthless conversations with potential clients. From a business perspective, small law-firm practice is an exercise in cash flow. While lines of credit are available, many small law firms don't like to go that route. So every potential client is important, especially when you haven't reached that stride where you can claim a "book of business." Saying "no" before the client makes it clear that it's a "no" is tough. Did you just give up money? Was there another way to get the client signed up?

I draw lines. I am criticized for that, but it's my practice and it's worked for me. Normally when I don't get the case these days, I hear about who got the case, which vindicates my choice to shortcut the conversation. What works for me may not work for you.

Here are some specifics, the things that end my interest in the conversation, or cause me not to even return the call.

1. **Incessant name-dropping.** I heard you the first time you said you were referred by what's-his-name. The fourth time, I lost interest. Now I don't care. I'm not giving you a discount, I'm not impressed that you know him—hell, I don't even know him, and it's worse if I know him, but have nothing good to say about him. Name-droppers want something. I have nothing for them.

2. **Chronic reschedulers.** These idiots are either shopping, or don't really care about their legal problems. After they hire you, they'll continue to shop and not care about their legal problems. I don't reschedule anyone who fails to appear (save for an emergency, which never happens). If you cancel before the meeting, I'll reschedule once. After that, you're wasting my time. Go play with another lawyer.

3. **People who say "money's not a problem."** People with money don't say this. Anyone who says this is someone you will wind up chasing down for the balance, after they've negotiated your fee, and after they've paid your bill late every time.

4. **People with a buffer.** Your mom is not my client, nor is your brother who knows a lot of lawyers, or your buddy who is a lawyer in another state. I am your lawyer, you are my client. Any other arrangement doesn't work.

5. **Clients looking for a ghostwriter.** No, I'm not going to let you pay me for my time to review the work you've done on your case, edit it, and let you file it. That's another lawyer. I don't ghostwrite, and I'm not having you use my incredible talent on your crappy work so when there is a problem you can accuse me of screwing it up. You want a lawyer, hire one.

Many of you take all these types of clients. They're all problems. I understand you may take them because you need the cash. When you don't, they are the first types of clients you reject, and reject quickly.

A CASE TOO BIG

Young lawyers just starting out with their own practice usually tell me the type of work they're doing is "whatever comes in the door." Of course the pedigree Biglaw types criticize that type of practice, but probably don't know that when the now-dead founders of their firm started, they most likely had a similar type of practice. They did real estate work, wrote a will, and maybe even (God forbid) found themselves defending a client in criminal court. At some point, they developed a practice and became known for a certain type of lawyering.

What I see today are lawyers doing any kind of work in order to eat, and lawyers who are lucky enough to have a niche, but are still taking cases in which they have no idea what they are doing. It's like the lawyer whose niche is probate, but has never stepped foot in a probate litigation case, or the lawyer who handles misdemeanor cases taking on a complex white-collar case because it's a good fee.

Those of us who suffer through lawyer e-mail listservs see these lawyers all the time. "Has anyone filed a motion for _____ who can send me a copy?" That same lawyer asks for multiple documents in a period of several weeks and then asks about procedure and whether anyone knows the opposing counsel. They've never handled a case like this, and worse, have no idea what they are doing. They'll never realize how pathetic they look to everyone else on the list, many of whom will have an opportunity to refer a case, and will remember not to send it to them.

There is nothing wrong with learning, unless you are learning to the detriment of the client. There is no doubt we've all unknowingly been on an airplane with a pilot who is in the captain's chair for the first time, but there is also someone sitting to the right of him.

This post isn't simply about asking for help; it's also about determining whether the case is something you should take. When you're starting out, or struggling, and someone comes in with more money than you received in the last three months, you're all too eager to pretend you know how to handle the client's case. You'll just take the retainer and start typing away on the listserv, or fake it and hope you can figure it out. You also hope the client will never know that she's hired a lawyer who has no idea what to do.

I'm not saying you shouldn't take these cases; I'm saying you should protect your client, and yourself, in that order.

Sometimes I'll get a call from a lawyer regarding a possible new case. "I have a client coming in this afternoon on a case I haven't handled before and wanted to see if you could answer some questions." I'm always willing to do that, and so are many other lawyers. These are the conscientious lawyers who are looking out for the clients, and themselves, before taking on the case. There is nothing wrong with being open and honest with a fellow lawyer in the community about your lack of experience—you'll gain a tremendous amount of respect, and it gives you an opportunity to develop a new relationship. I'll often end the conversation with "Let me know if you get the case; I'm happy to help you along the way."

As a result of the lawyer reaching out, they may determine they shouldn't take the case, or that they should be second chair. Keep in mind that the more experienced lawyer is getting calls for cases they don't want and you're now in the front of their mind.

In addition to reaching out to another lawyer before the meeting with the client, here are some more thoughts on evaluating "the big case":

1. **Big cases often suck.** When you get over the fee, you often realize you hate everything about the case. Don't ever forget that big cases can bring big headaches. A $250,000 case is not always ten times better than a $25,000 case.

2. **It's that one outlier case that can ruin your practice.** You may be excited that this new, different case has walked in the door, but six months into it, you may find yourself in a forum you don't practice, and doing things you never wanted to do. It can make you hate being a lawyer. At least if you have solid help in the form of co-counsel or a good mentor, you won't be stumbling through every stage of the case. I know you want all the money, but that can come with headaches as well.

3. **Don't be afraid to accept that this new case is not for you.** I remember being a young lawyer and everyone talking about the wonderful

white-collar defense world. That was the goal. The first time I sat in a conference room with boxes of documents and too many lawyers, I thought, "This is the practice of law?" The best type of practice is one you like, not one that others think you're supposed to want.

4. **Most (not all) of the time when you decide not to take a case that is generally outside your practice area, or level of practice, you've made the right decision, and will realize it down the road.** Forget about the money, and concentrate on the legal work involved in the case.

(ALMOST) NEVER BE THE SECOND LAWYER

Sorry to interrupt the circus of marketing advice out there purporting to show you how to get all the clients you want who have a few bucks and a problem, but the one thing no one ever mentions is that most of this advice comes from those without clients. Failed former-lawyers-turned-marketers can help you be the best neon sign on the Vegas Strip (they say), but have no concept about the real decisions that are required by lawyers who wish to run their practices, instead of having their practices run them. You know what I'm talking about. Most lawyers have a philosophy about client intake: if you have money and a problem, I'm your lawyer. Lawyers hear that the best case is the case you turn down, but does anyone really do that?

Most lawyers don't create policies that weed out the headaches that cause burnout and a general distaste for the profession.

Policies like, for example, talking to clients over the phone and quoting fees prior to bringing them into the office, where an hour later you realize the potential client has no money. We are car salesmen after all, aren't we? Come on in, kick the tires, and we'll sell you the car. Or, as another example, not answering your cell phone at all hours of the day so the client doesn't think he can abuse the ability to reach you at all hours. Make clients think they need to respect your after-hours and weekend time and you'll have no practice, right?

Or like the policy I want to talk about here, never being the second lawyer.

Yep, that's mine.

I don't want to be the second lawyer, for several reasons.

One, and most important, is that the majority of people who have a falling out with the first lawyer, will never be happy with any lawyer. Many calls I receive from lawyers with bar complaints begin with "I was the (second, third, fourth) lawyer on the case." While there are exceptions to this policy, they are rare. Sure there are lawyers who take a case and do no work, never return calls, and are truly the culprit in the breakdown of the attorney/client relationship. Mostly though, the problem is that the client is unhappy with news, or believes that the lawyer is not paying her enough attention, or wouldn't file a motion that no lawyer should file. I also rarely get a call from a second or third lawyer where there isn't a trail of unpaid legal fees.

What interests me is the controversy this policy causes. Lawyers express shock that I would have such a policy. These are the same lawyers who are all too willing to meet with a represented client and make the client believe they can do better. They would never think to recommend that the unhappy client try to reconcile with the offending lawyer. There is no money in that. Some lawyers also believe, assuming it's not just a case of a client with ridiculous expectations, that I have an obligation to a client who chose a bad lawyer.

Why?

There is more information about lawyers out there today than there ever has been. If the client is making a bad decision on bad information, perpetrated by scumbag marketers and not taking the time to verify the lawyer's credentials, why does that become *my* obligation? Disagree all you want. I'm not the savior for those who hire lawyers based on flash and buzzwords.

So yeah, I did it. I violated my policy.

It gets worse.

All the evidence was there not to do this. But it was going to happen. Sometimes human elements trump hard and fast policy. Now the search for the third lawyer commences.

Will I do it again? Probably. Soon? Not a chance. But I will tell you this: the practice philosophy of 24/7, any case, any client, any fee, any personality, is a recipe for burnout.

Not every client or case is right for every lawyer, regardless of the fact that the money looks the same.

LOOKING FOR "FREE"

I received this e-mail:

> Brian,
>
> We are running our annual survey to find out what real people really think about cloud systems, and we are entering everyone who takes part in a draw for a case of six bottles of our favorite Chablis from France. We'd really appreciate it if you could spare just 2 minutes to take the survey—it is only six questions, so why not take the survey now and maybe you'll win those six bottles? Just click here.

Translation: Brian, the Internet is such an easy place to convince people to spend their time on things for the hope of getting something back that we are spending zero dollars on market research and instead hoping that people who have opinions that can help our company make more money will donate their time on the hope of some vino.

My response:

> Whatever your name is, thanks for the offer.
>
> These days, 2 minutes of my time is worth about $X, and I don't really want to spend that money giving my opinion on cloud systems, which I understand is going to be all the rage among attorneys.
>
> I have an opinion though. Why don't you set aside some market research dollars and send each person who responds a bottle of wine? What does it cost? $20 or something. Let's say 100 people respond? I think a couple grand investment is worth it.
>
> Don't you?

Their response: none. I assume they were a little surprised. Wouldn't I be honored, excited, thrilled to be asked my opinion for the chance to win some cheap crap wine? Isn't everyone these days interested in giving away their time for the possibility of getting something back?

Before the explosion of the Internet, where those without credibility now travel to conferences for free so they can tweet what's going on and get lots of attention, or speak at some side conference down the hall where many who would never be asked to speak at the main conference huddle and videotape their session in the hope of becoming the next YouTube star, we had other ways of obtaining things for free. I used to hear "This case would be good for you." Translated: "I have no money, but the publicity will be worth your time."

I still get the e-mails:

> Mr. Tannebaum, I have a question. (The answer will determine whether I get this job, keep my job, get arrested, get into the bar, ever have a life.) The question is in four paragraphs and requires your immediate attention. I won't ask you if you will charge me for this or otherwise offer you anything to help me, and after you make me feel relieved over my situation, I will not send you even a thank-you card. You may get the standard one-word "Thanks!!!" and then you'll never hear from me again.

In this age of minor celebrity status being created by a few interesting ideas written on the World Wide Web, people are all too willing to seek free advice—and not just a quick answer to a simple question, but a detailed analysis to a scenario that has a significant effect on the questioner. I'm always intrigued by someone who may lose a $100,000 job, but won't spend a few thousand dollars to help fix the problem. More and more I realize that it's not that they won't, it's that they don't feel they should. Sure, some people offer to pay, or provide the appropriate thanks, but too many are trolling the Internet looking for "free."

I'm always happy to answer a question (not a five-paragraph hypothetical for which you've done not a stitch of research), and I'm always happy to spend some time with an appreciative soul who inquires as to whether my time is worth anything. (Hint: I usually reject the offer, but they come so infrequently.)

We lawyers see the search for "free" on listservs. Lawyers are hired on cases they know nothing about, or how to handle them, and start typing away: "Anyone got any case law on this scenario?" "Anyone know of a REASONABLY PRICED expert that will opine on whether my client is innocent? He is facing life and has a family of 12 but only wants to spend about $500, thanks!!!" My unscientific research says this is all getting much worse. People, lawyers, are not just looking for free, they're *expecting* free.

Why is that?

I think it's because many are willing to give it all away for the hope of something in return. Our value is becoming what we are willing to take. Our worth is becoming nothing.

NO, I WON'T HELP INCOMPETENT LAWYERS TAKE MY BUSINESS

When I first went into private practice, I was doing exclusively criminal defense. A lawyer I didn't know, who didn't practice criminal law, got my name and wanted to refer me a case. He told me his client was arrested and asked, because the client only spoke French and he had an assistant who spoke French, if I would come to his office and consult with the client.

Sure, no problem.

I went to his office and sat in his conference room with the client, the assistant/translator, and the referring lawyer. As I went through the substantive and procedural aspects of the case I noticed that the referring lawyer, let's call him "Joe" (because his name is actually Joe), was taking copious notes. A couple of days later, I called Joe to ask whether the client was going to hire me. "Actually Brian, I was surprised to hear from the client that he wants me to represent him."

Joe sat there, listened to my 90-minute road map of how I would handle the case, decided he needed to pay rent, and told the client he could do it. Maybe that was the intention from the beginning; I don't know. I do know that I no longer allow anyone to take notes during consultations, and I rarely go to someone else's office to meet with a new client.

Now you may be thinking, "Oh, Brian's one of those lawyers who doesn't share." Quite the contrary. If I could bill for the "Hey, can you just answer a question?" advice I give to other lawyers, or for the case law cites that colleagues need for their motions, or for sending over the motion I filed that a young, or even experienced but lazy, lawyer now needs to file, I wouldn't actually have to practice law. I share, and I'm happy to share with a lawyer trying to do a good job for a client. But I decided a while back that sharing is not the same as helping a lawyer take my business or commit malpractice.

I'll give you two examples: First, when you're starting out and trying to develop relationships, you believe it's important to let as many lawyers as possible know what you know. You think it will help you get business. It should. But there are lawyers out there starving who will take any kind of work they can get. These are the criminal lawyers asking for copies of civil complaints, and civil litigators asking if anyone has a copy of a financial affidavit for a divorce case. Those are lawyers on their way to screwing over a client, or at least stumbling through the case only because they need cash, and I'm not going to be a part of it. I'm not going to help bad lawyers do bad work. The answer is no, and it should be your answer as well. Sending a lawyer a rope to hang himself with is not help. It's stupidity.

Second, I'm not going to teach you what I do if you're just interested in learning so you can become a competitor. I'm a nice guy, not a moron. I know, harsh. Here's the call: "I have a friend who needs to hire you, but I really want to learn how to do what you do, so can you just tell me how it works or maybe I can co-counsel, because I want to learn how to do this work?" I didn't make that up, that's a real call. I said no. Candidly, I think in my early years, I may have said "yes." This is not an old lawyer versus young lawyer issue; it's an issue of doing the work to become competent.

To this caller, I said the better path was to send me the client and I would attempt to reciprocate (as he's a good lawyer in his field). I was happy to represent the client and would even pay a referral/participation fee in accordance with the ethics rules, but wasn't interested in teaching a lawyer in another field to do this work. Contrast that with a young lawyer doing this type of work and needing some assistance—that's different.

So go ahead and see this as a post from a 20-year lawyer who wants those kids to get off his lawn. It's not—and they're not just "kids." You're not doing your practice or the profession any favors by becoming the lawyer who shadows other lawyers just to make a buck. Law is a business and a profession, don't forget either one. Protect both.

THE PARTNERSHIP SPLIT

You and your partner are going separate ways. It sounded like a good idea—you left the same firm together, or quit the prosecutor's office at the same time. You got a little corner of another firm's space, a wood sign with silver letters, a nice desk, and those two chairs in front of it that would make the clients believe they were in the right place. You plugged in a new phone system and off you went. But your partner isn't bringing in business, or maybe it's you. Maybe a small law firm isn't for you and you're headed back to Biglaw or in-house. Maybe your partner can't seem to get in before 10:00 a.m. or your contingency cases are way too contingent.

Lawyers split up; they have issues like any other type of relationship. They fight about money, space, others (read: clients) in their lives, and who knows, maybe they even sleep together. Sometimes the split occurs over time, and sometimes it happens suddenly. Let's keep some things in mind.

Assuming the split isn't a result of death or disbarment, you and your partner are going to continue to practice law, and most likely in the same city. You will meet up again, you may compete for the same clients, you may wind up working together on another case. No matter how strong the resentment, anger, or hate is right now—never focus on now—always consider the future. You do not want your partnership dispute to be the talk of the town. You do not want it to consume you. No one looks good when the first thing that comes to mind about a lawyer is the war you just had with your partner. Your partner may make it a war, but if there was ever a situation where you should take the high road, this is it. Forget that you are a lawyer; forget that you can litigate, argue, and make people's lives miserable. Go into resolution mode and stay there.

Do not run to your state bar association for a map of how to deal with every single silly detail, or with every question you think is relevant. You are not the first partnership to split up. Find a lawyer who has gone through the same thing and learn from him or her. Do not think that getting the bar involved will make things easier. Here's a thought: maybe find a lawyer who handles contract disputes and has dissolved a partnership. Do not think that filing a bar complaint is a good way to resolve things. Yes, the bar has ethics opinions and rules and you should read all of them and follow them, but the people from the bar don't care about your stupid partnership—they care about your clients. Getting the bar involved in your petty disputes is a sure path to a trust account subpoena, and an inquiry into, well, your entire practice. You think you're in the driver's seat threatening or actually filing a bar complaint? Just wait until the letter from the bar comes addressed to you and your partner.

Speaking of clients, that's the focus.

I know, you think all the clients belong to you, or will want to stay with you because you are awesome and your partner is a piece of crap. But seriously, are these the only clients you will ever have? Do what's expected, tell the clients who have worked with you and your partner that you're splitting up, and let them make the decision. Some won't go with you. Grow up, get over it. Go get better clients. The fact that you made a bad decision on a partner should not wind up putting clients in a position where they feel they are in between two lawyers trying to kill each other. Jerry Maguire? Bob Sugar? Time to watch that movie again.

Here's another novel thought: sit down and talk about it. If the split is because you despise each other, bring in a mediator. In the end, you may wind up with each partner having his own lawyer, but do everything you can to resolve things principally between the partners. Your split likely has something to do with money, and bringing in lawyers just costs money. You're a lawyer; your job is to resolve issues, not create them. (Unless you need to meet your billable hours quota for the month.) Resolve what you can resolve, and bring in the lawyers only if you have issues that you can't agree on, or to draw up an agreement that makes the partners comfortable about the future after all the issues are resolved.

The goal of a partnership dissolution is—wait for it—to dissolve the partnership. It is not to enter into protracted negotiations, litigation, or a public war. There are costs to ending a relationship, and those costs are not just money. If your goal is to end the relationship for free or an even split of everything, well, good luck with that. You know the term we lawyers use, "go-away money"? Spend it to end the partnership if your overriding goal is to just get out. Yes, lose the ego, realize that being right costs money, and get out.

SPRING CLEANING FOR LAW FIRMS

After summer, I can see you all enjoyed your vacations. I see the 175 pictures you posted on Facebook of every single place you went, and I see that you "can't believe (your) baby is starting 7th grade." Now that it's time to get back to work and figure out what to do about all those clients calling you as a result of seeing you on the first page of Google, I will again offer you life-changing advice. This advice is all real, and in no particular order.

1. If you have an office, or even a desk, take every single thing off the top. Clean it, and then place everything back, except the stack of papers that belong in a file or the garbage, the magazines and articles you're never going to read, and the items that do nothing but take up otherwise workable space. This will cost you no money, take about 15–20 minutes, and you will thank me.
2. Read a bunch of articles from Lee Rosen's *Divorce Discourse*.[33] Particularly read his post from August 18, 2011,[34] on the basics of law firm financing. After you read that, put into play something that will save you money. Maybe things are slow and you can consider dropping off those filings at the courthouse yourself on your way to grab coffee with a referral source, saving yourself some money and finding a way to get outside and meet potential clients—unless you believe the virtual law firm model is in your future.
3. When you're done reading Lee's stuff, read "Law Firm Marketing Must Include Empathy and Understanding,"[35] by Dave Lorenzo.
4. Gents, if you actually do meet with those people we call clients, or have a practice that requires you to leave your den, consider an important investment: a shoe shine. (Yes, I just told you to get your shoes shined.) If you're feeling particularly interested in your appearance, go all out and get a new suit. Throw in a couple of new shirts and ties. A nice appearance makes you money (this goes for ladies

as well). If you don't understand that, find a lawyer who dresses well and ask him why. Then you can do the face palm.

5. Watch *Jerry Maguire*.

6. Make a list of all your clients, all your cases, all the tasks that need to be done, and which ones you don't want to do. Can a law student do any of them? I like having law students around. They remind me of why I love being a lawyer.

7. Number 6 does not apply to every law student. Find one or two who actually want to be lawyers.

8. Those business cards in a rubber band you've collected over the past year? Find three people and connect with them in person. Throw the rest out. (Here comes the "never throw out a business card" crowd.) Throw them out, now.

9. Figure out how to save $1,000 to go to an upcoming conference. Sign up for the conference. Not a tech or legal marketing conference, a conference of lawyers or other business professionals who may need your services.

10. Revisit your local bar associations. Would meeting a few more lawyers in your town kill you? You don't have to be on the board. You can go to a lunch or two, attend a few social events, or pick a project to develop.

11. Revisit your retainer agreements. I'm constantly revising mine, adding in more protective language regarding payment, scope of representation, and other areas where there are occasional disputes.

12. Clean your other desktop. Most of the stuff there was just easy to save on the desktop. Now it looks like your desk. Put Word and PDF files in folders. Delete those icons you never use or never will use.

13. Schedule a meeting with your CPA, financial advisor, and insurance agent. Ask each one of them to review your file or portfolio before the meeting. That $1 million life insurance policy seemed good enough when you didn't have a decent house and three kids.

14. Start making a list of who is getting holiday gifts. You're not buying cards because they are a complete waste of money. Pick the gift now. Obviously you'll have a few gifts that need to be special, but for the most part you can pick a big and a small gift. Someone who gave you

a $10,000 case gets the big gift. The person who answered your question that helped you resolve an issue gets the small gift. December 15 is a bad time to do this.

15. Speaking of the holidays, pick your "stop" day—the day you want to stop working in December. Pick it by September 30. My date is usually around December 17–18. If I can control it, I will not have any court hearings, depositions, or out-of-town obligations beyond that date through the rest of the year. I'll still meet with new clients and work on cases, but foreclosing other obligations gives me the ability to do things on my own time, like holiday shopping and going to school events. If you work for someone, you can't do this. I have to say that because some of you are so stupid that you'll actually tell me that you work for someone and can't tell your boss that after a certain date you're not doing certain things.

Try one or two of these things. At the least, watch *Jerry Maguire*. I love that movie.

CLOSING OUT THE YEAR

For those who have clients and spend their days surrounded by real people, I have some advice about year-end planning. I don't care if you do or do not do any of this stuff; I can only tell you that it's what I do and have done for years. Obviously, if you are part of the "man, I hope all these idiot consultants are right" future of law, much of it won't apply to you.

MEET WITH YOUR ACCOUNTANT

If you've made some money this year, you should meet with your accountant. I hope you have a good relationship with your accountant, and I hope you set a lunch or meeting in your office or coffee shop before the end of the year to discuss year-end tax planning. Next spring is a bad time to learn that you could have done some things to save yourself having to pay Uncle Sam more money. (By the way, for those of you getting a refund, you have bigger problems.)

CONSIDER TELLING CLIENTS TO PAY IN JANUARY

If you're not desperate for cash and you have clients who owe you money, consider doing this. Biglaw folks have to try and collect before year's end, so that leaves us small guys to give early Christmas gifts to our clients by telling them, yes, you will have money for that flatscreen you can't afford, just pay your bill by January 15. Trying to get money out of clients during the holidays (after Thanksgiving) just makes you the one who is crushing the client's mellow.

NO HOLIDAY CARDS, NO STAFF PARTIES

Cards: I think it was just after the kids were back in school when I got my first "time to order holiday cards" brochure. I stopped sending holiday cards years ago. I don't even look at the ones I receive anymore; I just ask for a list of who sent them, and hard copies of those with personalized messages. Cards signed by the entire bunch at the insurance company or law firm deserve a special place in hell.

If you want to say happy holidays, pick up the phone. No, not that phone with the text messaging app, the one with a wire. Maybe you can talk about next year.

Staff parties: You have a firm with lots of clients and referral sources you want to party with? Have a party—but tell your staff it's optional. Please though, for the love of all that is holy, do not have an office party for the people in your office just to have a party, or some lunch where the staff looks suicidal. And I know, there are those of you who can't think of anything more fun than a two-hour lunch or wild party with your staff. But if you're not that firm, take the money, buy gift cards for your staff, and give them a half-day off. That's right, on office party day, give your staff $500 each (this is not their bonus), and tell them to go shopping. Yes, I've done this; yes, they love it.

REFERRAL GIFTS

Anyone who thought to send you a client, whether or not you were retained, gets something. Wine and gift baskets are easy, but if you want to be more creative, consider signing a coffee table book or a book relevant to your practice area. Also, nothing says "it's the thought that counts" like personalized gifts, and don't forget the option to send breakfast or pizza to an office (these need to be coordinated with the receiving office). People who send you business like it when you help make their office happy.

One other thing about gifts: if it's been a particularly good local referral relationship, don't hesitate to tell the source that you didn't just want to send a gift, but rather offer to take the referral source and their significant other to dinner. Relationships need to be fed and bathed.

TIME OFF

December 17 is my date. What's yours? This is the date I want to stop working for the year. No, I don't close my office, but I don't want to have major deadlines or court appearances after this date. Every year, I miss this date by a couple days because there are things out of my control, but I try to get close. The way I do this is to start thinking about it after the summer. When I'm in court, or talking to opposing counsel, I listen for things like, "Can we set it for December 20?" No.

Whether or not you make your date, it's a good mental exercise to think about when you will start your holiday vacation. We all have ways to communicate and work during vacation, but if you set a date where the obligations can at least slow down, you'll better enjoy your time off.

THE MOST IMPORTANT GIFTS

Don't forget the people that take care of you—the guy at the restaurant that gets you in, the server at the deli who never screws up that complicated breakfast you order, the hairdresser that gets you in at the last minute, and the FedEx guy that just works his ass off. My list goes on, and yours will too if you think of all the people who make your day easier. Don't forget these people.

CHAPTER 11
REEVALUATING
THE WHOLE THING

FINDING MEANING

In 2011, I attended the first-ever Innocence Project of Florida dinner. I was invited by a board member, and upon acceptance, asked by the incoming chair of the Innocence Project to turn over a fairly large amount of cash to be a cosponsor. Apparently, while Holland & Knight was receiving an award for their thousands of hours helping to free the wrongfully convicted, money for the dinner wasn't pouring in from the establishment. Maybe next year.

As lawyer-type dinners go, it was a little different—poor lawyers representing alleged violent criminals mixed with Biglaw lawyers who spent the last decade doing the same, as well as three dozen judges, the elected state attorney, the appointed U.S. Attorney, and a slew of law students. Also in the crowd were a half-dozen exonerees. The exonerees included James Bain, who served more time than any other exoneree—35 years for a crime he didn't commit. He went to jail when I was four years old, and got out as I was planning a trip for my 40th birthday.

The night had its share of speeches and awards. One of the awards went to lawyer Marty McClain, whose client, Juan Melendez, was there among the suits wearing a T-shirt. Juan spent 17 years, eight months, and one day on death row before being exonerated. Marty's other client, Frank Lee Smith, couldn't make it because he died of cancer on death row before being exonerated. At Marty's table was his high school buddy, actor Tony Shalhoub, who looked like a stalking fan taking pictures on his phone when his lawyer friend was honored for being poor and a hero. While people were asking Shalhoub for pictures and autographs, he was busy being enamored with Marty.

The night then took a turn. Each exoneree was given the microphone to say a few words—how long they were in, what they're doing now, and then a video was shown. We saw pictures of their young children visiting them in prison, and then those same grown children, hugging them upon their release decades later. I lost count of the standing ovations. Juan Melendez was given the microphone, pointed at his honored lawyer in front of 250 people, and said, "I owe this man my life."

Yeah, it was pretty powerful.

I predict you haven't had this experience. Few have. To be the lawyer that discovers a client is innocent after decades in prison is as meaningful as it gets. But, the money isn't so good. This type of work, even on the side, doesn't pay for the Mercedes, or even the new iPad.

In the daily grind of practicing law, the results, good or bad, become just part of the job. Finding meaning in what we do is the exception. Sometimes, even in a practice where people's lives are affected, the question is asked, "What am I doing?" I imagine in other areas of law, it's asked with more frequency. The meaning of what we do as lawyers is mostly buried under the desire and need to make money, the next motion that needs to be filed, the next document that needs to be prepared or read, and the next client.

At this point, some of you are wondering what this post is about. Where are the tips on how to make money? How do you get clients from this? Is he telling us *again* that criminal defense is the only practice area that matters?

Here, I'll give it to you on a platter: the quickest way out of the practice, mentally or physically, is to believe that none of what you are doing has any meaning. If you're one of those insurance defense lawyers tired of spending your days trying to deny coverage to injured or sick people, or one of those civil litigators tired of trying to help one wealthy guy screw over another wealthy guy, then find something to do, even if it's just one case, that leads you back to the reason you became a lawyer. (Caveat: If the reason was "to make lots of money," well, you probably stopped reading after the first paragraph.) It doesn't have to be a criminal case. Help an old lady keep her home, help an immigrant prepare a document, do something where someone's life will change for the better because of something you did.

So many among us are miserable and wondering why—and what—we are doing. When you're done, the stories you will tell—that will be told about you—will be about the work you did that mattered, not the amount of hours you billed, or the cool gadgets you used.

There are people out there that need our minds, our thoughts, and our time. They have big and small problems that we can fix, and little to no money. They do have two things though. They have an ability to make you realize, to bring you back to, the core meaning of being a lawyer, and they may just tell a few (hundred) people one night that they owe you their life.

WHEN NOTHING IS WORKING

There is no lack of advice these days about what lawyers should be doing to get clients or run their practices. And you take it. You take the advice of the former lawyers with no clients or practices, or the perennial failures who understand that lawyers are gullible when it comes to advice about making money. But still, you take it, or, God forbid, pay for it.

So you create a Facebook fan page for your law firm and ask everyone to "like" your page. You go on LinkedIn and join groups. You go on Avvo. com and ask lawyers to endorse you. Your website is awesome and you've got an e-mail newsletter campaign going. Offline, you do the bar association networking circuit. You've met some people for lunch, and you even had an article published. By the way, you're also a good lawyer and have some happy clients. But the phone isn't ringing, or isn't ringing enough. You get to the point of frustration, and start thinking of discontinuing part of your marketing, or worse, closing your practice.

Let's be honest: Some of you won't make it. You're decent lawyers but have no business sense. Some lawyers need to work for someone else. That's why we have Biglaw—so really smart people with no ability to make a buck on their own can pretend they are superior.

Let's say though that quitting is not an option, but neither is continuing on this path. You're just trying to figure out which of the half-dozen things you're doing is worth continuing, and what else you need to do. I'll take a stab at it. My apologies for being a lawyer with clients and a practice, as I know I'm not the typical guru selling you on the dream.

The first thing you need to do is look at what you're spending every month on marketing. This includes that idiot SEO guy, lunches, drinks at happy hours, everything that is related to you trying to connect with others, online or offline. Next, I'm not going to tell you that you should spend a certain percentage of your income on marketing. Let the gurus try and sell you on that silly number. I have no idea what that number should be, but I do know that your money should be intelligently spent.

I would then look at your last 10 cases. Who sent them to you? Avvo? Facebook? Lawyer referrals? Your friends at Rotary? If you're getting cases, something is working. If the number of cases received, either directly or through an introduction due to your marketing strategy, is 2 out of 10 or more, I would consider an increased investment in that strategy. That's right, I'm telling you if your time or financial investment in social media is working for you, increase the investment.

You also need to determine how long you've been doing each form of online and offline marketing. I believe everything deserves a year before pulling the plug. So let's say you've been begging the world to like your Facebook page and although you're scared to tell me, it's done nothing for you over 12 months. Leave it there, don't abandon it, but let's get out the tissues and wipe the tears of reality that it's just not the future of your practice. Don't spend any more time on it. But let's say the bar association happy hours you've been going to have garnered you a few referrals. Try to sponsor a happy hour. Try to create some type of dinner group where you take people from the monthly happy hour to a nearby restaurant after-wards. Invest in that event and the people that attend.

While you may think nothing is working, when you evaluate your past cases, you will discover the source of your business. It may vary—it usually does—but when it appears to you that nothing is working, back away from the marketing strategies that have given you zero, and double up on those that have had some return. It sounds basic, but there is a difference between continuing successful marketing strategies and increasing your investment in those that work for you.

The other thing to do is consider marketing strategies you've avoided. This goes back to the idiot marketing gurus who "know" how to get you business. If you've gone all-in on networking and it's not working, consider doing some online marketing, and vice versa. There is no one thing that works for every lawyer or every practice area. You may be frustrated that your Google AdWords isn't bringing in the millions, but instead of kicking yourself for buying in to the dream, go join an organization or sponsor a charity event.

Or, try to go work for someone or do something else. I certainly don't profess to have all the answers; that's for the idiots from whom you actually take advice.

WHAT I DID ON MY SUMMER VACATION

I'm one of those lawyers that goes on vacation. Not just long weekends, real vacations. I pity those of you that pride yourselves in announcing, "I don't take vacations." Good for you, you pathetic drone. I didn't take vacations at first, as I was always fearful that someone would call to hire me and wouldn't wait until I came back. Now I don't care. If you can't wait until I come back, there are plenty of lawyers on the Internet to hire that can take your PayPal payment online and send you whatever documents you think you need to handle your case.

When was I able to take my first two-week vacation and not worry about business? After 14 years in private practice. I say that because I know how patient all of you are out there.

Anyway, when I'm on vacation, I think about my business. I think about what I love, what I hate, and what I want to change. There is nothing like thinking about your business (not the cases or the clients) while you are away from the phone calls (if your phone is ringing), other interruptions, the deadlines, and all the trappings of a lawyer's day.

One of the things I do a lot while I'm away is watch other businesses. I try to figure out how they make their money, why their employees are happy or unhappy, why their customers patronize the store, restaurant, or tour company, and how they handle problems. You're an idiot if you are trying to build your law practice solely by watching how other lawyers run their practices. Client dynamics can be found in many places, and ideas come from everywhere. Most lawyers are doing it wrong anyway.

Here is what I saw over two weeks in California.

BIG ADVERTISING, NO SUBSTANCE

We went to a restaurant with a banner touting a "World Famous Breakfast." It was full of people. Big bold banner, full of people, what could be bad? The food and the service. They were both awful. The next day I went to a place I heard people talking about in the hotel. I also found some detailed reviews online. The place had a small sign, it said "Home Cooking." We went back two days later. Even though it was more expensive, it was one of the best breakfasts I've ever had. It's called Hollywood Café. It's in San Francisco. The other place? I can't remember the name.

WHAT GOES UP, MAY NOT COME DOWN, BUT IF IT DOES?

We went to a winery with a stellar reputation for their wines. *Wine Spectator* had just named one of their wines at the top of a recent list. Those who have been to wine country know there are wineries that have big signs on the road advertising "free tasting," and there are those that you can't find because their sign is the size of a wallet-sized photo. They don't have free anything, and they aren't looking to attract the idiots that came to get drunk with $5—you know, those people (maybe you're one of them) who wouldn't know wine from grape juice and aren't buying anything anyway?

If you were at this winery, you were there to buy some wine with a well-known reputation. The staff wasn't overly friendly, because they didn't have to be—they're on top, and they know you know that. You didn't find them from a big road sign, you looked for them. I wondered, though, what may happen when their wine is no longer at the top of any ratings lists and they have to rely on those buyers that have been loyal to them because they feel like they are part of the family. Have they thought about their relationships with their customers? They surely weren't trying to develop any relationships deeper than the buy-sell relationship, and that's called a transaction, not a relationship.

THE IMPORTANCE OF THE RECEPTIONIST

Then there was the doorman at one of the hotels. This guy was a genius. Upon arrival, he immediately started joking around with my kids. Every single time he saw them he started up a conversation with them. One night we returned from dinner, said we were going to a big chain ice cream shop, and he literally took them by the arm and walked them down the street to the "best of the city" ice cream shop. When I checked out, I gave him a tip that reflected my appreciation for the attention he paid to my family. One of my daughters joked that he "loved his job too much."

As with any vacation, there were problems, mistakes, misunderstandings, and opportunities at every corner to watch business owners and managers teach me lessons, both good and bad. Yes, I took a vacation from my clients and my cases, but not from the recurring work of learning how to better run my practice.

When you run your own business, you either look for ways to do things better, or someone else will. And let me just add that none of what I speak of here had anything to do with owning an iPad.

There are those to whom only skills matter—those clients are few and far between. Most clients want skills, and they want you to deal with their quirks, they want you to pay attention to the concerns of their spouse, they want you to admit when you failed to satisfy them, they want brutal honesty (well, a couple do), and their loyalty to you is based on more than your ability as a lawyer. These are things you don't necessarily learn from other lawyers.

Enjoy your vacation.

GROWING

While self-anointed law futurists are competing for who can give the best advice on having a practice-from-laptop-sans-office and remain as small as possible (because happiness practicing law is being alone all day in front of a screen), some lawyers are still considering adding a lawyer as an associate, partner, or of counsel. The question is, how?

Hiring a lawyer can be expensive, and there is not always an extra chair next to you at Starbucks, so you'll probably have to put them somewhere with a wall and a desk. The bottom line is that even when you get too busy to handle everything yourself, the cost/benefit analysis of adding another lawyer can be scary. You're not just talking salary, but also benefits. And what about if that lawyer brings in business; how should they be compensated? There is no one way to do this, so here are some considerations for those who are contemplating adding on.

The first decision to make is whether you are looking for someone to do your work, bring in work, or both. Hiring someone who wants to be you—the rainmaker, the one that goes to court or meets with the clients—can often be a short-term proposition. That lawyer will learn from you, and then leave when they realize (or think) they can do it on their own. The reason nerdy law-review types are attractive to and work well as Biglaw associates is that they enjoy being in a small room all day, researching and writing.

If you are looking for someone only to do your work, you must make that clear. If you don't, and instead provide incentives for them to bring in business, they will not be focused on your work. At 4 p.m. when you are on a deadline, your associate will be meeting with a new client. At 10:30 a.m., that associate will be milling around the courthouse coffee shop. At lunch, they'll be at some two-hour networking event.

Nothing ends a relationship between lawyers quicker than a dispute over money. Whatever arrangement you make must be routinely reviewed. If your associate is good enough that you are able to be out of the office more or working on other matters without having to supervise much, reward that. We all hear "take care of the people that take care of you," but lawyers aren't very good at that. There is no rule that says appreciation is limited to a Christmas bonus or annual review.

Sometimes you don't have a choice—you have more work than you can handle, but not enough to hire someone. Consider creating a hybrid relationship. Bring in a lawyer who has some business who may be looking for a little help. Maybe your name is worth something to them and they believe if they are associated with you, that you can help them build their practice. It may not be a long-term relationship, but you never know. You can bring them in, with no salary, have them help you out, and you in turn help them build their practice. Maybe it will turn into a mutually beneficial relationship. If not, no big loss. This type of lawyer will probably work better in an of-counsel or just space-sharing relationship.

The options are many. There is no one way to add a lawyer, especially in today's economy. There is no reason to think the only way to add a lawyer is by paying a salary and benefits. Before growing your practice though, make sure you understand the reason why. Sometimes what appears to be a prohibitive investment will quickly become money well spent.

FUN AND HAPPINESS IN THE PRACTICE OF LAW

There is a lot of misery in our profession. Much of it occurs because lawyers didn't realize that the practice is not like a television show glamorizing our daily lives. We are also a miserable bunch because many of us do the same thing every day, we hate what we do every day, and we deem it useless. Even if you're one of those rare lawyers who loves what they do, you stand the risk of being around the miserable ones.

As I said in the beginning of this book, I love what I do. I don't love it every day, and like everyone else on the planet, occasionally think about doing something else. There are days when, like everyone else, I have to deliver bad news to a client, or wonder if every conversation I am having is a conspiracy to cause me to jump out a window. But because I generally love what I do and love you all so very much, I thought I'd give you some advice about how to actually enjoy lawyering.

I know you may be stuck in a job because of the salary and your lack of ability or desire to run your own shop. If you're beholden to the job, then you have to do what you are told. You can't work on the cases you want, and you don't have much freedom, so don't expect much from me on this issue. Perhaps you can focus a little on some pro bono work through which you can actually help a client do more than move to compel discovery.

This leads me to what I think is the most important factor in finding happiness in the practice—enjoying the satisfaction your clients get from your work. For example, one day I completed and filed a lengthy document for a local client. I e-mailed it to the client and received the following response:

"Good job, want to get a beer?"

I assumed this was one of those invitations to do something at some point that would be put off and never happen.

"Sure, let me know when."

"I can leave in 10 minutes."

It was 3:30.

Oh the horrors. This was not on my synced calendar. There were more hours to bill clients, make phone calls, and write, write, write. How could I imagine doing this?

And there I was, 15 minutes later, talking about all kinds of stuff—work, kids, life. I saw the relief on his face that my work was completed. I sensed his appreciation. The chicken wings were pretty good too. Whatever I had to do could wait until the next day. This was a time to take a breath, and be in the presence of what my work is really all about—affecting the lives of clients.

I sometimes do this with the delivery of good news as well. I've been known to walk or drive over to a local client's office to show them the letter I just received regarding their case. The story is not the news, it's "and my lawyer actually came over to tell me." This is something I do for the client, and myself. That's right—sometimes it's OK to be a little selfish. Ask a florist the favorite part of their job and they'll tell you it's seeing the look on people's faces when they receive flowers.

But you don't do anything in which you would ever imagine celebrating with a client in person, or taking the time to deliver good news in a method other than a .3 e-mail? You sit at home and pump out documents for people you've never met, or you have a practice where there is never anything to be happy about (other than the check every two weeks)? Here is my advice for you—maybe you heard it in elementary school: make better choices.

TECHNOLOGY AND THE LOST ART OF UNAVAILABILITY

Two lawyers pissed me off to the point that I need to write about why technology sucks and needs to be controlled like a screaming 2-year-old on an airplane.

I took a Friday off to chaperone a field trip with one of my kids to the Everglades. I promise if I ever get a Pinterest account I'll post all the pictures of the alligators. On that Thursday, I did everything but wear a shirt that said, "I Will Not Be in the Office or Available FRIDAY." I also e-mailed some annoying people that haven't been out of their office, ever. That day, one lawyer I e-mailed responded something to the effect of, "I know you're going to be out tomorrow but," and then asked me to do some work on our matter. The other lawyer called Friday morning, was told I was out, and said, "Can you have him call me to discuss a case even though he's out?"

Yeah, we all have smartphones, we're all getting e-mail in real time, and regardless of what we're doing, the other side can't comprehend that we are either really not available, or just don't want to be available. Maybe we're looking at alligators with our kids while our phone is back on the bus. Being out of the office (and for those that don't have an office, "being out of the office" is a concept, not a physical geographical location issue) is something lawyers need to do to avoid hating the practice of law, but it is becoming more and more looked down upon.

Today there is no such thing as unavailable. Being unavailable is a sign of weakness, and a good way for Biglaw associates to get fired and then be permanently unavailable. But I'm weird that way—I take a day or an afternoon here and there to do odd things like spend time with my family or friends and remind myself why I'm lucky to be a lawyer practicing law instead of a paper-pushing drone.

Your concern is that you may miss the opportunity for a new client, or that something will explode and you need to be available 24/7 to fix it, especially if you're a solo. The Internet is full of articles written by people full of crap that are promoting legal tech, as well as those giving us tips on controlling tech. I can only tell you what works for me.

1. Never respond to an e-mail immediately unless it requires an immediate response. If you respond to everything immediately, you are only training people to think that you respond immediately. When they send an e-mail at 8:30 a.m. and by 8:42 you haven't responded, they will stalk you. Back off, respond within 12 hours.
2. Do not let people contact you the way they want. You know those clients or others that have your cell and start texting everything? End that crap now (unless you love practicing law by texting). Tell people your preferred method of communication (call the office, e-mail me, call my cell, whatever). When people disregard that, ignore them.
3. Be OK with missing a new case. If your goal is to really convince the public that there is, in fact, a 24/7 lawyer, skip this advice. If you want to have a life, understand that you cannot be obsessed with every new case or client. If you haven't learned yet that good clients will wait to hire good lawyers, learn it now.
4. If you're going to be unavailable for a few days and you just can't bear being unavailable at all and have no staff, make a friend. Have your calls forwarded to your new friend. I did that when I started out, and I returned the favor when my friend went on vacation or was out for a day or so. As for e-mail, I used to be anti-auto-reply. I've changed my thoughts on that. And I appreciate when I see one that says, "If this is about a legal matter, please (call, text, etc.)."

Most importantly, if you're a lawyer and another lawyer says they're unavailable, show some damn respect and go work on something else. The sun will rise tomorrow. And don't start with the "what about those lawyers that are always unavailable." I'm not talking about those idiots.

BAD NEWS: TO REMAIN IN THE PROFESSION, YOU HAVE TO LOVE THE LAW

It shouldn't shock me that the headline of Brad Kane's piece in the *Hartford Business Journal* reads "Profession in Turmoil."[36] Why is the profession in turmoil?

> The price of admission is up and interest in being a lawyer is down. The passion that once marked the profession is fading in the face of business pressures as law firms race to be the biggest and most comprehensive, judging lawyers' value on the revenue they generate.

That's a long way of saying people are getting into the profession to make money, not to be advocates.

I say that all the time. Some tell me I'm wrong. Others tell me I'm right, and insist that this is the reason everyone becomes lawyers and they don't know anyone who became a lawyer because they wanted to be a lawyer— because the only reason to become a lawyer is to make money. Something like that.

But I love to see that it's not just me, as others would make me believe, that thinks a slew of law students in the '90s and through present time went to law school for one reason:

> "Lawyering used to be a profession. Now, over the course of time, it has become just a business," said Bill Crowe, partner at Hartford law firm Mayo Crowe. "A lot of people are disillusioned because they go to law school thinking they are getting into this dynamic,

lucrative career; and they've come to realize that often they are just pushing papers around."

"The large role money plays in today's legal market undermines the profession's higher goals," said Lee Hoffman, a member of Hartford law firm Pullman & Comley LLC. "The first job of a lawyer is to make someone's legal problem their own. The second job is to be an adviser. Once the profession becomes about the paycheck, those tasks are hard to fulfill."[37]

And here is the knife in the heart:

Although the pay is high compared to other professions—the median starting salary for a 2010 University of Connecticut School of Law graduate was $75,000—a law degree does not lead to a cushy lifestyle. Other professions such as entrepreneur or investment banker are more lucrative with a lower demand on time.

"*More* lucrative." "*Lower* demand on time." Now I have the attention of the slackoisie. See, you don't have to become a lawyer to make money—go do something else. Get out of the profession. Leave us advocates to try and bring it back up to par. Go start a business or become a stockbroker. Just go. It's already happening. Your friends are going elsewhere:

After a significant jump in law school applications in 2009 and 2010, law school applications dropped 11.1 percent nationwide this year. Connecticut's three law schools—at Yale University, University of Connecticut and Quinnipiac University—saw a 17 percent drop in applications in 2011.

Yippee!

"Those people who thought earning a law degree would lead to riches are taking a much broader scope and thinking about if it is going to pay off," said Karen Lynn DeMeola, UConn School of Law assistant dean for admissions and student finance.

So take that "much broader scope" and think about the long hard days of working in a profession that you never wanted to enter but for the cash.

> Passion is what keeps lawyers in the profession, said Jeff White, associate at Robinson & Cole and chairman of the Connecticut Bar Association Young Lawyers Section.

Passion.
Look it up.

WHO ARE YOU LISTENING TO?

I spent four hours at the home of a lawyer who had been practicing law for 64 years. I became friends with him when he'd only been practicing 48 years, and have had the opportunity to learn from him and even work on good cases together. We talked about law, lawyers, legal stuff, court, clients, and judges. The only time the word "computer" came up was when he told me his hands are having a hard time typing these days.

When I look around the Internet, and see the lawyers who frequent the place, I wonder from where other lawyers get their advice, tips, mentors, and philosophies. I see what I call "real lawyers," those with clients who get up every day and, whether it be in their home office, rented time-share office space, or an actual real office with a name plate on the door, spend their days practicing law. They take phone calls and e-mail inquiries about representation; they research, write pleadings, negotiate resolutions to cases, or stand in courtrooms and seek a jury's input on their dispute.

I see what I call "Starbucks lawyers." They don't necessarily sit in Starbucks all day, but they are lawyers who pray to the god of coffee beans and free Wi-Fi because they would otherwise be at home, typing about social media among the silence. Starbucks lawyers have law degrees and may have had a law job at one point, but for the most part spend their days being asked to or are begging to speak at conferences, spending money they don't have when they actually are asked to speak at a conference, and telling each other how great they are all day on the Internet. They may have wanted to be "real" lawyers at some point, but it was just too much to get up early, drive somewhere, and tax their brain with legal issues. Life is better trying to convince other real lawyers that they could have the life of a Starbucks lawyer, if they just would hire them as consultants.

When I see the dozens of Google searches a day for "how to make money as a lawyer," I realize that my conversation with this lawyer yesterday seems like a complete waste of time. He didn't look at my website, he didn't ask me about my social media strategy. He just talked, and I just listened. There are those reading this who know this lawyer. He is undoubtedly one of the most legendary lawyers this country has ever seen. I don't need to mention his name, even though the Starbucks lawyers out there couldn't imagine having a conversation with anyone they determine to be of some import and not spreading the word in order to make themselves appear relevant. Starbucks lawyers love to let everyone know that they "just had a conversation with _____" (insert seemingly important—but really not—person's name).

People ask me why I care about these Starbucks lawyers. Why does it matter that they falsely create this apparent celebrity life when in fact outside of a laptop screen, they are of no relevance to the practice of law?

I don't care. What I do care about is that I get the sense some of you out there who are real lawyers or want to be real lawyers are listening to them. They have no secrets; they know nothing that you can't find out yourself. They all need to go away. They demean our profession by making you think that a piece of technology or "10 tips to pumping yourself up on the Internet" will make you a better member of our profession.

What will make you a better member of our profession is spending time with those who *are* better members of our profession, even if they can't teach you how to use a toy.

ASKING WHY

In 2008, a lifetime ago in the legal economy, Professor Bainbridge asked if the law was a "mature" industry:[38]

> If law in fact is a mature industry, we face a problem of systemic oversupply. The rate at which demand for new lawyers grows has permanently leveled off. Economic recovery will help, but it will not change the fundamental structural changes in the market for lawyers.

Bainbridge believes "We have been growing the number of law schools as though the demand for lawyers would permanently continue to experience exponential growth." He thinks we should close the bottom third. Of course that will never happen—law schools are moneymakers. The fact that all law schools today are facing their own jobless graduates is of no moment.

When I began law school in Florida 22 years ago, there were six law schools. Now there are 11, I think. That's a new law school about every three and a half years, just in one state. But say there are too many lawyers and you'll get one of two answers: "There is always room for good new lawyers" and "Of course you say that now that you're a lawyer."

There *are* too many lawyers. More importantly, there are too many new lawyers and law students that have no idea why they went to law school. It wasn't to become an advocate, per se, it was to get a good paying job.

Society is much to blame. The reason a high school diploma today is worthless is because we now encourage everyone to go to college. I know some plumbers and electricians that do pretty well financially, but we no longer encourage high school students to learn trades. A sociology degree that leads to nothing is more important. Now that we encourage everyone to go to college, a college degree is worthless. An MBA used to be impressive—that is, until everyone started getting MBAs on the weekends.

Now it's law.

More lawyers don't create more cases. And don't talk to me about "frivolous" law suits—those are just cases with which you don't agree. More family lawyers don't create more divorce. More criminal lawyers don't create more arrests. More lawyers just create competition between more lawyers. We eat our own. Competition just makes legal services cheaper (which is not necessarily the same as affordable). There is nothing wrong with cheap and quality, as long as both exist, but they rarely do. You normally get one or the other—cheap, or quality. Sometimes you get lucky. Sometimes.

In today's economy, getting lucky with legal services is often all that matters. A client buys a will online and hopes it works. Of course they'll only know if there is a message left for them at the pearly gates. In my world, there are some new kids on the block charging 20 percent of what I charge. Are they good, quality, experienced lawyers? Does it matter? Yes, to some it matters. To most, it doesn't. People will always say that if they needed a lawyer, they would seek out the best and find a way to hire that lawyer. Those are people who are not typically clients. Remember, most people never need a lawyer, and if they do, it's usually for a transaction like a house sale, will, or divorce. Most people have a number in mind, and whichever lawyer they meet, or talk to, or e-mail with who says that number, is hired.

As the economy worsens (and yes, it's worsening), struggling lawyers will have to make a choice: lower your fees to the point where the increase in clients is borderline unmanageable, take on matters in which you have no experience, or get out and find another way to make money. Hopefully, by now most graduates are over the theory that going into massive debt in law school entitles them to a six-figure job. It ain't happening.

I've said before that the good part of this recession is that lawyers who never wanted to be lawyers will get out. If you were here to make money and you're not making money, you won't stay. Even those who are here because they wanted to be lawyers are getting out. Families have to be fed, mortgages have to be paid, and there of course needs to be money for Starbucks coffee and new iPhones.

The other good thing about a recession is that lawyers and law students are forced to ask a complicated question about their venture into this profession: Why?

LEAVING THE LAW

No, not me. I actually got into this profession for the right reasons. And although it's hard for many to admit, many of today's law students and lawyers didn't.

I call it the LA Law syndrome. It started right before I started law school. The TV show *LA Law* showed us that law offices were nice places, in tall buildings, with nice furniture, and beautiful people. *LA Law* caused a whole generation to go to law school. The work was tedious for those sent to Biglaw, but the golden handcuffs were tight. Where else could a 25-year-old make $100,000 the first year out of school? It wasn't about the profession, or representing clients, or building a practice. It was about the paycheck.

And like the last line in *Goodfellas*, "Now it's all over."

So to no one's surprise came an article[39] in the *ABA Journal* about a legal career consultant who claims 25 percent of her clients want to leave the law. The article is nothing to write home about, but the comments are.

Elena (whose name probably isn't Elena, nor is the comment probably real), writes:

> I would like to leave the law, but not the paycheck. So the only way I can leave the paycheck is to find a guy who will support me. I am having difficulty finding a guy willing to pay for me and my lifestyle. So I must continue to work, even though it is not as interesting as shopping and eating out in restaurants.

Dreamboat, probably a close friend of fake Elena, says:

> I would like to find a nice gal to support and pamper, too bad you are a lawyer. The thought of freely spending time with a lawyer makes me nauseous. Otherwise it would totally work.

Robert takes the first easy shot at Biglaw associates:

There's more to "law" than working in a big firm where one has to expect to be told what to do, and that some of what one is told to do is distasteful; after all, you have to figure that if the work employees do could be considered "fun," the Bosses would do it themselves, right?

You also have to figure that most employee-employer relationships will tend to degrade to "employer pays employee just enough so they won't quit, employer does just enough work to not get fired." That's not enough for everyone, but it's all a "career counselor" usually has to offer.

Then here comes the "wait, it didn't happen like I thought it would," commenting as "Looking for the right fit":

> I would like to find the right fit in the law, but I graduated right when the crash struck and so it has been a while since school. I've done some contract work here and there, but I'd really like to use my legal degree to help start-up businesses get off the ground. How do I transition into this? I'd like to stay in the law but have a more interesting and stable life!

A police officer who beelined back to being a police officer because the money is better there in this economy blames the ABA for creating and selling law school as a ticket to cash:

> From JD to PD:
> I just graduated, passed the bar, and will return to my previous field of law enforcement. I will get all of my loans paid off with 10 years of public service. Plus, get a great pension, start at 50k per year, and get a month's vacation.
>
> It is sad the ABA keeps accrediting more schools who publish misleading salary stats. Who thought you could make more money as a nurse having an AA degree than a lawyer.

And no comment section would be complete without the "get off your ass" cry that offends so many new graduates:

Hey JDtoPD

I think it's great you found a government job with good benefits. Good for you. To all those who are bitter about JDtoPD's good deal, instead of complaining, get up and do something about it. Instead of denouncing the public sector's reasonable pay/benefit packages, why not demand that the private sector provide the same. Yes, I know the Biglaw lawyers chained to their Blackberries 24/7 are well compensated, but most lawyer-employees in the private sector have a much worse deal, and calculated hourly probably do make less than a nurse. These lawyers need to demand more of their stingy employers or quit and open their own law offices and compete with their stingy former employers. That said, JDtoPD, don't get too caught up in the nurse-with-an-AA comparison. You with your law degree have a much greater upside. Ten or 20 years from now you could go into the private sector, hang your shingle, and command many times per hour what a nurse makes.

Just bringing this up infuriates today's law school graduate and young lawyer. Some who know they went to law school for the cash and aren't making it, or aren't making much of their career as a lawyer, don't like to discuss this. Others will admit with righteous indignation that "Yeah, I went to law school for the $160,000 salary first year out." Who I feel sorry for are the few who actually thought about becoming a lawyer before entering law school.

Ever wonder why ethics are more and more of a problem? Because more and more law students see law school as career school, not professional school. They see law as a business, not a profession. It is a means to a nice living, not a high calling.

I've written before about the lack of shame a lawyer should have in deciding to get out. The question always is, "And do what?"

My answer?

Something else.

REINVENTING YOURSELF AS A LAWYER

I've watched lawyers reinvent themselves, both successfully and unsuccessfully. It can be done, but like anything else in the legal profession, it takes thought and time. (I just lost half the audience.) For those left here, there are only two reasons you want to reinvent yourself. One is money, and two is that you hate what you're doing.

Let's take two scenarios. First, you're a former prosecutor turned criminal defense lawyer who after three years of defense work wants to do personal injury. You've been practicing six years and the dream of going from $40,000 as a prosecutor to $250,000 as a defense lawyer just hasn't happened yet. You also hate all your clients, and hate the work. Everyone says there is more money in PI, and you're convinced that $5 million verdicts are readily available for the taking.

You are a lawyer who has not become "the man" (or woman—oh, you were getting ready to pounce) to see, and therefore you don't have a lot to lose by shutting down the defense shop and moving into the world of PI work.

But if you're this lawyer, I wouldn't recommend you open up shop as a PI lawyer. I'd recommend going to do insurance defense for a couple of years. There is a steady salary that's probably about or more than you were making, and no one will really miss you for a few years. This is not to say you can't just wake up tomorrow and say you're no longer doing criminal defense, but remember that when you reinvent yourself—especially if you're going to be doing contingency work—the money won't start coming in right away.

Go do insurance defense, meet all the people in the practice area, and then emerge on the plaintiff's side. I suggest this for other practice areas as well—if you're relatively young in the practice, it's easier to reinvent yourself by learning on someone else's dime. You're probably not making the kind of money that is tough to walk away from, and if your goal is to be competent rather than just taking money from clients and pretending, or sending embarrassing e-mails asking 300 lawyers for "a copy of a complaint for negligence," it's a better move to learn how to practice in your new area while not having to worry about making rent.

For the lawyer who has developed a multi-decade practice and well-known reputation in a certain discipline and decides it's time to do something else, it's not necessarily more difficult—it's just different. This type of lawyer has been his own boss for a long time and going to work for someone is generally not an option. My advice for this lawyer, or the younger lawyer that doesn't want to get a job to learn the new practice area, is to find a lawyer that does this type of work. You've got to be careful here. No lawyer wants to teach another lawyer to take his business, unless he's close to retirement. Find a lawyer who does something similar. Going back to the PI example, I would find a lawyer who concentrates on medical malpractice. I would tell this lawyer that I am looking to get into PI, but don't want to do med mal. This sets up an immediate referral relationship. Not every lawyer will be interested, but those that understand the benefit of having someone around that does something similar will at least consider the possibility of working together. I would tell this lawyer that I want to work together on my cases and will pay co-counsel fees in accordance with my bar rules.

There is, of course, a marketing aspect to reinventing yourself. There are two things to consider. One, I've seen the "now accepting personal injury cases" ads. I guess that works if you're a lawyer who does mass advertising. The other way of course is to mine your list of current and former clients. One thing lawyers are bad at is understanding the value of relationships with clients after the case is over. I don't care what you practice, every client leaving your office when a case ends should be told to contact you for any legal issue. It's not that you practice in more than one or two areas, but you want to be the person the client calls so that you can maintain contact and put them in good hands. If you do this as a matter of course, you now have an easy path to communicating your new practice area.

One last thing: Reinvent yourself if you hate what you do. If you are reinventing yourself because you think you'll make more money, I hope you do—because if you don't, you'll hate what you do.

EPILOGUE

THE CAUSE OF THE DEFENSELESS OR OPPRESSED— 15 YEARS LATER

I will never reject, from any consideration personal to myself, the cause of the defenseless or oppressed
   —Oath of Admission to the Florida Bar

I wrote this post on the fifteenth anniversary of my admission to the bar. I wrote it for myself, so that one day my kids would read it, but it received a ton of feedback, so I included it here.

On the evening of April 28, 1995, I entered the courtroom of the Honorable Stanford Blake to be sworn in as a member of the Florida Bar. I first met Judge Blake when he was criminal defense lawyer Stan Blake, and I was his 19-year-old client. The irony was apparent. I had already been working at the public defender's office for five months under the certified legal intern program, but from this moment on I would be official. I could talk in court without the supervision of another lawyer.

Fifteen years is not 20 years, it's not 40 years, not a half century of practice, but it is 15 years, a decade and a half of practicing criminal defense law. I think it's something to talk about. Fifteen years ago after graduating from the only law school to which I was accepted, I took the only job offer I wanted, to become an assistant public defender. I went to law school to become a criminal defense lawyer. My salary was $28,000. After passing the bar, I would receive a raise to $32,500.

I began in the county court division—DUIs, misdemeanors, homeless clients, drunks, and minor screw-ups. I learned everything I could about DUI, tried as many cases as I could, and did that for 18 months. It was there I had my first high-profile case representing a Santeria priest who was charged with animal cruelty resulting from a videotaped ceremony. It was there I learned that no evidence can result in a conviction if the arrest is on Christmas Eve and a juror says, "Well, we just thought if someone was arrested on Christmas Eve, the cop must have thought they were really guilty." I also learned there that a seriously drunk guy who hits a pole on a sidewalk and then pisses all over himself can be acquitted due to overwhelming evidence if the jury "thought the cop was arrogant."

After 18 months, it was off to juvenile. I went kicking and screaming. I left after eight months and three weeks. I hated it. I hated the parents who enabled and made excuses for their kids, and I hated the notion that there was something wrong with every kid, other than they were just being kids by getting into fights and doing stupid things. After my stint in juvenile, I went to "felonies." I tried some cases as a "C" lawyer, and then started to think about how long I would stay in the office. I didn't want to do death penalty work, and I really didn't see the benefit to staying more than three years. I loved the job, I just became a little bored and wanted the challenge of learning how to be a private lawyer.

My salary was about to be raised to $39,000 when I was offered a job at a DUI boutique for $50,000. I took it, and spent nine months there. I learned how to run a business, and how not to run a business. I learned I didn't want to just do DUI work. We need those lawyers, lawyers who are experts in a particular crime, but it wasn't for me. I quit. I had no money. I had the car they leased me, a new townhouse, and $10,000 coming in from court-appointed cases.

I had made friends with a partnership of 20-year criminal defense lawyers who offered me a free office, free desk, and free computer. My professional association (PA) was born. These guys referred me their "junk" and taught me how to practice in federal court. They became mentors in all aspects of my life.

After five years I wanted to start a small firm. I got some furnished space, and my firm was born. After a year, we left and rented the space we are currently in, and the rest is history.

I've experienced every high and low of private practice, times when the phone didn't ring for weeks, good clients, great clients, nightmare clients, good judges, terrible judges, outstanding lawyers, awful lawyers, fascinating cases, and not so fascinating cases that became fascinating as the case proceeded.

Do I miss working at the public defender's office? Every day. Best job I ever had.

What have I learned in 15 years of practicing law?

1. I love what I do. I could not imagine doing anything else but defending those in trouble, criminally or before the bar.
2. You can make money as a criminal defense lawyer. You can make money doing anything you love. What matters is that you do it well, and that your clients see your commitment to your chosen practice area. There are criminal defense lawyers, and lawyers who take criminal cases. The difference is immense.
3. One word-of-mouth referral is worth a year in the yellow pages, in-your-face Facebook ads, and mailers to homes of those arrested.
4. If you have decided the type of lawyer you want to be, it doesn't matter what anyone else thinks. Those who handle traffic tickets with zeal and professionalism deserve the same respect as a lawyer who handles complex "bet-the-company" litigation. Anyone who advocates for a client and does it well is a lawyer deserving of respect.
5. No case or client is worth your reputation.
6. Honesty that hurts your position is the best kind.
7. Hearing that a judge is a bad judge never matters, unless you hear it three times, from three different people.
8. Most lawyers are unhappy because they are not practicing in an area that inspires them.
9. Your reputation as a lawyer can be cemented within 90 days of admission to the bar.
10. If you are in private practice, work *on* your business, and not just *in* your business. There are people out there—go meet them.
11. The length of time someone has been a lawyer has no bearing on their skills, ethics, or reputation, unless proven otherwise.
12. A phone call is always better than a letter.
13. There are three places where cases are resolved: counsel tables, conference tables, and restaurant tables. Use them all.
14. As to number 13, breaking bread with opposing counsel does not show weakness.

15. Never lie.
16. If you burn a bridge, make sure you burn it to the point that it is unrecognizable, otherwise, expect it to come back to bite you. It will.
17. Some people don't matter. Never treat them like they don't matter.
18. Most people you deal with have a family, a child, a personal issue, or something else that makes them just like you. If you need me to explain the relevance of this, just move on to . . .
19. Your obligation is to the bar rules first, and your client second. If you reverse that, you won't need to worry about it.
20. People hate lawyers, think they are greedy, and don't respect them. That will never change. Don't waste your time trying to convince society otherwise. Spend your time convincing your client through your work that they shouldn't hate lawyers, lawyers aren't greedy, and lawyers deserve respect.
21. The best case is the one you don't take.
22. "Money's not a problem" is never true. If money is not a problem, you won't hear that statement.
23. Don't ever practice law at the level of your sleazy opponent.
24. Immediately cease using the word "immediately" in correspondence with other lawyers.
25. Threats are worthless.
26. Take every opportunity you can to teach a young lawyer something, regardless of their response.
27. If you have a bad feeling about taking a case, don't.
28. If you are asked to be the second lawyer and you agree with the work the first lawyer has done, don't.
29. Never take a case from a friend.
30. Never bad mouth the competition, even if they deserve it.
31. If you want to be a lawyer that makes good money, gets good clients, and does great work, then dress like you are a lawyer that makes good money, gets good clients, and does great work.
32. Remember that what your client told you is what your client told you—nothing more.
33. A client who won't tell you the truth should be fired.
34. Some of the best lawyers you've never heard of.

35. The people you walk by and ignore, notice.
36. People who want you to represent them and will scrimp and save to retain you are better people than those who think they own you because they wrote a check.
37. Always make time for a colleague who needs advice, and asks you for that advice.
38. Never say "same shit, different day." I hate that.
39. You never know where your next case is coming from, or who can afford your fee.
40. Those who insisted I "don't go into criminal law," I'm laughing at you.
41. There are cases you are not right for—admit it.
42. The best advice I've received on case theories is from non-lawyers.
43. Many lawyers follow none of these "rules" I've listed.
44. As long as students enter law school to obtain a ticket to a job, our profession will dwindle into nothing but a trade.
45. As Larry Pozner, past president of the National Association of Criminal Defense Lawyers (NACDL) said once, you make your worst decisions when business is slow.
46. When business is slow, get the hell out of the office.
47. The best way to get to know your client is to get to know his family.
48. Never object to a continuance for a family issue or a vacation. Never.
49. In court, always let someone go before you if they ask. You'll ask one day too.
50. Speaking and writing is a better advertisement than your angry photo next to the words "Aggressive" and "Available 24/7."
51. Most white-collar cases are boring.
52. A $250,000 case is not 25 times better than a $10,000 case.
53. Whenever you argue with a non-lawyer, they will tell you to stop "cross-examining" them, and that they are not "on trial."
54. I have no interest in judges who are "nice off the bench."
55. Lawyers who brag they don't go on vacations are miserable human beings who I never want to deal with on any level.
56. There are three reasons people hate lawyers: advertising, the perception that they charge too much and make a lot of money, and that they sometimes win.

57. Most people think a judge's job is to keep bad guys in jail.

58. There are three types of conversations not worth having: one with a potential client who thinks hiring a lawyer will make them "look guilty;" one with the girlfriend, wife, sister, other family member, or friend of someone who was arrested and is not in jail; and one from a marketer who wants to help take your practice "to the next level."

59. Payment plans will consume you.

60. Regardless of what others think of what you do, remember, there are three branches of government, and you're an officer of one of them. Pretty cool.

ACKNOWLEDGMENTS

Writing, call it "blogging," starts with inspiration. Much of mine comes from a group of instigators known in the computer age as "bloggers." Some I've never met nor ever heard their voice, while others now know my deepest confidences. Some have jumped on a plane to share an important moment with me. As I finish this book, I've just left a chance meeting in Paris with the Texas Tornado, Houston's Mark Bennett, author of the aptly titled *Defending People* blog, and my good friend. We met through blogging.

In no particular order (because they are egomaniacs), the bloggers that have inspired (and often criticized) many of my writings, are:

Matt Brown, Keith Lee, Jordan Rushie, Leo Mulvihill, Scott Greenfield, Ken White, Mark Bennett, and Lee Rosen. It's no coincidence that they are all practicing lawyers, each with reputations and successes that warrant reading (and stealing) their thoughts and ideas. If I left you out, I do not apologize. It was intentional.

Not knowing if I'll write another book, this seems like as good a time as any to also thank the teachers, mentors, critics, partners, friends, and family who helped get me to a place to turn thought in to the printed word: My parents Ned & Rhoni Tannebaum, Albert Krieger, David Rothman, Judge Richard Hersch, Judge Marilyn Milian, Judge Stan Blake, Steve Anderson, Marvin Pickholz, Dan Weiss, Dave Lorenzo, Brian Cuban, Professor Steve Everhart, and my first employer as a lawyer, Retired Miami-Dade Public Defender Bennett Brummer. From my first employer came my first trial partner, later CIA Agent killed in the line of duty, and one of my greatest mentors, Gregg David Wenzel (1969-2003). He would have been proud to see this book, although he would have told me "it's fine."

Thanks to the captain of Above the Law, David Lat, and everyone at Breaking Media for giving me a platform to express my (often despised) views of "the practice." To the Editor of Above the Law, and resident troublemaker, Elie Mystal, who made the initial invitation (3 times) to me to write for "ATL," I love you dude.

Over the years I've heard "you should write a book," but one person actually took it a step further. Miami attorney Frank Ramos introduced me to the ABA's Jonathan Malysiak who, after a breakfast meeting in Chicago, would become my editor and who I thank for his honesty and willingness to be my partner in this endeavor.

It's a cliché for men to thank their wives, but anyone who is married knows—hell, I don't have to explain it. I'll just say this—Thank you Lisa, for every time you walked by me while I was typing with my headphones on, asked "are you writing," and kept walking. That's true love.

Finally, to my dear mother-in-law, Diana Montalbano, who lost her second battle with cancer during the writing of this book, but even in her last days would always greet me with: "How's the book coming?"

"It's done Mama."

Brian

NOTES

1. www.sfgate.com/sports/article/LeBron-James-carries-the-look-of-a-champion-3656991.php

2. www.law.com/jsp/law/careercenter/lawArticleCareerCenter.jsp?id=1202427937942

3. www.divorcediscourse.com/crappy-lawyers-happy-clients/

4. www.law21.ca/

5. http://www.law21.ca/2013/08/ready-for-the-future-your-survival-kit-survey-results/

6. http://thecareerist.typepad.com/thecareerist/2013/04/advice-for-law-students-anna-ivey.html

7. www.divorcediscourse.com/struggle-year-practice/

8. www.bni.com

9. http://en.wikipedia.org/wiki/Hobby

10. www.governing.com/

11. www.simplejustice.us

12. www.law.com/jsp/article.jsp?id=1122368711858&slreturn=20140114084036

13. www.rainmakerlawyer.com/index.php/site/permalink/do_internet_directory_services_work_for_lawyer_marketing

14. www.thomsinger.com/

15. http://thomsinger.blogspot.com/2011/06/how-to-refer-thom-singer.html

16. http://en.wikipedia.org/wiki/Self-fulfilling_prophecy

17. www.entrepreneur.com/article/217507

18. www.lawsitesblog.com/2010/08/the-art-and-science-of-lawyer-bios.html

19. http://online.wsj.com/news/articles/SB10000872396390443517104577571453933076304 "In Email, Scammers Take Aim At Lawyers," *Wall Street Journal*, Jennifer Smith, August 5, 2012

20. http://blogs.hbr.org/2011/11/separate-social-media-from-mar/

21. http://blogs.telegraph.co.uk/technology/author/miloyiannopoulos/

22. www.telegraph.co.uk/technology/8152012/Time-to-ditch-the-blood-sucking-social-media-gurus.html

23. http://onwardstate.com/2012/01/21/a-letter-from-the-managing-editor-of-onward-state/

24. http://www.cbssports.com/collegefootball/story/16960572

25. www.mylawlicense.blogspot.com

26. Dictionary.com

27. American Heritage Dictionary, fifth edition

28. USLegal.com

29. www.imdb.com/title/tt0116695/

30. *Nuts! Southwest Airlines' Crazy Recipe for Business and Personal Success*, by Kevin L. Freiberg and Jacquelyn A. Freiberg. Copyright 1996.

31. Ibid., 269.

32. Ibid., 268.

33. www.divorcediscourse.com/

34. www.divorcediscourse.com/simple-basic-law-firm-finance/

35. www.rainmakerlawyer.com/site/permalink/law_firm_marketing_must_include_empathy_and_understanding

36. www.hartfordbusiness.com/article/20110509/PRINTEDITION/305099992

37. www.rainmakerlawyer.com/site/permalink/law_firm_marketing_must_include_empathy_and_understanding

38. www.professorbainbridge.com/professorbainbridgecom/2009/07/is-law-a-mature-industry.html

39. www.abajournal.com/news/article/legal_career_consultant_says_up_to_25_percent_of_her_clients_want_to_leave_/

INDEX